of that examines how such a widely
with its inevitable clash of egos, wa
against rather long odds."
— **Kirk Victor**, *National Journal*

"*The People Rising* is and absorbing inside account of
one of the most significant domestic political events of
recent years. The book provides a fascinating bird's-eye
view of the coalition that successfully blocked the Reagan Administration's most visible effort to bring about
fundamental change on the Supreme Court. The story
is lively and well told and provides solid practical advice to all who would challenge efforts to turn back the
clock on civil rights and justice."
— **John Shattuck**, *V.P., Government, Community
and Public Affairs, Harvard University*

"President Reagan nominated Robert Bork to remake the
Constitution. *The People Rising* is a fascinating account
of ordinary citizens saying, 'Reject this nomination, we
like the Constitution the way it is'."
— **Senator Howard Metzenbaum**

"Liberals will find *The People Rising* inspiring because
it shows that you can beat the establishment at its own
game; right-wingers will find it essential because of
what it indiscreetly reveals about left-wing strategy;
middle-of-the-roaders will merely find this unique
behind-the-scenes tour of public interest lobbying an
enthralling political thriller."
— **Victor Navasky**, *Editor, The Nation*

"Essential reading for anyone who wants to understand
the decision-making processes in the United States
Congress today. And happily, the authors reveal that
the people count."
— **George C. Lodge**, *Professor of Business
Administration, Harvard University*

"This timely and illuminating book shows why progressive activists should be grateful to Ronald Reagan.

Without his courage and determination—culminating in the nomination of Robert Bork to the Supreme Court—there would have been no resurgence of leadership of the American left. Bork was the spark that touched off the wild fire; Reagan was the arsonist. It's a great book."

— **Robert B. Reich**, *Kennedy School of Government, Harvard University*

"The citizen campaign to defeat the Bork nomination was inspired by love of liberty and justice. It marked the flowering of women's leadership in the mainstream of American political life, seizing the potential for democratic grass roots mobilization in a new era. *The People Rising* captures the innermost workings of the campaign and confirms the best of American traditions."

— **Arvonne Fraser**, *Senior Fellow Hubert H. Humphrey Institute of Public Affairs, University of Minnesota*

"*The People Rising* is one of the best books available that describes and dissects lobbying, organizing, and media strategies for social change. There are critical lessons here for the novice and the veteran activist."

— **Gene Karpinski**, *Executive Director U.S. PIRG (Public Interest Research Group)*

THE
PEOPLE
RISING

THE PEOPLE RISING

The Campaign against the Bork Nomination

BY

MICHAEL PERTSCHUK

AND

WENDY SCHAETZEL

THUNDER'S MOUTH PRESS

Published in the United States by

THUNDER'S MOUTH PRESS

54 Greene Street, Suite 4S, New York, NY 10013

First printing, 1989.

Library of Congress Cataloging-in-Publication Data:

Pertschuk, Michael, 1933–

The people rising.

Includes bibliographical references.

1. United States. Supreme Court—Officials and
employees—Selection and appointment.   2. Judges—
United States—Selection and appointment.   3. Bork,
Robert H.   I. Schaetzel, Wendy.   II. Title.

KF8742.P337   1989   347.73'263   89-20274

ISBN 0-938410-88-1   347.307263

ISBN 0-938410-89-X (pbk.)

Text design by Loretta Li.

Printed in the United States of America.

Distributed by Consortium Book Sales

and Distribution, Inc.

213 East 4th Street, St. Paul, MN 55101

T O

the unnamed citizen

who gave up the summer idylls of 1987

to fight for her Constitution and her rights

Contents

Acknowledgements

To anyone who reads this book, it will be evident that it draws its greatest sustenance from the words of those, in Washington and beyond, who worked to defeat the nomination of Robert Bork. More than seventy campaign participants were interviewed, some two or three times.

Some were wary. Some doubted we would do justice to the campaign; others were reluctant to disclose strategic insights which might be turned against them in future contests. But most were proud of what they had accomplished and secure in the ethical standards to which they had held themselves. And so they readily provided documentation, campaign memos, press releases, reports. They opened their files to us. We are delighted that the texts of their interviews, and the materials which they provided, will be placed in a special archive at the Library of Congress.

At our request, many of them reviewed sections of our drafts for accuracy—though none reviewed the final manuscript, for which we take full responsibility. To the extent we got it right, it is because of their patience and caring. To the extent we got it wrong, it is because we did not ask enough of them.

It is hard to know how to thank them, especially how to single out those who responded with patience and wisdom to our every inquiry and puzzlement. Those who find our portrait of the campaign accurate will find that reward enough. Those who are less than satisfied will prefer anonymity. So we limit ourselves to this collective acknowledgement.

Several years ago, a colleague of ours ghost wrote a book for a noted politician. She not only wrote every word of the text, but also the acknowledgements themselves. Of her own role, she wrote with total accuracy, and becoming modesty, "Without the help of _____ [herself], this book would not have been possible." So we say of all those in the campaign who helped us through their words and deeds.

Anita Stearns, who brought to this venture a deep social consciousness nurtured in the civil rights movement of the sixties, transcribed more than 100 hours of taped interviews. And as she listened, she not only typed, but heard. And she counseled us to explore apparent inconsistencies and undeveloped leads. We soon learned that both the quality of our interviews and the precision of the transcripts took a leap forward if she joined us in conducting the interviews. Finally, Stearns undertook for us a series of extensive phone interviews with field organizers throughout the country, which helped greatly to reinforce our determination to avoid excessive Washington-centeredness.

Several students at New York University Law School joined us in the early exploration of the Bork campaign. They prepared papers on aspects of the Bork campaign which provide useful and diverse insights, and will be available through the Library of Congress archive. In particular, **Sharon Rennert's** excellent—and mammoth—paper on the grassroots campaign helped guide us to many of the richest grassroots sources.

Philip Simon, another NYU law student, and a former Common Cause research associate, performed a series of critical research tasks for us, including an exhaustive survey of editorial content. We make reference to his independent findings and insights at several points in the text. More than that, his scholarship and dedication to our joint undertaking were reflected in his exhaustive, line-by-line critique of our early drafts. He was almost always right.

Jill Cutler, as she has done before, brought an editor's clear eye and a citizen advocate's soul to the editing of three successive drafts of the manuscript. The excessive verbiage, the endless sentences, the awkward syntax you will not be forced to endure are only part of her contribution.

Bill Byler brought the fresh perspective of a master of the craft of public interest lobbying in a parallel field—the interests of Native

Americans—to his scrutiny of the penultimate draft. **Laura Tracy**, a feminist literary theorist, heightened our sensitivities to the treatment of women in the manuscript.

Daniel Sofaer, a young scholar, served as an energetic and resourceful researcher and reader, offering lively and challenging insights in response to the earliest drafts.

Pursuant to this world of the computer and word processor, most of the typing and editing of this manuscript was accomplished with our own fingers. But we sometimes made a mess of things, and emergency aid was needed. Ever cheerily at the ready were **Konny Daley** and **Helen Lichtenstein** and **Frieda King** at the Advocacy Institute.

For its financial support for our studies of the role of media advocacy in the campaign, we also thank **The Benton Foundation**, which has become a preeminent force for examining and achieving the potential of the mass media in America for enhancing participatory democracy.

The book would also not have been possible without the support of the **Advocacy Institute**, and its other staff members. The Institute is dedicated to capturing and disseminating learning about citizen advocacy in order to strengthen the capacity of all citizens groups effectively to pursue their own visions of truth and justice.

We especially thank our colleague, the co-director of the Advocacy Institute, **David Cohen**. David had the extreme patience and caring to read every one of our drafts. Only through his vast experience as the dean of public interest lobbyists could he bring his understanding and perceptions of the world of issue politics to guide us closer to the truth about the campaign. Typically, he never mentioned his own role in the campaign; it was only at the tail end of an interview with several of the campaign's principals, that we thought to ask, "What kind of role did, and does, David play?" The answers are revealed in the last chapter, and we commend them to you.

THE
PEOPLE
RISING

INTRODUCTION

This is not a book about Robert Bork; it is a book about the campaign to defeat the appointment of Robert Bork to the Supreme Court. It is the story of citizens rising in defense of their vision of the Constitution and the Court.

The book begins in the early summer of 1987. For twenty-five years Ronald Reagan had railed against the liberal evils of the Supreme Court. After seven years as president, he had been able to name two conservative Supreme Court justices, Sandra Day O'Connor and Antonin Scalia, and he had elevated conservative justice William Rehnquist to chief justice. There were now, on the Court, four solid votes for restraining or reversing many of the landmark Court cases of the last four decades which had strengthened constitutional protections. On June 26, President Reagan received the resignation of Justice Lewis Powell, who had often been the fifth vote for preserving the Court's established constitutional doctrines.

As Supreme Court scholar Herman Schwartz observes, in *Packing the Courts: The Conservative Campaign to Rewrite The Constitution*, Powell was probably the Court's "single most influential member. . . . He was the only justice to be on the winning side of every affirmative action case on which he sat . . . and was the swing vote on many of the 5–4 decisions so common in this area."

"Because the Court was so polarized into two nearly equal blocs, Powell was frequently the swing man in other civil rights and civil liberties contexts as well. He was on the winning side in every church-state separation case during his time on the Court. . . . His views also prevailed in every case granting rights to illegitimate children, on every abortion-related issue, and in many decisions affecting education, food stamps, welfare, and capital punishment . . . In eleven First Amendment cases during [Powell's last] term, in which government action was invalidated seven times, and six of the eleven decisions were 5–4, Powell was in the majority in all eleven."

Powell, in contrast to Reagan, had affirmed "the irreplaceable value" of judicial review by the federal courts, which, he said, "lies in the protection it has afforded the constitutional rights of individual citizens against oppressive or discriminatory government action."

"At the eleventh hour," writes Schwartz, "Powell's departure . . . offered a weakened lame-duck president and his scandal-enveloped attorney general a chance to obtain with one stroke what they had not come close to achieving in the preceding six and a half years."

On July 1, 1987, President Reagan announced his intention to replace Powell with Robert H. Bork, Judge of the U.S. Court of Appeals for the District of Columbia. By contrast to Powell and the majority of the justices with whom Powell served, Judge Bork was known as an apostle of "judicial restraint," the intellectual and moral compulsion to confine—and reconfine—the Court to "the original intent" of the framers of the Constitution. And that intent, as divined by Judge Bork, would not admit the modern Court's expansive defense of citizens' rights.

Judge Bork was among the most prominent of constitutional

scholars. He had taught antitrust and constitutional law at Yale Law School for seven years, holding two named chairs, as Chancellor Kent Professor (a chair once also held by Chief Justice William Howard Taft), and as the first Alexander M. Bickel Professor of Public Law. During the Nixon and Ford Administrations, he had served as solicitor general of the United States, in which capacity he submitted hundreds of briefs and personally argued thirty-five cases before the Supreme Court. As a Court of Appeals judge, he had written about 150 opinions and participated in over 400 decisions.

As his former colleague Professor Bruce Ackerman of Yale observed,

> [W]hen judged by normal personal and professional criteria, Robert Bork is among the best qualified candidates for the Supreme Court of this or any other era. Few nominees in our history compare with him in the range of their professional accomplishments—as public servant, private practitioner, appellate judge, legal scholar. Few compare in the seriousness of their lifelong engagement with the fundamental questions of constitutional law.

Yet, on October 23, 1987, the U.S. Senate voted to reject the nomination of Judge Bork by a vote of 58–42, the largest margin of defeat for a Supreme Court nominee in history. That vote followed twelve days of hearings by the Senate Judiciary Committee. Through the testimony of many leading constitutional scholars and lawyers, the committee—and an attentive nation—were drawn into a great national seminar and debate about competing visions of the Constitution, about the meaning and significance of the Court to the lives of ordinary Americans.

But neither the vote nor the extensive confirmation hearings would have been as they were, had it not been for the campaign to defeat the Bork nomination. And it has been the campaign itself, more than the Senate's rejection of Bork, which has since evoked the greater controversy. Reagan declared Bork the victim of a "lynch mob." Bork himself claimed to have been "tarred, feathered, and ridden out of town on a rail."

As the common public memory of the campaign fades, conservatives who still seethe over the Bork defeat increasingly yield to the temptation to twist the historical record. So, on May 31, 1989, columnist George Will lumped the Bork campaign with other instances of crude neo-McCarthyism, as follows:

> [I]n the Robert Bork affair, nastiness was covered with a cloying incense of ethical pretense. It clicked when some of Bork's critics in the media laid their muddy hands on a list of movies he had rented. That they were disappointed (Bork's taste involved nothing kinkier than Fred Astaire) does not alter the disgusting nature of their partisanship; any stick will do to beat a dog with, and any one we want to beat can be considered a dog.

The facts are as follows: On September 25, 1987, a reporter for Washington's *City Paper*, who had never written previously about Bork and had no discernable position on the Bork nomination, wrote what was intended to be a whimsical article celebrating his own (misguided) genius in obtaining a copy of Bork's videocasette rental records from his local video rental store. No one associated with the coalition, nor any journalist who had criticized Bork's nomination was in any way associated with this misadventure. Those who commented on it had nothing but condemnation for the *City Paper's* invasion of Bork's privacy. Mort Halperin and Jerry Berman of the ACLU immediately wrote the *City Paper*, charging the paper with a "wholly unethical practice . . . Judge Bork is entitled to live certain parts of his life outside of the public eye, and not even our curiosity about him justifies this intrusion into his private affairs." Arthur Kropp, the executive director of People for the American Way, called upon the D.C. City Council to make the unauthorized release of such information illegal. "Unlike Bork," he wrote, "we believe in the right of privacy."

It is, of course, not surprising that both Reagan and Bork, along with their partisans, would attribute his defeat not to a repudiation of their constitutional vision, but to the know-nothing savagery of mob politics.

Those who participated in the campaign to defeat Bork have a different view. They insist that their efforts were a necessary and measured response to Reagan's politicizing of the judiciary, and to the extensive and energetic campaign of the Right. They celebrate their campaign as an extraordinary mobilization of those citizens throughout the country for whom the Constitution lives as a dynamic defensive shield against civic harms. They see their opposition as high democracy, not low politics.

We were drawn to this study by its significance — and its drama. It had to be a great story, an historic story: the unimaginable defeat of a powerful, popular president by a guerrilla band of citizen activists lobbying for liberty. On July 1, 1987, few were predicting a Bork defeat; indeed, the first, and perhaps the most crucial task for those who would challenge the nomination was to convince their own potential leaders, both inside and outside the Senate, that the fight was winnable. And from that point on, given the traditions and inclinations of the Senate, which dictated great deference to the president in judicial nominations, it was all uphill.

We knew from our studies of past citizen lobbying campaigns that the story of this effort to challenge the president would crackle with the tensions of grand alliances, struggles for leadership, warm bonds and persistent enmities, bold strategies, near-fatal missteps, and intricate maneuvers. We also knew we would find clashes of institutional "turf" and outbreaks of what David Cohen of the Advocacy Institute calls "column inches envy," that scourge of frail egos who measure their worth by the newspaper columns which bear their name. And, in the end, a triumph over great obstacles.

That would have been enough; but there was also much to be learned from the political skills of the campaign, the lessons to be extracted from it. The campaign brought together in common purpose a vast, diverse array of organizations and activists. We knew that such coalitions are balky and unwieldy political instruments. Yet no other citizen campaign within memory seemed more skillfully conceived and implemented, more prudent and wise in its advocacy strategies, more adept at addressing critical tactical problems, or more unified and steadfast in purpose.

So we undertook this study in large part to help those who would understand or be effective citizen advocates to learn the lessons drawn from the campaign. There would be rich lessons in the advocacy skills of coalition-building and networking, lobbying, research, grassroots organizing, and media advocacy.

And we sought to examine questions raised about the campaign. Given the quality of the testimony opposing Bork and the attentiveness of the Senate, was the campaign, after all, necessary? Could it be that it was really the "Beard of Bork" that beat Bork? Might not that unruly appendage with its Mephistophelean aura have disquieted the American public more than all the research, all the coalition-building, all the grassroots lobbying, and all the skilled media advocacy that the campaign marshalled?

Or, again, might not Reagan justly lament that, "for want of a cigarette, the Court was lost?" Plainly, Bork failed to seize the hours of his testimony to wrest the mantle from his accusers with the wit and the warmth, the aplomb and the avuncular charm which his White House followers insisted were their ultimate weapons. Ralph Nader startled us with the observation that Bork, as a heavy smoker, may have been suffering the stresses of acute nicotine withdrawal as his hours testifying without a smoke wore on, marring what would otherwise have been a masterful performance at the televised committee hearings.

The "beard" theory, or the "nicotine fit" theory, hardly account for the Senate's historic rejection of Bork's nomination. But these speculations illustrate the treacherous shoals we navigate as we seek to determine the relative significance or impact of the anti-Bork campaign, and of the host of contributing factors that, converging, led to Senate rejection.

Nonetheless, it needs to be done. If outside opposition did indeed play a major role in the defeat of the nomination, then we need to assess that role, and its implications—not only for future Supreme Court nomination struggles, but also for issue politics in the Bush era. But if it amounted largely to "sound and fury, signifying nothing," then it teaches other lessons.

Ironically, both Bork's supporters and those who opposed him share a common interest in seeing to it that the anti-Bork effort gets full credit for Bork's defeat. Thus, Reagan was generous in assigning responsibility for Bork's defeat to the campaign "lynch mob." *New York Times* columnist William Safire credited the "militant Left," led "nationwide by a hyper-politicized American Civil Liberties Union." Reed Irvine of Accuracy in Media insisted, "there is no doubt that the Communists played an important role."

There is method, as well as malice, in this feverish rush to write-off the Bork defeat to the effectiveness of a left-wing mob. As New York University law professor Ronald Dworkin wisely observes, "The right-wing charge . . . is interesting only because it suggests how fearful right-wing commentators are that Bork's loss will be interpreted as a jurisprudential as well as a political defeat." So we can't safely take Bork's word that it was the organized opposition alone that did him in.

The campaigners themselves are of mixed minds. On the one hand, some of them are truly modest. But they are *strategically* modest: they would have us see the campaign not as an independent force, but only as a humble servant to their Senate leaders' proper role in safeguarding the Constitution from radical assault.

On the other hand, institutional and ego needs prompt them, in the very telling of the story, to claim or suggest a less than modest role for the campaign, and for themselves. So the campaign unavoidably assumes a larger significance in the eyes of the campaigners than it may merit.

There are other important issues raised by the campaign of opposition to the Bork nomination. Was it measured, or excessive? Did it inform, or merely inflame? Did its leaders deliberately distort Bork's views in order to manipulate "grassroots" constituencies? Or did the campaign fairly alert, inform, educate, respect the truth, address real issues?

Did the campaign simply force the Senate to take seriously its "advise and consent" responsibility—and pay heed to the great constitutional issues at stake? Or did the campaign's massive lobbying efforts, both in Washington and at the grassroots, chill the Senate's freedom to vote independently on the Bork nomination?

What of the institutional concerns raised about the campaign? In legitimizing Senate inquiry into a Court nominee's ideology, did the campaign elevate or debase the Senate's role in future nominations? When it opened the gates to lobbying, grassroots organizing, and media advocacy, did the campaign unduly politicize the confirmation process, endangering the integrity or independence of the judiciary? Or did it broaden democratic participation in the process of judicial selection and confirmation—a process which had previously been the undemocratic domain of legal elites—not less political, but simply less open?

These questions are important, if only because in their answers lie much of the meaning of the Bork defeat. And so we seek to address them, too.

But let us be clear: we were drawn to this study not by its controversy, but by its achievement; not because we believed the campaign to be nasty and brutish, but because we believed it to be expansive and empowering—giving life to the abstractions of the Constitution and, perhaps, holding promise for broad and effective progressive issue campaigns in the Bush era, and beyond.

We have sought, throughout, to be accurate, fair, and objective in chronicling the course of the campaign. But we are not neutral. Our beliefs, our sympathies, and our biases (where they cannot be contained) lie with those who opposed Reagan and who opposed Bork. One of us played a brief role, modest though it may have been, in counseling the campaign. Many of its leaders are our professional colleagues and friends.

That collegiality and friendship led directly to what may be this book's principal contribution: it helped us to convince most of the leaders and many of the participants to share with us their stories of the campaign—spontaneously, in the aftermath of their triumph. The foundations of this book are the more than seventy interviews we conducted with them. Had we more time and stamina, we could have profitably conducted twice as many interviews, especially among the hundreds of grassroots spark plugs throughout the country. Our portrait of the campaign is thus, unavoidably, illustrative rather than comprehensive.

This is not an "authorized biography" of the campaign, not an unabashed celebration. But it partakes of both genres, and therein may lie some of its gaps and flaws. It is not an authorized biography because we yielded none of our autonomy as authors to any of the participants. We did not avoid the dark side of the campaign, its internal conflicts, tensions, and rivalries, but we tended to treat these generically, rather than trace individual feuds and complaints. That can be seen either as an avoidance of needless gossip, or as a form of self-censorship.

We have not undertaken to tell "the whole story" of the Bork nomination. Our interest and focus have always been more modest: to chronicle the citizens campaign against Bork. Thus, we have only sketched the story of the nomination as it was played out in the Senate itself, focusing on the roles of those senators—such as Biden, Kennedy, Metzenbaum, Leahy, Cranston, and Johnston—who were among the principal leaders of the fight to deny Bork confirmation. We have written of them only in relation to their interaction with the "outside" campaign — in which, of course, they played a central role.

Perhaps a more serious gap is the absence of direct testimony from the other side, the pro-Bork forces. Their voices are absent except through their published utterances. There are two reasons for this absence. First, our primary interest lay with the opposition, not the White House and the Bork partisans. Second, given our own public identities as members of the liberal public interest community, it was exceedingly unlikely that Bork or his supporters would have shared with us privately any insights about the anti-Bork campaign that they had not already revealed publicly.

Still, we believe that we follow in a respected tradition. Herodotus may not have interviewed Persians, and certainly displayed what Thucydides scorned as "deficient partiality" toward his Greek heroes. Yet he occupies no mean place among historians.

We have tried to tell the story of the campaign largely as it unfolded, though we vary that chronological pattern in order to weave in the distinct parts of the campaign. We trace the creation of the "mega-coalition" in Washington, and its early struggles; the process of researching and analyzing and educating the public and the Senate about the Bork record; the rising of the grassroots opposition beyond Washington; the sorting out of the relationship between the coalition and the Senate; the framing of the campaign's message, and the struggle between the anti-Bork campaign and the White House "spin controllers" to gain access to the media with their competing themes and messages.

We then move into the second phase of this popular uprising: the building of the campaign's momentum; the resolving of structural tensions between "Washington" and "the field;" the ability of the campaign to stay the course as the White House seeks to make the opposition "lynch mob" the central issue; and finally, the grand denouement of the Senate Judiciary Committee hearings, and the role of the outside opposition as the hearings unfold.

More than fifty characters move in and out of the pages of this history play, so we've included a "cast of activists" (Appendix A) and a list of organizations opposed to the nomination and their ubiquitous acronyms (Appendix B), to help orient the overburdened reader. And to compensate for our occasional leaps forward and backward in time, we've also provided an orderly chronology of key events at the end.

We close with two chapters of reflection. In chapter 12, "Hard Questions," we ask ourselves such questions as we and others have put to the campaign, and offer our judgements. And finally, we seek to assess, with some humility, the legacy of the campaign, and its meaning for the future of progressive issue politics.

We begin in chapter one, "Fears and Obstacles," with a summary portrait of the legal mind of Robert Bork, including those words and ideas which so alarmed those who rose to resist his confirmation. And we suggest why, nonetheless, at the date of his nomination, the prospects for denying Judge Bork confirmation as the 104th Supreme Court justice seemed far from auspicious.

1

FEARS AND OBSTACLES

It was the Book of Bork that defeated Bork.
JACK ROSENTHAL
New York Times editor

The Fears

Many constitutional lawyers and scholars and civil libertarians were only moderately concerned on July 1, 1987, when Judge Robert H. Bork was nominated by President Ronald Reagan to the Supreme Court. From what they had heard, or casually read, they believed Judge Bork to be a conservative scholar and judge much like other conservative scholars and judges, and so they did not greatly fear his confirmation.

Then, between July 1 and September 19, 1987—the close of Bork's testimony before the Senate Judiciary Committee— thousands of lawyers, legal scholars, and concerned citizens read more carefully what Robert Bork had said and written. They read his scholarly articles as a law professor, his formal opinions as a judge, his speeches, his prior congressional testimony.

Some constitutional scholars, moderate as well as conservative, were reassured, especially by what they perceived as Judge Bork's evolution towards moderation and judiciousness. But the more deeply many others read of this "Book of Bork," its end chapters as well as its provocative opening salvos, the more they came to fear him.

What was it about this scholar of the law that so evoked fear and outrage? What could be troublesome about Bork's intellectual commitment to seek out and be guided only by "the intentions of those who framed and ratified our Constitution?"

Other scholars, as we shall see, have challenged the intellectual force of Bork's theory of "original intent," and his application of that theory. But the opposition to Bork's confirmation was not moved by disputations over abstract theory, but by his passionate, relentless, assault on virtually everything the Supreme Court had done in the latter half of the twentieth century to strengthen the equality of citizens before the law and the defense of individual rights against the power of the state. Bork's challenges came early in his career — and late. The *Legal Times* of April 17, 1989 reported, "Bork said, in response to a reporter's question, that the United States today would be a better country if the Warren Court had never existed."

Wielding "original intent" as an intellectual club, Bork had, early and late, assailed more than three decades of landmark civil rights cases. "[T]he Court . . . began in the mid-1950s," he complained in 1986, "to make . . . decisions for which it offered little or no constitutional argument . . . Much of the new judicial power claimed cannot be derived from the text, structure, or history of the Constitution."

"Restrictive covenants" that forbade homes being sold or leased to blacks, for instance? There was nothing in the Constitution that Bork could find to support the Court's 1948 decision that state enforcement of such covenants was unconstitutional.

Nor could Bork accept the Court's decision striking down a Virginia poll tax that a lower court had found was "born of a desire to disenfranchise the Negro." Bork scorned the Court's opinion as intellectually barren. At his confirmation hearings in 1973, when President Nixon appointed him solicitor general, he belittled the issue: "As I recall," he commented, "it was a very small poll tax, it was not discriminatory and I doubt that it had much impact on the welfare of the nation one way or the other."

His aversion to decisions which forged civil rights progress was not confined to the Supreme Court's role. In a 1963 *New Republic* article, Bork attacked the Congress for seeking to outlaw discrimination in hotels and restaurants in the historic Civil Rights Act of 1964. Legislating morality in this way invaded property rights and was, he said, "a principle of unsurpassed ugliness." He unleashed no comparable rhetoric to condemn the unsurpassed ugliness of discrimination.

Bork lamented the judicial evolution of free speech to encompass literature and the arts, and the efforts of the Court to extend the Constitution's promise of "equal protection" to women and other minorities. To a gathering of Federalist Society conservatives at Yale in 1982, he criticized "a radical expansion of the First Amendment," and "a radical expansion of the Equal Protection Clause," in "the last twenty-five years."

He was offended by the Court's "one person, one vote" rule that abolished "gerrymandering"—the practice of manipulating voting districts by which ruling minorities systematically denied power to emerging majorities. As recently as 1987, Bork complained that the Court had "stepped beyond its allowable boundaries when it imposed one man, one vote under the Equal Protection Clause. That is not consistent with American political theory, with anything in the history or the structure or the language of the Constitution."

For the Court to hold that women, as well as blacks, were entitled to equal protection under the Constitution was, according to Bork, not only "historically not intended," but also *unworthy*, reflecting merely "current fads in sentimentality," the judicial invention of an "equal gratification" clause.

A constitutional right to privacy? Not in Bork's Constitution. When the Court ruled, in 1965, in *Griswold v. Connecticut*, that the State could not breach the privacy of the bedroom to ban the sale or use of contraceptives by married couples, Bork called it, "an unprincipled decision, both in the way in which it derives a new constitutional right and in the way it defines that right, or rather fails to define it."

And as for a woman's right to choose whether or not to seek an abortion, upheld by the Court in the 1973 *Roe v. Wade* decision, Bork simply dismissed the Court's painstakingly wrought decision, along with those in other unnamed civil rights cases: "[N]obody believes the Constitution allows, much less demands, the decision in *Roe v. Wade* or in dozens of other cases in recent years." He labeled *Roe v. Wade* "an unconstitutional decision . . . by no means the only example of such unconstitutional behavior by the Supreme Court."

Would Bork, as a justice of the Supreme Court, seek to impose these views to overturn decades of settled constitutional law?

"Certainly at the least," he told the Federalist Society as late as January 1987, "I would think an originalist judge would have no problem whatever in overruling a non-originalist precedent, because that precedent by the very basis of his judicial philosophy has no legitimacy. It comes from nothing that the framers intended."

Not even Bork's strongest supporters deny that he had campaigned for nomination by Reagan to the Supreme Court. He maintained a rigorous speaking schedule as a Court of Appeals judge, appealing, largely to conservative audiences, as the apostle of that form of judicial restraint which would restore conservative values and traditions to the country. His attacks on the Supreme Court's established doctrines were his campaign platform. He certainly led his audiences to believe that he was prepared to lead the crusade to cure what both he and Reagan clearly saw as its false path. As he told the Senate in 1982 at his confirmation hearing for the D.C. Court of Appeals, "The only cure for a Court which oversteps its bounds that I know of is the [president's] appointment power."

Although Bork appeared to modify some of his views over

time, acknowledging at his hearings that some constitutional precedents were so well established that they should not now be overturned, he still resisted the dictates of precedent. "Supreme Court Justice[s] always can say," he wrote in 1985, that "their first obligation is to the Constitution, not to what their colleagues said ten years before." And in the same year, when Bork was asked whether he could identify any Supreme Court doctrines that he regarded as particularly worthy of reconsideration in the 1980s, he responded: "Yes I can, but I won't."

As an appeals court judge, Bork had been confined by Supreme Court precedent and review of his decisions. "When he was a circuit court judge," warned Massachusetts senator Edward Kennedy, "there was always a Supreme Court to keep him in line." Senator Bill Bradley (D-N.J.) put the matter tersely, and well: "A law school professor dissects precedents. A circuit court judge applies precedents. A Supreme Court Justice sets precedents."

We are not constitutional scholars, and these excerpts from Bork's writings and speeches are selective, not the product of a dispassionate or comprehensive analysis of his writings and record. Judge Bork had eloquent champions—not the least of whom was himself—who argued that his more extreme utterances as a scholar were deliberately designed to provoke and challenge discourse and debate, that his views had tempered over the years, and that the record of his performance as a judge, where he exercised the responsibility of upholding the law, was the record of a jurist well within the constitutional mainstream.

At his confirmation hearings before the Senate Judiciary Committee, Judge Bork articulated his judicial philosophy in a way which reassured some who feared that he would seek to overturn many of the civil liberties protections extended by the Court in the past. He told the committee:

The past includes not only the intentions of those who first made the law, it also includes the past judges who interpreted it and applied it in prior cases. That is why a judge must have great respect for precedents. It is one thing as a legal theorist to criticize the reasoning of a prior decision, even to criticize it severely, as I have done. It is another and more serious thing altogether for a judge to ignore or overturn a prior decision. That requires much careful thought . . . "

"Overruling should be done sparingly and cautiously," Bork testified. "Respect for precedent is a part of the great tradition of our law, just as is fidelity to the intent of those who ratified the Constitution and enacted our statutes. That does not mean that constitutional law is static. It will evolve as judges modify doctrine to meet new circumstances and new technologies."

He embraced the Court's obligation to protect those freedoms which are found embedded in the Constitution: "A judge who refuses to see new threats to an established constitutional value and hence provides a crabbed interpretation that robs a provision of its full, fair, and reasonable meaning, fails in his judicial duty."

At the same time, Judge Bork reaffirmed his commitment to judicial restraint: "When a judge goes beyond [the powers and freedoms the framers specified] and reads entirely new values into the Constitution, values the framers and the ratifiers did not put there, he deprives the people of their liberty. That liberty, which the Constitution clearly envisions, is the liberty of the people to set their own social agenda through the processes of democracy."

Judge Bork observed pointedly that rigid adherence to precedent would have foreclosed "the primary example of a proper overruling . . . *Brown v. Board of Education*," the unanimous Supreme Court decision outlawing school segregation, which overturned previous precedents.

And he also said, in his opening statement, that the proclivity of judges to recognize new rights not expressly contemplated by

the Constitution can harm the very persons his opponents
sought to protect—as when "conservative judges . . . [used]
the concept they had invented, the Fourteenth Amendment's
supposed guarantee of a liberty of contract, to strike down laws
designed to protect workers and labor unions."

These views, and their own scrutiny of Bork's intellectual
evolution, convinced such moderates as Carla Hills—former
chief of the Justice Department's Civil Rights Division and cabinet secretary in the Ford administration—and Lloyd Cutler—
former counsel to President Jimmy Carter and a founding member of the Lawyers' Committee on Civil Rights. After reviewing
Bork's record and testimony, Cutler concluded, "I believe that if
Judge Bork is confirmed, the journalists and academics of 1992
will rank his opinions as nearer to the center than the extreme
right, and fairly close to those of the very distinguished justice
whose seat he would fill."

It is not our purpose, nor within our competence, to argue that
Judge Bork and those who supported him were wrong. It *is* our
purpose to show that others, many others, were driven to the opposite conclusion. We now turn to their testimony—not to
reconstruct the case against Judge Bork, but to demonstrate the
passionate fears which his record evoked. These fears remained
even after Bork's testimony—not among the easily misled
"mob," as Reagan and Bork would have it, but among the most
learned.

What they drew from that record, taken as a whole, frightened
even moderate and conservative men and women—many of
them former teaching colleagues and even friends of Judge
Bork. Overcoming tradition, peer expectations, and personal
reticence, they appeared before the Senate Judiciary Committee
to express their fears of a Justice Bork.

One who based his judgment on "personal acquaintance with
his mind and intellectual framework, as well as on his public

writings and speeches" was Burke Marshall, professor of law at Yale Law School, who had taught alongside Bork from 1970 to 1973 and from 1977 to 1981. He told the Senate committee:

> The basic reason that I believe that the Senate should not confirm Judge Bork's appointment is this. He has shown himself in his writings over and over again to be adamantly opposed to the long and well established judicial role of protecting individual liberty and disadvantaged and unpopular minority groups against government coercion. At the same time he has appeared to me to favor uncontrolled executive power, free from congressional constraints. He finds support for these positions in his view of the Constitution, and of the judicial function under it . . .
>
> He does not appear to believe in an important aspect of the principle of government limited by law. That is to say, in the proposition which I believe to be a basic to constitutional government, and especially to the Bill of Rights, that is the special role of the judicial branch vigorously to protect the people against the command of their government that controls or interferes with their rights to behave as they choose, to speak and write as they choose, to read what they choose, and to make freely their own decisions about their personal affairs.

As Marshall observed, Robert Bork condemned these "basic" propositions in terms not of ideology, but of reasoned discourse. The nominee had scorned decades of Supreme Court decisions as "lawless," "unconstitutional," "improper," "utterly specious," "pernicious," "unprincipled," and "deficient" in "candor," "logic," and legitimacy." And he did so not only in 1963 and 1971, writing as a scholar, but as late as June of 1987, speaking as a U.S. Court of Appeals judge.

Another witness was John Frank, who has taught, practiced before the Supreme Court, and written ten books on constitutional law. In 1969, he was invited by the Senate Judiciary Committee to testify on President Nixon's nomination of conservative Judge Clement F. Haynsworth, Jr. to the Supreme Court.

Frank did not oppose Haynsworth's confirmation, though the Senate ultimately rejected it. Indeed, in appearing in opposition to the confirmation of Judge Bork, Frank declared, "I have never before in my life appeared here to oppose an appointment to the Supreme Court." He said that he did so because he found Bork "is the extremest judicial activist I have personally observed in a lifetime study of judges."

After reviewing Judge Bork's decisions and opinions as a Court of Appeals judge, Frank concluded:

> If you pull together his whole career as a judge, there is a remarkable void. The life of no average American who works for a living, or his family, is better, richer, happier, safer, or in any way more secure because of Judge Bork's opinions in his years of judicial service.

As for Judge Bork's claims to be an apostle of judicial restraint, Frank concluded that he was, in fact, "a loose cannon in an area where care is required. He clearly regards it as his proper function and duty to make law, either precedents or acts of Congress notwithstanding. In a profoundly intellectual sense, Judge Bork is a profoundly willful man."

Frank also highlighted the contrast between Bork and the justice he would replace, Lewis Powell: "Justice Powell was a conservative judge who restricted his necessary lawmaking to new situations. Judge Bork, quite truly, makes law as though precedent were meaningless and the Congress were in permanent recess."

Robert Pitofsky, dean of Georgetown Law School and a distinguished antitrust scholar, augmented the portrayal of Judge Bork's lack of judicial restraint. Pitofsky chronicled Bork's zeal to defy the plain will of Congress and upset nearly a century of judicial precedent in enforcing the antitrust laws—because he considered much of antitrust law as interpreted by the Supreme Court irrational. Pitofsky testified:

Now, how does he get to this position? The linchpin of his argument is that only economics counts; that any "political considerations"—for example, the possibility that massive concentration will threaten the stability of the political process—is irrelevant. And when it is pointed out to Judge Bork that there are cases and much legislative history that go the other way, he is again quite candid. He says that only economics counts and that is all he is going to pay attention to.

Pitofsky observed that Bork felt free to ignore Congress's manifest fear of concentrated economic and political power, because, in Bork's own words, Congress is "incapable of the sustained, rigorous and consistent thought that the fashioning of a rational antitrust policy requires." "It is odd," concluded Pitofsky, "that these are the views of a judge reputed to advocate 'original intent and judicial restraint.'"

Shirley Hufstedler served as a state and federal judge for fourteen years, rising to the U.S. Court of Appeals. She was also the first secretary of the U.S. Department of Education. She feared and deplored Bork's "crabbed" constitutional views as wholly at odds with "the spirit and grandeur of the Constitution." She told the Judiciary Committee:

> "Justice," "liberty," "welfare," "tranquility," "due process," "property," "just compensation," are neither neutral nor static concepts or principles. They are words of passion. They are words of dedication. They are words that cannot be drained of their emotional content and carry any meaning. None can be cabined without destroying the soul of the Constitution and its capacity to encompass changes in time, place, and circumstances. To limit the search for meaning to the thoughts of colonial gentlemen as applied to the conditions in the seventeenth and eighteenth centuries would destroy the hopes of its draftsmen to write a charter of government for their posterity and, I might add, our own. It is as futile to discern the meaning of these words from a crabbed "originalist's" point of view as it would be to know the meaning of marriage solely from the words of the nuptial vows and the thoughts of a bride and groom on their wedding day.

Adhering to his "originalist" credo, Judge Bork has caustically criticized all of the Supreme Court decisions recognizing a constitutionally protected right of privacy. He has been unable to find a definition of privacy in the Bill of Rights to satisfy his requirement of certitude. He can find no meaning for the grand words of the Ninth Amendment ["The enumeration in the Constitution of certain rights, shall not be construed to deny or disparage others retained by the people."] Applying his criteria, he has denied the existence of the right, and discarded the Ninth Amendment altogether.

In phrases that echoed with many of those who followed the hearings long after the hours of fine analysis had faded from memory, Hufstedler pierced the essence of what many had found troublesome about Bork, but few had named. Bork's lifelong "quest for certitudes," she observed, served largely to enable him "to avoid having to confront the grief and the untidiness of the human condition."

Even Judge Bork's dogged committee advocate, conservative Republican senator Orrin Hatch of Utah, conceded that Professor Philip Kurland of the University of Chicago was a bona fide legal conservative. Yet Kurland joined those witnesses opposing the nominee, and was no less fearful of the impact of Bork's confirmation than the others. He warned that Bork's "original intent is not a jurisprudential theory, but, like Nixon's 'strict construction,' and Roosevelt's 'back to the Constitution,' it is merely a slogan to excuse replacing existing Supreme Court judgments with those closer to the predilections of their expounders." Kurland concluded, "Bork's current constitutional jurisprudence is essentially directed to a diminution of minority and individual rights."

Bork was feared as a threat to those individual rights which potentially affect all Americans. Thus Kathleen Sullivan, who teaches constitutional law at Harvard and served as co-counsel before the Supreme Court in six cases involving constitutional issues, testified on the impact of Bork's view that the Constitution contained no right to privacy, despite a line of cases to the contrary extending back as far as 1923. She told the Committee:

> He says there is no right in the Constitution of privacy that pro-
> tects parents' rights to educate their children in private schools; no
> right of privacy in the Constitution that says a married couple is en-
> titled to use contraceptives in their own bedroom; no right of
> privacy in the Constitution not to be sterilized by compulsion of the
> State; no right of privacy in the Constitution to marry someone
> whom you love but who is of a different race; no right of privacy in
> the Constitution to marry someone if you are a debtor and the State
> does not want you to marry. In every one of those instances, the Su-
> preme Court has said there is a right of privacy that protects those
> activities. He has said there is not.
>
> There was no other sitting justice currently on the Court and no
> other justice on the Court in the last three decades—the period in
> which he has been writing and speaking on the subject—no other
> single justice that has taken that absolute and categorical and ex-
> treme a position—if I may use that word—on the right to privacy.

But perhaps Bork was most feared by those who most owed the redemption of their constitutional rights in this century to the Fourteenth Amendment's Equal Protection Clause. No wit-nesses were more persuasive than those legal scholars who were also women or members of minority groups.

Vilma Martinez is a distinguished lawyer and litigator, and a former chair of the Board of Regents of the University of California. She is also a former president and general counsel of the Mexican American Legal Defense and Educational Fund. Martinez told the Committee:

> Supreme Court decisions have had particular importance—life
> and death importance—for American citizens of Mexican origin . . .
>
> Many poor Americans, black Americans, women, Hispanics,
> have gained a foothold on the ladder of opportunity and equality
> only by attacking very small poll taxes; securing reapportionment
> based upon one person, one vote; striking down literacy tests; and
> all Americans have benefitted as a result . . .

Through his writings, speeches, and testimony before this committee, Judge Bork has demonstrated his disagreement with some of the most crucial equal protection decisions of our lifetime, announced his adoption of a reasonable basis test which would provide less equal protection to racial minorities and women than they currently enjoy, and announced his opposition to constitutional protection for racial minorities and women from discrimination by the federal government . . .

William T. Coleman, Jr. is a brilliant legal scholar, and former law clerk to Supreme Court Justice Felix Frankfurter. He is also a Republican and a member of the leading Los Angeles law firm, O'Melveny and Myers. President Ford named him secretary of transportation, and Ralph Nader lamented his caution and conservatism in resisting aggressive regulation of the automobile industry. Coleman had not publicly opposed confirmation of any other Reagan Supreme Court nominee. He cannot, by any stretch of the imagination, fall within Senator Hatch's characterization of the anti-Bork witnesses as "occupying a narrow niche on the Left." He was, despite his strong feelings, a reluctant witness. "I have tried very hard," he told the Committee, "to avoid this controversy."

Coleman is also a black civil rights advocate. He has been chairman of the board of the NAACP Legal Defense and Educational Fund since 1977, though he testified as an individual, and not on behalf of any organization. He may have been a reluctant witness, but he was not an uncertain one. "As one who has benefitted so greatly from this country's difficult but steady march towards a free, fair, and open society, the handwriting on the wall—"mene tekel upharsin"—would condemn my failure to testify against Judge Bork." Shunning the fate of the Old Testament king, whose indictment he had quoted, Coleman would not be "weighed in the balances, and found wanting."

Coleman submitted a fifty-two-page statement to the committee, a detailed legal brief on Judge Bork's unsuitability for the Court. Coleman had read and analyzed what Bork had written and said, as well as much of what had been written and said about the nominee's views. He concluded his testimony to the committee:

> We are held together as a nation by a body of constitutional law constructed on the premise that individual dignity and liberty are the first principles of our society. In this day and age, can we really take the risk of nominating to the Supreme Court a man who fails to recognize the fundamental rights of privacy and substantive liberty . . .
>
> Having come this far towards a free and open society, we should not stop, or turn back the constitutional development that slowly and steadily is removing the vestiges of slavery, of 350 years of legally enforced racial discrimination, and of centuries of irrational discrimination against women.

Ironically, the worst fears of Bork's opponents were mirrored in the hopes of Bork's most ardent partisans, and in the campaign pledges of President Reagan and Attorney General Edwin Meese. As Reagan was nominating Bork, the founder of the conservative Washington Legal Foundation, Daniel J. Popeo, hailed the "opportunity now to roll back thirty years of social and political activism by the Supreme Court." "He's going to begin turning the Court back," predicted Daniel Casey of the American Conservative Union. And the fundamentalist scourge of the Court's waywardness, the Reverend Jerry Falwell, proclaimed, "We are standing on the edge of history." And though he spoke in his hearings with humility about the importance of settled precedent, Judge Bork himself never abandoned critical, fear-evoking tenets of his originalist theories, including his refusal to find any generalized right of privacy in the Constitution.

There were many witnesses of high rank and academic distinction who opposed Bork. But there were even more who were prepared to vouch for the moderate Bork—including a former president (Ford) and chief justice (Burger) and three former attorneys general (William Rogers, Griffin Bell, and Edward Levi).

Of course, numbers of witnesses, no matter how distinguished, are hardly a sound measure of truth or probable consequences — although it is not insignificant that the fears of Coleman and the others were publicly shared by the nearly 2,000 law school teachers who petitioned the Senate to reject the nomination. Ronald Dworkin, a legal philosopher who teaches at Oxford and New York University Law School, observed, "the opposing witnesses seemed to have the better of the argument, mainly because they talked about the substance of Bork's announced views while his supporters mainly praised his character and mental ability."

In the end, the vast divide between the Bork supporters and opponents rested, at least in part, upon a series of unanswerable questions: Would Justice Bork, freed of the political necessity to satisfy concerns about his extremism which faced nominee Bork, emerge as the moderate of his testimony or the extremist of his extra-judicial writings and speeches? Was the scorned "confirmation conversion" — the turn to the center which marked Bork's testimony — a reflection of the true tempering of his constitutional vision, or the mere trimming of his ideological sails to achieve confirmation? Would his vision of justice remain "crabbed," as Shirley Hufstedler and others found it, or would he eschew such "crabbed interpretations," as he himself pledged? And to what extent would he feel truly bound by his sworn fealty to "the great tradition . . . of respect for precedent," rather than his declaration that "non-originalist" decisions "have no legitimacy"?

For the purposes of this book, we need not conclude whether the worst of the fears of Bork's opponents or the most generous hopes of his supporters would have prevailed had he been confirmed. No one can truly know what is in the heart and mind of another. Predictions of future behavior, especially by Supreme Court justices appointed for life and freed of political res-

traints, have proved notoriously unreliable—though no nominee before had so thoroughly exposed his or her thinking in
writing and testimony.

It is enough, for us, to establish that the fears were not
ungrounded—that fair-minded moderate and conservative legal scholars could and did conclude that Bork posed a great risk,
and that they did so not because they were inflamed by an ignorant "lynch mob," but because they were inflamed by their
own, painstaking analysis of the Bork record.

Final witness to the reasonableness of the fears comes from
the one member of the Judiciary Committee whose studiousness
in reviewing the Bork record, in preserving an open mind
throughout the hearings, and in remaining immune to political
pressure were never challenged: Republican senator Arlen
Specter of Pennsylvania.

Having listened as closely as any member of the committee,
having questioned and challenged each key witness, Specter
concluded, at the close of the hearings:

> My judgement on Judge Bork is based on the totality of his record
> with emphasis on how he would be likely to apply traditional con-
> stitutional principles on equal protection of the law and freedom of
> speech.
>
> I am troubled by his writings that unless there is adherence to
> original intent, there is no judicial legitimacy; and without such
> legitimacy, there can be no judicial review. This approach could
> jeopardize the most fundamental principle of U.S. constitutional
> law—the supremacy of judicial review—when Judge Bork concedes
> original intent is so hard to find and major public figures contend
> that the Supreme Court does not have the last word on the Consti-
> tution . . .
>
> In raising these doubts about Judge Bork's application of settled
> law on equal protection and freedom of speech, it is not a matter of
> questioning his credibility or integrity, which I unhesitatingly ac-
> cept, or his sincerity in insisting that he will not be disgraced in his-
> tory by acting contrary to his sworn testimony, but rather the doubts

*persist as to his judicial disposition in applying principles of law
which he has so long decried.*

What is perhaps most striking about the record of the hearings
is the contrast between Bork's antiseptic vision of service on the
Court as "an intellectual feast," and the passion of witnesses like
William Coleman, Barbara Jordan, and Andrew Young, whose
lives as minority citizens had been deeply touched by the
Court's redemption of civil rights.

As Coleman summarized his prepared statement for the committee, he digressed, momentarily, into personal reflections on
the impact of the Supreme Court *Shelley v. Kraemer* decision,
striking down restrictive racial covenants in deeds—a decision
that Bork had scorned:

> At some time, you get affected by your own life experience. There
> was a beloved man in Philadelphia, an outstanding lawyer, Judge
> Raymond Pace Alexander. He wanted to move to a neighborhood in
> which there were restrictive covenants. He wanted to see a particu-
> lar house before he moved into it, and that gentleman—an under-
> graduate from Central High School, which, with all due respect to
> you, Senator Kennedy, we think is as great as Boston Latin School,
> an undergraduate from the University of Pennsylvania, a graduate
> of Harvard Law School, his wife a Ph.D. recipient and a member of
> the Law Review at University of Penn—could get in and see that
> house only by dressing as a painter and getting in that way. *Shelley*
> comes along and changes that. We cannot have that type of decision
> be undone.

Then there was a moment of drama, which the official stenog-
rapher missed. Veteran civil rights lawyer Bill Taylor and People for the American Way's Melanne Verveer describe the scene
from memory. "Bill [Coleman] was complimented by [Senator]
Biden and others for his contribution to the civil rights movement," they recall, "But he said, 'thank you, but look at the people around me.' There was a young black lawyer and an Asian-

American lawyer and he said, 'Look at the people with the brief-cases here — these are the people who are the future.' We talked to Bill about it — we think it was spontaneous, we don't think he had calculated doing it. It brought home the message that we must look to the future, not undo the past."

The Obstacles

If there was so much in the Bork record for even moderate legal scholars to fear, and if those fears would be presented elo-quently to the Senate Judiciary Committee, and if that commit-tee would embark on an intensive inquiry into Bork's constitu-tional views, *why* was the launching of a political campaign of opposition to Bork necessary at all?

The answer lies in the inauspicious prospects of July 1, 1987, the day Bork's nomination was announced by President Reagan. On that day, there appeared little likelihood that the nominee would even be subjected to a rigorous Senate inquiry — much less that the Senate would deny him the nomination.

As we have noted, Robert Bork was, by consensus, among the most professionally qualified and competent candidates ever nominated for the Court. Few could match his lifelong dedica-tion to the study and practice of the law. His personal integrity was not in question. Indeed, the Standing Committee on the Federal Judiciary of the American Bar Association had given him its highest possible rating — "exceptionally well qualified" — when it unanimously recommended his confirma-tion six years earlier to the nation's second highest court, the U.S. Court of Appeals. And the Senate had responded by unani-mously confirming him.

To be sure, in earlier years, the Senate openly and frequently rejected Supreme Court nominees when their views on the great issues of the time conflicted with those of the Senate's majority. Senators took their constitutional duty of "advise and consent" seriously, reflecting the original intent of the founders that the Senate play a coequal role in the shaping of the Supreme Court.

But by the latter half of the twentieth century, the Senate had come to view its role far more modestly, as one limited largely to a check on fools and scoundrels. Since the Second World War, the Senate had only denied confirmation to one Supreme Court nominee on the basis of ideology: sitting justice Abe Fortas, nominated by President Lyndon Johnson in 1968 as chief justice and denied confirmation not by majority vote, but through a conservative filibuster. And Senate Democrats had defended the Fortas nomination by declaring the nominee's ideology off-limits. Joseph Rauh, general counsel of the Leadership Conference on Civil Rights, believes "the liberals made a terrible mistake" in declaring that it was illegitimate for conservatives to challenge Fortas on his judicial philosophy. They had insisted that the Senate's evaluation must be limited to inquiry into the nominee's legal credentials and qualifications. Rauh was right. That insistence would return to haunt those who now challenged Bork on the basis of his judicial philosophy.

The Senate's dramatic rejections of Nixon nominees Clement F. Haynsworth, Jr., and G. Harrold Carswell, in 1969 and 1970, were not based upon their conservative ideology but upon questions of ethics and competence. Even the forceful opposition in 1986 to the confirmation of Justice Rehnquist as chief justice was only partially grounded upon charges of his ideological extremism. Those who opposed him also raised issues of character, integrity, and truthfulness. Yet three of the Judiciary Committee's Democratic senators still voted for Rehnquist. (Interestingly, Rehnquist had far more reason to resent the personal nature of the attacks on him than Bork, whose personal integrity would not be challenged.)

"It was, at least until the Bork hearings," writes Robert Katzmann of the Brookings Institution, "generally considered inappropriate and even unseemly to delve into a nominee's views about specific areas and doctrines."

President Reagan, on the other hand, made ideology the litmus test of his judicial appointments. He campaigned in 1980, 1984, and 1986 as if the Supreme Court were an outpost of the Reagan social and political revolution. During the first years of the Reagan presidency, Senate Democrats were too decimated by losses, and too cowed by the breadth of Reagan's apparent "conservative mandate" to challenge his restructuring of the courts. And though the Democrats had regained control of the Senate in 1986, despite Reagan's pleas to the electorate for a Republican Senate to safeguard conservative appointees, it was not yet clear, on July 1, 1987, whether the Senate majority was prepared to assert itself to resist even the extremity of a Bork appointment.

What *was* clear was that, in its waning days, the Reagan White House and the Meese Justice Department would deploy all the political forces they could muster for the confirmation of Robert Bork — the last hope for the Reagan social agenda, the last chance to achieve what Ralph G. Neas of the Leadership Conference on Civil Rights terms their "counter-revolution on civil rights."

If past practice was to be followed, many members of the Senate would feel compelled — on the basis of Bork's scholarly eminence and past unanimous approval by the Senate for the Court of Appeals — to publicly announce their support for the nomination even in advance of the hearings. By the evolving folkways of the Senate, such a rush to favorable judgement was not considered unseemly, while an early announcement of opposition was looked upon as premature, unfair.

The Democratic leadership of the Judiciary Committee, which would lead the opposition to Bork, was handicapped. The Judiciary Committee chairman, Joseph Biden, was chairman by virtue of seniority, not choice. He had been reluctant to challenge Reagan's transformation of the federal judiciary. In particular, he had appeared to rule out ideology as a legitimate ground for challenging a Supreme Court nomination. In 1986,

he had even cited Judge Bork as the model of a credentialed conservative for whom, if nominated, he would feel compelled to
vote. "I'd have to vote for him," he declared, "and if the groups
tear me apart, that's the medicine I'll have to take. . . . That
kind of vote may turn out to be a liability for the presidential
nomination process, but it would happen whether or not I was
chairman." In July, 1987, he was in the midst of that presidential
campaign.

Biden would change his mind and become a leader in the
fight against Bork. But many agreed with conservative columnist George Will, who confidently predicted, "the bad news for
Biden is that . . . [Bork] will be more than a match for Biden
in a confirmation process that is going to be easy."

Senator Edward Kennedy, the second ranking Democrat of
the Judiciary Committee, had instantly declared his impassioned opposition to Bork — a declaration which, we shall see,
served a critical strategic purpose, but was nonetheless seen by
critics as reckless and intemperate.

The pillars of the Bar, lawyers and scholars alike, could not
be counted upon to oppose Bork. Lawyers rarely oppose judicial
nominees, especially those likely to be confirmed. They shrink
back, at least in part because they never want to find themselves
representing a client in front of a judge whose nomination they
had (unsuccessfully) opposed. To the contrary, there is a great
temptation for a nominee's peers to rush to endorse him or her
as early as possible, thereby generating eternal good will. At the
very least, lawyers who might come before the Supreme Court
would feel constrained to remain silent.

While Judge Bork's legal views may have been immoderate,
he was socially moderate. Though his nomination may have
delighted the far Right, he was not *of* the Right, but moved socially well within Washington's establishment. He seemed to
enjoy the company of liberals, and they, in turn, often found
him warm and engaging. So it was not surprising that promi-

nent moderate and liberal Washington insiders, such as Lloyd Cutler, rose to proclaim him one of them.

By contrast, the voices of opposition to Bork would appear to come mainly from those whom the Reagan administration had succeeded in portraying as "special interests": advocates for civil rights, women's rights, abortion rights, gay and lesbian rights, consumer rights. And no matter how just their cause, nothing was more likely to drive moderate and conservative senators into Bork's arms than the association of his opposition with the issue agenda of such "special interests," especially abortion or gay rights.

In short, as of July 1, 1987, it was not at all certain that the Senate would even open the pages of the "Book of Bork." And even if it did so, and found the constitutional views therein abhorrent, it seemed unlikely that a majority of the Senate would consider it appropriate to reject Bork on that basis.

That is why, on July 1, 1987, those who would oppose the nomination of Bork knew that a campaign had to be mounted — a campaign of unprecedented breadth and political strength, as well as intellectual force; a campaign not so much against Bork — or Reagan — as for a shared vision of the Constitution.

2

NURTURING THE COALITION:
From Chaos to Consensus

> I got a sense that things were going to be
> different in mobilizing around Bork just by
> the electricity in the room, by the fact that
> so many people turned out. I had never seen
> that collection of people and organizations
> in the same room at the same time.
>
> JO BLUM, Lobbyist, Planned Parenthood

Formed at the turn of the century, the National Association for the Advancement of Colored People (NAACP) is the nation's oldest and largest civil rights organization. In 1950, its leaders helped found the Leadership Conference on Civil Rights (LCCR, "the Leadership Conference"), the coalition which coordinated the lobbying campaigns which have led to all the civil rights laws of this century. The NAACP remains squarely focused on traditional civil rights issues; it has no position on abortion. Indeed, within the Leadership Conference, it has long worked in close harmony with the U.S. Catholic Conference, which most assuredly has a position on abortion.

An advocacy organization born of the feminist movement of the late sixties, the National Abortion Rights Action League (NARAL), has dedicated its energies to a single cause: women's reproductive rights. It is not a member of the Leadership Conference, though it has joined with the Leadership Conference on certain issues.

Althea T.L. Simmons has been director of the NAACP's Washington Bureau and its chief lobbyist since 1978. Before that, she spent twenty-six years as an NAACP field worker, adept at grassroots mobilization. Now she calls herself "one of the senior citizens in the coalition." A lawyer, born in Shreveport, Louisiana, Simmons's formidable eloquence, in intimate negotiations or in rousing a crowd, evokes echoes of Barbara Jordan.

Kate Michelman had been the executive director of NARAL for less than two years. No Washington insider, Michelman had trained as an archeologist and a developmental psychologist. Less than a decade ago, she was designing a therapeutic program for young, handicapped children in a rural Pennsylvania county on the fringes of Appalachia. In the winter of 1985, she had leapt from executive director of Planned Parenthood in Harrisburg, Pennsylvania to the center of the national abortion rights stage in Washington. Michelman is warm, direct, and pragmatic. The reaction of her three grown daughters reflected her chill at the prospect of the Bork confirmation. They were each, she said, "shocked at the reality they faced."

At the onset of the anti-Bork campaign, Michelman felt herself still outside the Washington advocacy community. She had grown comfortable speaking out in the media and rallying NARAL's 250,000 activists throughout the country, but felt less comfortable with "inside" lobbying. On most issues, she was also uneasy at the constraints of coalition: "I don't want a huge hundred-plus member organization [the Leadership Conference] speaking for NARAL. For a cutting-edge women's organization, that would not work."

Despite these differences, Simmons of the NAACP and Michelman of NARAL shared a common passion on July 1, 1987: stopping the confirmation of Judge Bork. NARAL and the NAACP also shared a resource which could prove vital to the campaign: they were leaders of extensive and highly motivated networks of grassroots activists in "swing" states.

So, at the July 7th organizational meeting of the anti-Bork coa-

lition, Simmons and Michelman would be asked to serve as two
of the four co-chairs of the Grassroots Task Force.

Michelman was pleased. Joining the coalition's leadership
offered the potential for yoking NARAL's political resources
with others joined in a common cause. It also represented an opportunity for NARAL, and Michelman herself, to enter the established network of national civil rights leaders, and for the
abortion rights issue to enter the mainstream of civil rights.

Simmons was not pleased:

> I was at our national convention when the first meeting was held
> at the coalition. When I came back I learned that I was a co-chair of
> the grassroots operation and then when they told me one of the other
> co-chairs was Kate Michelman I said, "Oh my God!" I went to the
> first meeting of the Grassroots Task Force and decided no. I said, "I
> haven't accepted yet; I want you to know that."

But Michelman was prepared to reassure Simmons and others
who feared that she would pursue NARAL's abortion rights
agenda at the risk of jeopardizing the effort to deny Bork confirmation:

> They didn't know what kind of player I would be, they didn't
> know my philosophy, they'd never really seen me at work and so
> they were worried. Is she going to be a loose cannon on deck? I had
> to prove to them that I wasn't going to make this effort to defeat Bork
> a referendum on abortion.

Simmons agreed, reluctantly, to co-chair the task force, but
she remained wary of Michelman. Says Michelman of
Simmons, "The tone of her voice was very clear, she just did not
trust me." But Michelman was not content with a cool, arms-
length relationship. She sought out Simmons. "We discussed
our views on how to plan and implement a successful grassroots
campaign," she recalls. We commiserated frequently regarding
the tactics of other groups and whether they were effective or

not—and found that we agreed. Slowly but surely we forged a really tremendous relationship."

Simmons agrees: "We found that even though we disagreed on some stuff we were able to reach an accommodation. That really led to tremendous respect for each other, even though we are miles apart on some issues."

This unlikely alliance and friendship did not end with the defeat of Bork. Says Michelman,

> We formed both a personal and professional relationship that's been one of the few that I've experienced since I've been in Washington, and it's wonderful. I've asked for Althea's help on how NARAL can build permanent bridges with groups in the progressive community and she's been willing to assist me with suggestions for strategy. She's been sharing her wisdom, which is invaluable. It is amazing how our relationship evolved.

That Robert Bork brought NARAL and the NAACP, Kate Michelman and Althea Simmons together is testament to the transcendent passions he evoked in groups and individuals. The Bork nomination proved a great centripetal force. "Everybody wanted to get into the act," says Simmons.

The strength of the anti-Bork movement was its passion and its diversity. But in that diversity also lay potential division: as between NARAL and the NAACP, there were conflicts among issue agendas. Even among women's groups, only NARAL and Planned Parenthood were focused single-mindedly on reproductive rights. Other women's rights advocates were concerned at least equally with the threatening implications of Bork's unwillingness to afford women equal treatment in the workplace, with sex discrimination, and with a broad range of privacy issues.

There were conflicts between those who focused squarely on the challenging task of stopping this nomination, and those with a larger vision of the possible, who saw the struggle against Bork's confirmation at the close of the Reagan era as the trigger for a long-awaited progressive revival. There were clashes of organizational cultures and public styles, conflicts between those who preferred the "inside" strategies of low-profile lobbying and those who were more comfortable with full-throated "outside" advocacy—rallies and demonstrations.

There were conflicts in institutional imperatives: some advocacy organizations need media attention to attract and mobilize members—and to raise money and survive. Leaders have different needs, institutional and personal, especially for public attention and recognition. There were underlying racial, ethnic, class, and sex-based tensions.

There would be tension between the coalition's need for leadership and timely decision-making and the demand for consultation and consensus. And there was that curse of all coalitions, "turf-mindedness." Joe Rauh, general counsel of the Leadership Conference and, at seventy-eight, still the great lion of the civil rights movement, laments, "I think one of the sad parts of this city is the turf battles. It's getting uglier and uglier."

Some of those who came together in common purpose to defeat Bork had never before worked together, and so shared no history of trust relationships forged in earlier campaigns. Yet the time was short; the pressures were continuous, and there would be no respite.

What was needed was a flexible, well-wrought coalition framework, capable of mobilizing substantial but unwieldy political resources. There had to be leadership capable of facilitating and steering the campaign, while providing the maximum feasible participation and consensus-building by coalition members.

That coalition had to be capable of hammering out a common strategy, subordinating potentially divisive issue agendas, solving tactical problems and seizing tactical opportunities. It had to map out common ground but allow room for diversity and spontaneity.

It had to be wise enough to make Kate Michelman and Althea Simmons co-chairs of the Grassroots Task Force; it had to have the legitimacy to persuade them to try to work together; it had to nurture trust and confidence so that they and their organizations, together, could mount an effective joint effort.

The first step was to get organized.

Building Blocks

Ralph Nader had to stand in the anteroom; the upstairs meeting room at the Leadership Conference on Civil Rights was filled to overflowing. It was July 2, the morning after President Reagan announced his choice of Judge Bork for the Supreme Court. Two days earlier, reacting to the threat of a Bork nomination, the leaders of more than forty groups had met to begin the process of forming a coalition to resist the nomination. Today, eighty came. Before the nomination was defeated, more than 300 national organizations would join the national Block Bork Coalition.

Most of the people in the room were not strangers. A substantial majority of the groups who joined the coalition opposing Bork had worked together before. Many had come together in efforts to extend the Voting Rights Act in 1982, and to preserve the executive order on affirmative action. Together, they had helped deny Senate confirmation of William Bradford Reynolds as one of Edwin Meese's top deputies. (Reynolds, as assistant attorney general for civil rights, had been the architect of the Reagan administration's most regressive civil rights policies.) And they could take some satisfaction in lobbying for the thirty-three votes cast against William Rehnquist's nomination to be chief justice of the Supreme Court the previous summer, when Republicans controlled the Senate.

In each of these contests, the coordinating mechanism was the Leadership Conference on Civil Rights. It was also the LCCR that orchestrated the campaigns that led to the rejection of Haynsworth and Carswell as President Nixon's appointees to the Supreme Court. It had brought into coalition virtually all the civil rights and organized labor groups, as well as leading women's, ethnic minorities', disability people's, senior citizens', education, and religious organizations.

Since Bork's record of persistent resistance to civil rights doctrine was a core complaint against him, it seemed foreordained that the Leadership Conference would become the major building block of the anti-Bork coalition. It certainly seemed natural to Althea Simmons:

> First you decide that you're going to work cooperatively, and when we decided that, the best vehicle for doing that is the vehicle we already had, which was the LCCR. And any organization that was interested in being involved, whether or not they had been involved before, could just come in and say, hey, we want to be included.

However, a number of the groups, like NARAL, were not members of the Leadership Conference. Many of them were members of another smaller, preexisting coalition formed in 1980, the Alliance for Justice ("the Alliance").

"The Alliance," says Estelle Rogers of the Federation of Women Lawyers, "had an institutional history of laboring for years in the vineyards of judicial selection." Since the beginning of Reagan's second term, through its Judicial Selection Project, the Alliance had coordinated much of the research which unmasked the highly partisan, ideological, and even racist records of the more extreme Reagan administration nominees to the lower federal courts. Indeed, the Alliance had succeeded in derailing White House nominations of several potential judicial nominees, by building a forceful case that threatened a difficult confirmation battle.

In 1986, in the nearly successful campaign to deny confirmation on the Seventh Circuit Court of Appeals to Daniel Manion, an ill-equipped and inexperienced conservative lawyer, the Alliance had proved itself a pioneer in reaching out and involving law deans and law teachers throughout the country. In the vigorous, if short-fallen, campaign to deny Rehnquist confirmation as chief justice, the Alliance had reached out in coalition to citizen groups concerned with issues beyond civil rights. Each of these outreach innovations was to provide a model for the anti-Bork campaign. The Alliance was thus also a logical building block for the Block Bork Coalition.

Yet the edges of these two blocks were not precisely aligned. Not unexpectedly, the leaders of each considered their respective claims to preeminent leadership in the Bork campaign self-evident. But this early edginess was resolved by those who were active in both coalitions. "Essentially," says Judith Lichtman, executive director of the Women's Legal Defense Fund, who serves as a board member on both the Leadership Conference and the Alliance, "we melded together the two operations."

But not without the most delicate diplomacy. Ambiguity being the occasional midwife to agreement, the delicacy of the task can be glimpsed in the assignment of titles to the leaders of the coalition. Those who saw the LCCR as the senior and preeminent force, and the Alliance as a junior partner, told us that Ralph G. Neas, the LCCR's executive director, was the chair of the coalition, while Nan Aron, executive director of the Alliance, stood a half-rung lower, as the co-chair. Bill Taylor, a seventeen-year officer of the LCCR, and the first chair of the Alliance, considered it appropriate that, when it came to a national campaign, the LCCR's broad political resources and experience would give it the lead role. Others associated with the Alliance's Judicial Selection Project believed that the Alliance's sharp focus on judicial nominations should place it in the forefront of the anti-Bork effort. They understood Aron and Neas to be co-equal co-chairs.

In practice, some leadership roles were shared, while both directors served as leaders in different arenas of coalition activity. Most LCCR member groups, and most senators and their staff members, viewed Neas as the coalition's leader. Many groups unaffiliated with the LCCR looked to Aron for leadership, especially those women's groups which were not members of LCCR, and one of her arts was recruiting unaccustomed allies.

The Leaders

Neas and Aron each brought distinct strengths to the coalition. By demographics, Neas would seem an unlikely leader of a civil rights coalition: white, Catholic, male, Republican. But, coming of age in the sixties, he had confronted daily the graphic evidence of pervasive discrimination in our country. "You could watch the evening news," he recalls, "and see the results of the Birmingham church bombings. You could see the march to Selma. You could see "Bull" Connors beating up blacks before your very eyes. You could see state troopers using cattle prods on human beings. You could see Martin Luther King and the Kennedys and witness their leadership."

Once aspiring to the priesthood, Neas early on chose, instead, a lay priesthood of civil rights advocacy. By 1981, when the LCCR sought its first full time executive director, Neas, though only thirty-five, had made a strong mark as a force within the Congress for civil rights advancement. He did so through eight years as a chief legislative assistant to two Republican senators—Edward Brooke (R-Mass.), an early champion of civil rights, and David Durenberger (R-Minn.)—who, with Neas's support and guidance, had led congressional moderates toward more open and active civil rights advocacy.

Neas's commitment to political leadership as a vocation had been deeply reinforced by a searing and debilitating illness, Guillain-Barre Syndrome, which struck him on Valentine's Day, 1979. Over a period of weeks, he became completely paralyzed and was on a respirator. He lost fifty pounds, suffered constant pain, was on the critical list for three-and-a-half months, and was given general absolution. A seventy-three-year-old nun who, twenty-five years earlier, had herself contracted the disease, helped guide him and sustain him through his complete recovery. She also helped him renew his faith and recommit his life to service.

When he was approached for the Leadership Conference job, he was ready. "I had been given certain gifts for some reason," Neas believes, "and the Leadership Conference job was a once-in-a-lifetime opportunity to put these gifts to use. My work with Ed Brooke had prepared me professionally, and my experience in the hospital had certainly prepared me psychologically."

But Neas does not wear his vocation heavily. There is abundant zest and playfulness to accompany his good works. His colleagiality spawns ready and lasting friendships, which serve him well under fire. But his legendary patience hardly approaches saintliness. He can redden in displeasure, as well as with mirth, and that mirth is not infrequently triggered by pleasure at a strategic misstep of the opposition.

He knows the Congress, and enjoys deep and tested relationships with all the congressional players—members and staff alike—on civil rights issues. His instincts for the rhythms of the legislative process, and how to stretch the art of the possible, are as sound and tested as anyone's. No one has better mastered the techniques of leading without seeming to lead, of seeking and achieving consensus without succumbing to a flabby lowest common denominator.

The process is not unlike that of the patient child building a sand castle for hours—adding, granule by granule, layer upon layer, until a firm structure emerges. Just so, Neas consults now this, now that small group or member of his coalition, steadily moving from meeting to meeting, phone call to phone call, until a firm consensus emerges.

Neas is "the master facilitator," says Elaine Jones, Washington Director of the NAACP Legal Defense and Educational Fund, a close ally on many key fights. "What Ralph Neas does very well is to recognize what might need to be done, and then ask various ones of us to get it done. He independently cannot do it because he doesn't have the staff to do it. Then each one of us, in our own strengths, become our own individual facilitators."

The Taoist sage, Lao-tse, defines the ideal leader as one whom those who are led barely know exists. Ralph Neas is not quite invisible.

A colleague, who admires Neas, calls him a "supreme manipulator," not a term of unalloyed praise. Yet, at the end of a sixteen-hour day of talk, greeted by an explosion of discontent from one quarter or another, he is prepared to begin again to channel the disruptive energies toward the common goal.

There are critics who suspect his habit of consulting, first, with a small group of trusted counselors; they challenge his commitment to truly democratic, shared decision-making. But those who have lived through many seasons of issue campaigns most value and respect his qualities. "Ralph always stands out," says Joe Rauh, "because he is such a magnificent organizer and lobbyist."

"Ralph was the engine," says Bill Taylor of the anti-Bork campaign. "He was both Wright brothers. Once it got off the ground, there were lots of people who helped to keep it airborne."

While Ralph Neas took a giant, unmanageable coalition—the LCCR—and managed it, Nan Aron built the Alliance for Justice, and made it a force. In 1979, at the age of thirty, she sought out the leaders of thirty diverse public interest legal organizations —from the Consumers Union to the National Education Association and the Women's Legal Defense Fund—and convinced twenty of them to form the Alliance, from the shell of a moribund Council on Public Interest Law, to take on those issues which affected the public interest community broadly. And, since most citizen groups look to the courts as well as the legislatures to redeem the promises of this nation, the courts were from the beginning a central focus of Aron's and the Alliance's work.

Social activism is in Nan Aron's blood. "Many of my female relatives were involved in social movements," she asserts with pride. "They were very feisty women." Now her daughters give every indication of following the same path. (One is named for social reformers Emma Willard and Emma Lazarus. The other is named for an aunt who was active in the civil rights movement in the South.)

By high school, Aron was tutoring disadvantaged children and picketing against a school edict barring an appearance by folk singer and activist Pete Seeger. She chose Oberlin College in Ohio because it was "a politically active campus;" and at Case Western Law School, in the early seventies, she was counseling women prison inmates, writing briefs for welfare reform and prisoners' rights, and representing women in family law matters.

She joined the U.S. Equal Employment Opportunity Commission, developing and trying sex and race discrimination cases against major employers, then moved on to the American Civil Liberties Union prison reform project, where she brought legal challenges to brutal prison conditions in New Mexico, Tennessee, and New York.

But the Alliance best suited her strengths. If Neas's special genius lies in managing coalitions, Aron's is as a champion outreacher, a bridger of diversities, a tempter and persuader of the reluctant ally. A conservative opponent of the Alliance confessed that he was "fascinated by the number of liberal social agenda items she tries to fit under the umbrella of public interest."

When pressed for a comment on Aron, Bruce E. Fein, a visiting fellow at the Heritage Foundation, archly complimented her "excellent soprano." That remark may have been intended to diminish Aron's capabilities, but in fact it highlights one of her great strengths: the warm voice, the enthusiasm, and the persuasive skills to bring ever larger circles of groups into the fold.

"Nan was always on the phone to consumer groups, environmental groups . . . trying to stir up something with small business. Nan somehow lassoed them in," recalls Carol Foreman, a veteran political strategist whom Aron also lassoed in to the coalition.

She was also both talent scout and recruiter of the right talent for the right job. It was Aron who drew into the campaign Foreman and her partner Nikki Heidepriem, who, as we shall see, helped articulate the campaign's themes for the grassroots organizers. And it was Aron who sought out the redoubtable Ann Lewis to help counteract the White House's media campaign to direct attention away from the Bork record.

In the course of seven separate campaigns challenging Reagan appointees to the bench, Aron, as Neas, had developed a series of close working relationships with many senators and Judiciary Committee staff. Capitol Hill staff had come to rely on Aron for background information on nominees to federal judgeships that was fuller—and often damning—than the Justice Department's information.

Steven Metalitz, a Senate Judiciary Committee staff counsel, paid credit to Aron and the Alliance for building a national network of legal experts across the country who could be called upon to shed light on otherwise little-known nominees and potential nominees. That network was set aquiver by the announcement of the Bork nomination, and was fully ready to be called on by Aron and the coalition.

Neas and Aron presided over both a formal and an informal leadership structure. At the coalition's second organizational meeting, which was held six days after Bork was named, four task forces were organized, each with four co-chairs: Lobbying, Research/Drafting, Media, and Grassroots. These working units reflected both the breadth of the human resources available to the coalition and the broad taxonomy of tasks and necessary skills which make up a state-of-the-art political issues campaign. A formal steering committee, whose membership included representatives of seventy groups, was also formed and charged with decision-making responsibility for the coalition.

Each group in the coalition was assigned membership on at least one task force, and each task force regularly reported to the Steering Committee. Since either Neas or Aron, or both, attended many of the task force meetings, each group was assured continuing access to at least one of the coalition's leaders.

As we have seen, the co-chairs of the task forces were selected with great care and diplomacy. Thus the decision to name Michelman and Simmons—along with the American Federation of Labor and Congress of Industrial Organizations' (AFL-CIO) Ernie DuBester and the United Church of Christ's Faith Evans—as co-chairs of the Grassroots Task Force reflected a deliberate effort both to apportion visible leadership roles as broadly as possible among the participating groups, and to enhance the possibilities for just such synergy as occurred between Michelman and Simmons, NARAL and the NAACP.

Who made that decision? It carried the authority of the Steering Committee, but, plainly, a committee of seventy or more is all thumbs, no fingers. In practice, that choice, and the other painstaking choices of task force co-chairs, were worked through in informal planning sessions by Neas, Aron, Judith Lichtman, Elaine Jones, Bill Taylor, and one or two other coalition strategists. Such informal small-group planning sessions reflect the informal leadership structure that carried through the day-to-day, hour-to-hour operations of the coalition. They are what Bill Robinson, executive director of the Lawyers' Committee on Civil Rights, calls "the efficient part:"

You've got to have an efficient part that is represented by the people who take leadership responsibilities and who don't rely on having been elected. They are, indeed, leaders and when these leaders—and everybody knows who they are—in unison say, "here's the way it has got to be," then that is so.

Ralph Neas probably does that better than anybody in Washington. He will convene a meeting with all the right people there. There is usually some kind of a pre-meeting, where you pull out the issues and start tentatively identifying who should do what. Then you have the meeting and invariably you make some additional assignments on the same issue and you identify additional tasks, and you make more assignments. You don't even have to be in the room to get an assignment. And then Ralph is the key coordinator, the facilitator. There are other people who play key leadership roles . . . That's the way the organization of the stars goes. Then as you report back you identify holes, gaps, the need for other stars, and you develop strategies and approaches for obtaining those people.

Who made up the informal leadership, the "efficient part," of the Block Bork campaign? They were to be found both inside and outside the formal leadership structure. They were the veterans upon whom Ralph Neas and Nan Aron had grown, over time, to rely. But they were not only the veterans; there were also younger and newer leaders whose personal qualities commanded attention and respect.

They included the leaders of the most deeply involved groups in the coalition—but not only those leaders. As befits a coalition committed to human rights, they were not predominantly white and male—though more so than some believe they should have been. They were no fixed group; they changed with the nature of the problem to be solved, or the opportunity to be seized. They are to be found throughout this book—as we examine those called upon to guide (and be guided by) the grassroots, to frame the message, to develop the media strategies, to organize the research, to direct the Washington lobbying, and to respond to Judge Bork's testimony.

It was more than a handful; this campaign was blessed with collective leadership in each of its components, as we shall see in succeeding chapters. Judith Lichtman of the Women's Legal Defense Fund, herself a leader, celebrates the campaign's talent pool, which included "so many strategic thinkers who were superb, and they had a flair for how to be effective politically. The fear of Bork was a mobilizer and a tremendous impetus to us to work together, and we were lucky enough to have some of this genius about strategy on the same side."

Bridging "Insider" and "Outsider" Networks

Networks are simply those webs of informal working relationships that form, over time, as people reach out and work toward common goals with those who share their values. If the formal coalition structure can be seen as the skeleton of the campaign, its sinews — its connecting tissues — were its activist networks.

One veteran networker in the environmental movement once estimated that he maintained a personal network of 500 activists. Conservatively estimating that each of them also maintained a network of at least 100, he calculated that, in the right cause, his network was capable of mobilizing 50,000 activists — no mean political force.

Though networks do not form tidy boundaries, it is possible to see at work in the Bork opposition two distinct networks: an "inside" network and an "outside" network. The leaders of the Block Bork Coalition speak often of "the inside campaign," by which they generally mean the hands-on lobbying by the veteran lobbyists, and "the outside campaign," which usually refers to the grassroots coalitions within each state.

But the terms "inside" and "outside" have other meanings, which hold clues to both strengths and fissures in the campaign. As used by participants in the coalition, "inside" can mean all

those who work in Washington, whether they are the national
leaders of organizations headquartered in Washington or lobbyists. But many of those who work in Washington still see
themselves as outsiders. This may be a matter of choice, as with
the leaders of the National Organization for Women (NOW),
who believe lobbying Congress is a waste of time, and choose
instead to advocate to a broad national public through the mass
media, or to activate and support networks of grassroots activists. But there are others who use the term "insiders" to speak
of what they perceive as an inner, "clubby" network of lobbyists,
members of Congress, and their staffs, from which "outsiders"
are effectively excluded.

The terms "inside" and "outside" can also carry an implicit
judgment about legitimacy or respectability. Certain groups and
certain leaders are seen by the media, by the Congress, and by
themselves, as operating within the circle of recognized players
upon the national scene, while others, by ideology, social
norms, or styles of advocacy, are seen as outsiders.

In these senses, the terms "outside" and "inside" are terms of
exclusion and inclusion, and they reflect tensions and conflicts
within the broad reach of the campaign. For the coalition to
function both effectively and with a minimum of conflict, therefore, different networks had to be brought into play: the network
of Senate "insiders," the network of leaders and activists both in
Washington and at the grassroots who operated "outside" the
Senate, and the network of those who operated in both spheres,
and could be called upon to bridge tension and conflict between
them.

In chapters 4 and 9, we focus on the networks which functioned "outside the Beltway," and the interface between
Washington-based Grassroots Task Force leadership and "the
field." In chapter 5, on the coalition and the Senate, we take note
of the priceless political resource represented by the "insiders"
network of coalition lobbyists, senators and Capitol Hill staff

members. But here we examine the downside of the insider networks, and the mechanisms by which the coalition coped with insider-outsider tensions.

For not every member of the coalition viewed the innermost networks benignly. The more closely the insiders worked with "the Hill," the more discomfited some members grew. The egos of involuntary outsiders were bruised. Others were dogged by a sense that, no matter how frequent and extensive the lobbyists' briefings were, things were going on that were not being shared.

Those who wore their outside status as a badge of rectitude felt that the closer the lobbyists' collaboration with senators became, the greater the risks grew that the defeat of Bork would take second place to the separate political agendas of the various senators. Ralph Nader believed that Chairman Biden, especially, used his relations with selected coalition strategists to choke off the more spirited attacks on the Reagan agenda which, Nader still argues, could have launched a national progressive revival.

Some critical outsiders were less substantively motivated. Some with an elevated sense of self-importance harbored thinly disguised resentment against the coalition's casting directors, who chose to cast them in lesser roles. As Bill Robinson noted ruefully, "The people who wind up becoming the efficient part are indeed stage center . . . there is certainly some envy. In a large coalition, it's just that we cannot all be leaders."

These tensions—added to the ego and turf conflicts mentioned above, and magnified by the masses of groups and strong egos that made up the coalition—were a serious challenge, if not a threat to the campaign. Ralph Neas characterizes these conflicts, with characteristic aplomb, as "creative tensions." And he prescribes, as the only known cure, communication: "Communicate, communicate, communicate. That's the only way to hold the coalition together; and it's not just the Steering Committee meetings, it's those conversations in between."

Communication as Balm

Both the formal structure of the Block Bork Coalition and the informal networking served as channels of communication. The
Steering Committee was the designated forum for sharing information, and a psychically rewarding opportunity to "show and
tell." "There was a concerted effort," says Nan Aron, "to put as
much information out at the meetings, because it was critical to
have everyone feel part of the coalition . . . a shared experience".

The Steering Committee met regularly—first weekly, then
daily. It was also the locus of consensus-building for all major
decisions. And all participants who wanted to attend were encouraged to do so. Simmons recalls,

> It really wasn't a steering committee, because anybody who
> wanted to come was welcome. Initially, it started out being the lob-
> bying group but it was really anybody who wanted to come. People
> knew there was a meeting and they knew where it was being held,
> often at the headquarters of the National Education Association. If
> they were interested they were there; they didn't have to be part and
> parcel of the coalition.

Inclusivity, not exclusivity, was the operating principle—
with regard to both the participants and the sharing of information. So, too, with the task force meetings, especially the Lobbying and Grassroots Task Forces, whose meetings were regular,
and long. The Lobbying Task Force provided a forum for individual organizations to gain intelligence about the concerns
and leanings of each member of the Senate. Printouts providing
details on each targeted senator were frequently circulated
(though to protect the lobbyists from being accused of spilling
unauthorized beans, they were undated and unattributed). At
the Lobbying Task Force meeting, the coalition's grassroots

coordinator, Mimi Mager, also reported intelligence from the field—including responses from senators and their offices to their constituents, and other clues which might sharpen the Washington lobbyists' perceptions of how each senator was leaning, and why. And at each Steering Committee meeting, a co-chair or staff of each task force would report on its latest intelligence and activity. After even the new participants came to know and trust each other, and to be trusted, there appears to have been relatively little hoarding of knowledge, however "inside." There remained exceptions, however, where disclosure would have violated a confidence, or jeopardized a senatorial decision strategically held secret.

The coalition meetings were relatively free of paranoia, a more than occasional affliction of unaccustomed coalitions. Still, Ralph Neas puzzled some Steering Committee members by taking up precious time at the second meeting by patiently asking each person in the room to identify himself or herself, and his or her organization. The reason soon became clear: the roll call was both a socializing process and a security check. Judy Lichtman recalls a murmuring undercurrent of concern at the presence of two unfamiliar, suspiciously "clean-cut looking" men. Could clandestine "moles" from the pro-Bork camp have penetrated the inner sanctum? Not this time—or, apparently, ever: the two unfamiliar figures identified themselves as dedicated representatives from Americans United for the Separation of Church and State.

Trust built slowly. At first, Michelman of NARAL observes, "meetings were called and I wouldn't get invited, because they didn't trust me. Initially, we were just kept out of the loop. But the inner working of the Leadership Conference—which really was the decision-making body—finally opened up. It took them a little while to trust and accept me."

Although President Reagan spent August at his California ranch and reportedly had no contact with senators, and those who managed the administration's confirmation campaign fled the heat of midsummer Washington, the weekly meetings of the anti-Bork Steering Committee continued right through the month-long recess, building cohesiveness. During the twelve days of confirmation hearings in September, the Steering Committee met every morning, and sometimes one or two additional times each day.

Communication also meant a constant flow of paper. There were copies, excerpts, and synopses of Bork's own published writings and speeches, and a flow of reports analyzing those writings. There were strategy memos; there were "message" and "themes" memos. There were packets of editorials and press clips, reports of grassroots activities, calendars of events, and, of course, there were notices of more meetings.

But most of the nurturing and healing communications did not take place at meetings or through the mail. For the most part, to communicate meant sitting down together, as Michelman and Simmons did. It also meant "a thousand and one phone calls every day," as Carol Foreman says.

Melanne Verveer, vice president of People for the American Way, was one of the coalition's indefatigable communicators — so much so, that, at an annual Christmas party, her fond and amazed co-workers presented her with a mock proclamation, declaring, "It is hard to think about Melanne without thinking about the telephone." As a Christmas gift, they presented her with a toy telephone.

Network leadership requires communication with those who are "difficult," prickly, garrulous, petty, negative (and draining), distrustful (if not paranoid), righteous, self- important, unlovable. To build unity in any coalition effort, counsels Bill Robinson, "you don't simply say I'm willing to work with the people who are easy to work with, but there's also a commitment on the part of the coalition toward working with people who are acknowledged as being difficult to work with."

You can't communicate with a stone; and even the most heroic efforts to bridge the coalition's gaps could not have succeeded without networks built up over time, which reached into each corner of the coalition. As Ralph Neas explains,

> Achieving a coalition consensus is a monumental process, day by day, meeting by meeting, conversation by conversation. Thousands of discussions over years of fighting together on behalf of causes build trust relationships. We've been through great times and we've been through rough times and I think, essentially, among the people in the coalition there is a very strong trust relationship."

The Trust Builders

Within the core group of national coalition leaders, there were perhaps a handful who were especially adept at calming fears and inspiring trust — overcoming division or suspicion. Melanne Verveer was one. As we shall see in chapter 4, Mimi Mager was another. None played a more central role than Judith Lichtman, whom Neas called "the glue to hold such a coalition together."

Lichtman, of the Women's Legal Defense Fund, is a passionate civil rights advocate, and, in her own words, "unabashedly a feminist." She is, equally, an advocate of the politics of inclusion, and of the role of sweet reason and thoughtfulness. She refuses to write out of the human race those who may waver or backslide. "Cultivating alliances rather than attention," is how Charley Roberts of the *Los Angeles Daily Journal* characterized Lichtman's reputation as "an honest broker and consensus builder."

She is notoriously late to meetings — but quick to anticipate political brush fires and to arrive in time to douse them. She is so open and disarming, so lacking in malice or ego, that no one ever seems to take offense at her late arrivals. At key points, she was to give critical counsel to Aron, Neas, Jones, Michelman. Yet one key to her effectiveness is her disinclination to accept praise for her role in the Bork campaign: "I'm not so sure I should get any credit. The spectre of Bork on the Court upset such a broad constituency that it was a natural."

It was not natural. As Nan Aron says, "Judy helped to define and set up the coalition in such a way that most of the major organizations who felt the strongest and had resources to bring were involved right at the beginning." Others recall that it was Lichtman who first suggested the pairing of Simmons and Michelman as co-chairs of the Grassroots Task Force. Typically, she says she doesn't remember who came up with the idea.

When trust broke down, as it invariably would from time to time, the need would arise for a diplomatic mission to a dissident or outraged leader, or a skittish potential new coalition member. Again the coalition found peacemakers within its ranks—often among the most outspoken, most forceful coalition advocates. Joe Rauh, for example, disagreed with Neas's strategy on "two out of three" major strategic decisions. But he was still willing and able to modulate, for a while, the sharp strategic differences which arose between the coalition leadership and Molly Yard, president of NOW.

Labor lobbyist Ernie DuBester was a co-chair of the Grassroots Task Force and also active in the Lobbying Task Force. Though he represented the civil rights "establishment" in the form of the AFL-CIO, it was DuBester who was able to gain the confidence and ease the doubts of some of the more skeptical "movement" activists.

Public Citizen, an organization on the front lines of consumer, public health, energy, and environmental advocacy, was not a member of either the Leadership Conference or the Alliance for Justice. Its president is Joan Claybrook, for many years Ralph Nader's closest and most formidable ally, and the former administrator of the National Highway and Traffic Safety Administration under President Carter. Claybrook had not worked closely before with many of the constituent organizations active in the anti-Bork coalition.

Joan Claybrook is a public interest force field, moving with great sweeping energy, the only human who can make Nader appear to be moving in slow-motion. Her acerbic wit, turned often upon less vigorous upholders of the public weal in Congress and the administration, is balanced by her helpless delight in people, even wicked people—her connoisseur's appreciation of scoundrels.

Claybrook enjoys a justly earned reputation as a formidable adversary when crossed. The automobile industry, which owes as much of its subjection to strong safety regulation to her as to Nader, has mythologized her as "the Dragon Lady" of auto safety. A good fight "does gin you up," she admits, with a grin.

Characteristically, Claybrook was among those most outraged by the eventual "consensus" decision that none of the groups would testify at the Senate hearings. Yet the leaders of several of the task forces found her outsider's perspective, insights, and tactical judgments sound and very helpful. She proved equally capable of great tact when it was called for, and she was especially effective in dispelling the distrust and easing the integration into the coalition of groups who had never before worked with the Leadership Conference or the Alliance.

To Consensus

Formally, all major coalition decisions were made by the Steering Committee. But no one can recall any issue coming to a formal vote of the Steering Committee. If a vote had been required, it would have meant that no decision should have been made, because a coalition in practice can only move when a consensus is reached. Yet, as we shall see, there were clearly decisions made that not everyone agreed with. So consensus evidently means more than majority rule, but less than unanimity. What *is* clear is that on the way to consensus, all the coalition's leader-

ship groups and networks hum with consultation and deliberation. And then?

Joe Rauh, as the Leadership Conference's general counsel, has
often had to address the question of whether consensus has or
has not been reached. Rauh, more than any other active leader,
has nurtured the growth of the Leadership Conference and the
civil rights movement. His character and personality, as much
as his unflagging liberalism, are clues to his ability to thread his
way through the quagmires of coalition politics. This is why the
noted historian Arthur M. Schlesinger, Jr. saluted him as a
"great-hearted, generous minded, robust, combative, and incor-
ruptible force . . . Joe's always stood for liberalism without
solemnity and liberalism without self-pity."

Rauh discusses the process of determining when consensus
has been reached. The answer borders on the metaphysical, but
it provides a fitting close to a chapter dedicated to finding out
how a coalition of 300 groups ever got anything done:

> It is impossible to always know what a consensus is. I've been try-
> ing to find how you separate consensus from unanimity. Consensus
> means that if all the Jewish groups say no, okay, no. If all the black
> groups say no, no. Even if the NAACP alone says no, no. But you
> have to use judgment. I'd even say that consensus means substantial
> unanimity.

Getting to "substantial unanimity" does take organization,
leadership, communication, networking, nurturing of relationships; it takes Michelman and Simmons trusting each other;
Jones, Taylor, Verveer, Lichtman, and others of "the efficient
part" meeting into the night; Neas and Aron on the phone at
dawn; the statesmanlike untangling of a knotted problem by
Ben Hooks, Neas's ultimate boss as chair of the Leadership Conference. It takes the magnanimity of Joe Rauh—and the dark
shadow of Robert Bork.

For simplicity's sake, we will say, "the coalition did this," or "the campaign did that." This usage may convey an image of an orderly flock, as of geese flying in close formation—veering together, resting together, all heading in the same direction in the same way. More lifelike would be the image of a swarm of uncharacteristically independent-minded geese, constantly biting the tails of their leaders, heading generally in the same direction, but with some wandering off never to be seen again, and others actually heading determinedly in the opposite direction. The great achievement was not precision flying, but the amazing fact that the entire crowd didn't fly about in a circle, exhaust itself, and fall from the sky. However inelegantly, the coalition, and the campaign, did manage to stay together and arrive successfully at its destination.

3

PROPAGATING THE "BOOK OF BORK"

"We took him at his word."

RALPH NEAS

When Christian fundamentalists denounced and picketed *The Last Temptation of Christ*, many did so without reading the book or viewing the film. They learned of its supposed evils by rumor, prejudice, or dictate. By contrast, many of those who worked to oppose Robert Bork read his writings deeply. Many, for example, read such source documents as his 1971 *Indiana Law Review* article which denounced the Court's landmark decisions broadening the reach of the Fourteenth Amendment in striking down discriminatory practices.

Civil rights attorney Bill Taylor confesses that he had not read the *Indiana Law Review* piece until the week Bork was nominated. He knew quite enough about Bork's record to fear him, but he was still shocked by the brutality of Bork's attack. "He was prepared to trash the Fourteenth Amendment . . . his language was so extreme and so intemperate." Taylor believes:

> If you took Bork's *Indiana Law Review* article and his other writings and pronouncements in recent years, including speeches . . . and you gave that body of material to the United States Senate and

62

said, "Please, sit down and read this, and then, based on this alone, come to a conclusion," I think that the answer of a clear majority of the Senate would have been no.

If you gave that material to ten, or a hundred, modestly informed American citizens, my guess is that eight out of ten would reach the same conclusion. Now if that is right, then what this campaign was all about was seeing that information got to people and that people did not get deflected from the main issues.

Janlori Goldman, of the American Civil Liberties Union's (ACLU) Washington office, recalls her first reading through a sampling of Bork's writings and speeches: "I thought, 'My God! This man is going to put the nails in his own coffin. All we have to do is put forth his record and contrast it with what we would consider to be the mainstream judicial thought."

And Bill Schultz, who led the effort by the Public Citizen Litigation Group to analyze the impact of Bork's judicial decisions, adds:

It's very tempting to be strident and go on the attack, but in this case the basic material was so strong that if we could just stick to that we could make not only a very strong case, but a very credible case. The more people read of what Judge Bork had written, the more they took the view that we didn't need to characterize him, we just had to get across the message of what he had said.

"There existed," Ralph Neas reminds us, "a twenty-five year paper trail that couldn't be altered, forgotten or shredded." Robert Bork's paper trail included his seventy-nine law review articles, newspaper and magazine articles since 1954, a book on antitrust law, prior congressional testimony, eighty-four speeches in the past decade and 150 appeals court decisions.

The day Bork was nominated, however, there existed no published, comprehensive compilation of Bork's utterances, no guided tour through Bork's Constitution and its consequences.

But because Robert Bork's nomination had been feared ever since Reagan took office, the work was already underway.

In 1986, the "Supreme Court Watch" supported by the *Nation* magazine's Nation Institute had made a good start of analyzing Bork's record in anticipation of the dreaded event. This anticipatory research, and that done by People for the American Way (PFAW) and other groups, helped the coalition stake out the issues arising from Bork's record from day one. Based on PFAW's research, Bill Taylor was able to produce a "Talking Points" memo on the risks of a Bork confirmation within the first week after Bork's nomination.

But that was only the beginning. It was clear to leaders of the coalition that the politics of a Supreme Court fight against someone even opponents acknowledged to be an "outstanding legal scholar" required outstanding legal scholarship. "We issued statements describing our initial concerns," recalls Melanne Verveer of PFAW. "Now we had to build on that foundation; the studies and analyses of Bork's record were critical."

Ironically, the coalition both knew and did not know Bork. Many of the organizations had watched Bork's progress up the Reagan judicial ladder with genuine foreboding. The Alliance for Justice Judicial Selection Project, PFAW, and a number of other groups had been compiling data on Bork ever since they became aware of him as the model Reagan judicial candidate in the early eighties. What they knew, they knew they did not like. But what they did not know was whether the intellectual framework of the "old" Bork, the rampaging academic critic of radical law professors in the sixties and seventies, remained hidden just beneath the facade of the "new" Bork, the seemingly temperate and open-minded appellate judge.

The sudden resignation of Justice Powell, recalls Estelle Rogers of the Federation of Women Lawyers, "placed many organizations which had the real legal research capability on notice that they were going to be needed and needed fast."

As the news spread of Powell's resignation, Senator Nancy

Kassebaum (R-Kan.) was speaking to a conference convened by the National Women's Law Center (NWLC). She predicted that Reagan's choice to succeed him would be either Senator Orrin Hatch or Judge Robert Bork.

In the past, the NWLC had scrupulously adhered to a position of neutrality on judicial nominees. Still, many of the lawyers attending the conference urged their managing attorney Marcia Greenberger and her colleagues to examine Bork's record. When they began, they intended only to provide a quick, summary insight into his judicial philosophy. Six weeks later, they produced a detailed, thirty-nine-page report, which concluded that Bork was uniformly hostile to women's constitutional rights.

The Block Bork Coalition Research and Drafting Task Force became fully operational within three weeks of the nomination. Five of the ten organizations which volunteered in this research effort had worked together before. At first, the American Civil Liberties Union did not participate, since its board had not yet determined to break with ACLU tradition against involvement in Supreme Court nominations to oppose Judge Bork. The legal department of the ACLU national office, however, immediately began to compile its own "Compleat Robert Bork."

The Alliance for Justice, and its Judicial Selection Project, headed by Nancy Broff and aided by five summer interns, started assembling their Bork library. But People for the American Way, superior in resources to most other public interest groups, assumed the role of epicenter for tracking Robert Bork's massive record. Melanne Verveer recalls:

> There was so much on Bork it gave paper trail a new definition. As a legal theoretician, he had written exhaustively. We, at People for, became the Bork archives and information center. We had all kinds of stuff pouring in and we knew it was just the tip of the iceberg. There were hundreds of speeches, articles, interviews, and opinions, and all of this had to be digested, analyzed and organized into a meaningful case against the nomination.

People for the American Way dispatched eight researchers to the Library of Congress, most of them summer interns and law students. They undertook painstaking manual searches to acquire a complete set of every major newspaper article in which Robert Bork's name had appeared. This chronicle, in turn, furnished clues to the judge's indefatigable podium-hopping and enabled the coalition to track down such treasures as his commencement speeches, his address to the Attorneys General Conference on Federalism, a Brookings Institution lecture, a seminar on antitrust policy, and transcripts of dozens of other unpublished speeches. Additional manual checks of indexes back to 1970 retrieved magazine articles authored by Bork and documented his participation in debates and interviews. On-line searches of computerized databases identified all Bork's judicial decisions and all his law journal articles. Ricki Seidman, PFAW's legal director, was at the center of the research effort, and relentlessly pursued every hint of a Bork pronouncement. "The more information you have," she said, "the more likely you are to have the information that will matter. The earlier you have it, the more of a difference you can make with it."

And the information was not hoarded, as is sometimes the case in coalition politics, but generously shared. Althea Simmons of the NAACP recalls how she never did an on-line search once during the Bork campaign "because people gave me stuff from the LEXIS [legal] database."

Seidman admits, "we went overboard," but it is quite clear that if the research had been limited to the routine Library of Congress search, some significant statements might never have surfaced. For instance, the search turned up the United States Information Agency Worldnet interview, broadcast less than one month prior to his nomination, in which Judge Bork reaffirmed his long-argued view that the Equal Protection Clause of the Fourteenth Amendment was not intended to, and did not, proscribe unequal protection of women. Marcia Greenberger confirms that "if it hadn't been for People for the American Way, we would not have been able to do the report that we did, as quickly or as thoroughly. They had all of Bork's speeches and the Worldnet interview."

The intensity and meticulousness of this research venture strengthened the mutual respect and interdependence of the coalition and the Senate Judiciary Committee. "Redundancy is not a weakness during battle," observes Jeff Blattner, a key Judiciary Committee aide to Senator Kennedy. The complementary effort in the Bork research operation is illustrated by an anecdote recounted by Verveer:

> One year prior to the nomination we sent a staffer to attend a meeting of the Federalist Society at which Judge Bork spoke. Later, while looking over her notes, I came across a reference indicating that Bork had stated in his speech that there was a need to overturn precedent if the case had been wrongly decided. I spoke to Ricki Seidman about this and she told the committee staff about the reference and suggested they obtain the speech. It was important to have the complete statement, but the notes we had in our file were our first clue that this speech even existed, and it was a very important clue.

As a result of this lead, Chairman Biden's investigators requested and obtained a copy of the prepared remarks Bork made to the Federalist Society in 1987, making certain to get the version that contained, in marginal notations in Bork's own hand, his disregard for precedent: "no problem w/originalist judge overruling non-originalist decision".

It was this speech, perhaps above all others, that fed the fear that a Justice Bork would seek to overturn settled precedents, whose legitimacy he had challenged—even those stretching back over four decades.

The Exegesis of "the Book of Bork"

The mammoth excavation of Bork's record would be of little utility unless it was analyzed, organized, interpreted, and presented as the core of the campaign against the nomination.

The presentations had to meet the informational needs and the skeptical scrutiny of the undecided senators. They had to establish both Bork's judicial philosophy, and the appropriateness of basing a vote against him on that philosophy. Simultaneously, the presentations had to educate and empower lawyers and lay persons within the coalition who would be its frontline advocates — not only with the U.S. Senate, but also with the media. Their materials had to establish the gravity of the case against Bork and the *gravitas* — the seriousness of intellect and purpose — of those opposed to him.

In the first weeks following the Bork nomination, there were many groups with special concerns about the law — environmental and senior citizen advocacy groups, for example — who did not readily conclude that this appointment was of any concern to them. But in the ten weeks prior to the confirmation hearings a process of coalition-building took hold. More than twenty groups and dozens of individual experts, inside and outside the coalition, abandoned families and summer vacations to prepare in-depth analyses and reports that addressed their specific individual or institutional concerns. Estelle Rogers, a significant force in the Alliance for Justice's Judicial Selection Project, says:

> The Drafting Task Force were people from a lot of different subject areas who were either capable of, or interested in, making sure the right pieces of paper were circulating, and we sort of kept reevaluating. Do we need a piece on such and such? It was this ongoing group that kept its finger on the pulse.

Reports met, head on, the preliminary questions facing the Senate, such as, "is the nominee's ideology an appropriate issue for the Senate to address?" (e.g., Yale Law Professor Gewirtz's treatise on "The Senate's Role in the Appointment of Supreme Court Justices").

Unsolicited calls came from law professors, constitutional

scholars, and leading members of the Bar (as well as law students ready to assist them), who volunteered to research and draft memoranda and papers on specific aspects of the Bork record. American University's Herman Schwartz, for example, prepared a line-by-line examination of the implications of Bork's *Indiana Law Review* article. Other papers were designed to address the particular concerns of individual Judiciary Committee members and their staffs, and to serve in briefing them for the hearings. John Frank of Arizona, whose testimony we sampled in the first chapter, submitted such a briefing paper to Judiciary Committee member Dennis DeConcini (D-Ariz.).

Drawing upon his experience in earlier campaigns, Bill Robinson of the Lawyers' Committee on Civil Rights explains,

> Senators need high-quality legal advice and they cannot rely only on their staff or only on civil rights advocates. They want somebody who is eminently respected whom they can view as more detached and objective.

The research products also were packaged and presented in formats designed to meet the special needs of senators and their staffs. Eric Schnapper understood those needs. When he himself served as a congressional staff member, he learned that the pace and pressures of the work left little time for the quiet contemplation of legal texts and source documents.

Now with the NAACP Legal Defense and Educational Fund, Schnapper sequestered himself at his home in rural Connecticut throughout July, reading. At the end of that retreat, he produced, together with Ricki Seidman of PFAW, a spiral-bound reference notebook, "Judge Bork's Views Regarding Supreme Court Constitutional Precedents." Schnapper and Seidman strove to be "balanced, complete, reliable, not argumentative," and *useful* to Senate staff.

Elaine Jones of the NAACP Legal Defense and Educational Fund believes it succeeded because, "it was almost like a glossary. You could flip through and see all the Bork cases. It was just a synopsis of each case and his view and it was something that was easily used and the Senate staff all referred to it."

But the key was its reliability. Schnapper and Jones were grounded in the litigation side of the civil rights movement. "We practice law," says Schnapper. "Lawyering isn't like lobbying . . . you have to document every little thing . . . Rule number one for Elaine and myself: If you don't stick to the facts, you'll lose. You cannot be wrong. It's like the thirteenth chime of the clock; it's all the other side will ever talk about." This work of arduous scholarship reached "a total audience of thirty people—the committee staff," says Schnapper.

The loose-leaf binder labeled "Background Book Briefing Papers: The Nomination of Judge Robert H. Bork" was inspired by Public Citizen President Joan Claybrook, who had herself also served in a Senate staff position, and was an experienced lobbyist. Claybrook persuaded Nan Aron, Janet Kohn of the AFL-CIO, Michael Ratner of the Center for Constitutional Rights, and several other coalition legal experts to boil down the lengthy analyses of Bork's positions on each key issue to two to three-page synopses, alphabetically arranged. Distribution of this work was similarly limited to senators and their staff members.

There are large numbers of Americans who are populist in sentiment. They may or may not care about progress in civil rights, but they share a concern about concentrated economic power. A 123-page report by Public Citizen, developed under Bill Schulz's direction, analyzed Judge Bork's record on the U.S. District Court of Appeals and documented an apparent pattern of decisions which favored business over workers, consumers, and ordinary citizens. The report's authors reached out for populist response by skillfully garnering wide press coverage of its release.

Civil libertarians were not neglected. Both the National Women's Law Center's (NWLC) report on Bork and women's rights and the ACLU's *Report on the Civil Liberties Record of Judge Robert Bork* similarly received wide and respectful attention in the media.

These reports also proved helpful in aiding others to see the danger to their civil liberties inherent in Bork's judicial approach. For example, in preparing a statement for the National Urban League, Washington lobbyist Bob McAlpine relied on the ACLU's report, as well as on studies by PFAW, as a broad foundation, adding his own analysis of problems raised by Bork's views of the Thirteenth, Fourteenth and Fifteenth Amendments.

"A lot got written," says Schnapper, "but mattered in different ways. What is useful to Mark Gitenstein [Judiciary Committee chief counsel] and to Al Kamen [*Washington Post*] are two entirely different things."

While there was no master plan or scheduled strategic timing for the release of each report, the coalition's Drafting Task Force guided the traffic of converging reports. This insured that each study received its day in the media sunlight, and on the Hill. Such a strategy contributed to the campaign's momentum and built a sense of mounting public condemnation of Bork's record. One notable impact of having individual organizations release their own reports and conduct their own Senate briefings was to demonstrate, in the public's mind, the breadth of the institutional opposition to the nomination. As Jerry Berman of the American Civil Liberties Union puts it, "Not simply the ACLU, but the unions were out there, and the churches . . . a hundred flowers bloom."

This steady stream of reports, papers, and fact sheets with which the coalition deluged the Senate conveyed an almost physical sense of the substantial case against Bork. NWLC, Public Citizen, and the AFL-CIO all had reports ready for release in August. They were released in orderly succession, each gathering media attention, and each contributing to the sense of intellectual momentum.

The scholarly output by Bork partisans was meager, by comparison. Judith Lichtman was grateful for "the vacuum the White House left for us . . . We were affirmative. We made the case . . . We were the headlines. August is slow; they're not here. Long after the hearings began, Carla Hills and her pro-Bork group began issuing reports. By that time it was too late." Many columnists remarked how stacks of materials from opposition groups dwarfed those of Bork supporters. Neither conservative organizations nor the Reagan team maintained the quality or the steady flow of legal analyses to the Hill and the media.

As the coalition drew the portrait of an eccentric Bork, the administration sought strenuously to portray Bork as a mainstream conservative. The seventy-five-page White House briefing book, released August 4, was the chief instrument for making the case that Bork "would not change the balance of the Supreme Court" because of his belief in judicial restraint. The White House dismissed Bork's earlier criticisms of Supreme Court rulings as those of the professor *provocateur*, not of the mature judge. Supporters argued that Bork certainly fell within the centrist sphere of Lewis Powell.

By this stage in the campaign, the coalition had the "Book of Bork" at its command, and, as Ricki Seidman recalls with satisfaction, "We were prepared, so that when their salvo that Bork was a moderate came off, we had amassed the materials to say, 'no, he's not!' and, 'here's why,' and to immediately undercut them." People for the American Way responded quickly with a memorandum to editorial writers that challenged the administration's portrait of Bork's judicial mindset.

Exactly one month later, Senator Biden released an exhaustive rebuttal to the White House's position, which Verveer calls the "dictionary of Bork." Biden's response was straightforward: Judge Bork's record over the past twenty-five years reveals "an extremely conservative activist rather than a genuine apostle of judicial moderation and restraint." The eighty-five-page response was drafted by committee investigators Jeffrey Peck and Duke law professor Chris Schroeder and approved by Biden's formidable *ad hoc* "brain trust," which included constitutional scholars Laurence Tribe of Harvard, Philip Kurland of Chicago, and Walter Dellinger of Duke. It marked a turning point in the opposition's campaign. Biden's rebuttal succeeded in maintaining the opposition's offensive posture going into the confirmation hearings.

The Justice Department finally issued a 213-page broadside attack on the coalition three days before the hearings. It assailed various coalition analyses as "illegitimate and unwarranted attacks" on a distinguished and fair-minded jurist, and offered an extensive defense of Bork's views.

The coalition did not respond. Its leaders believed they had already won the battle of dueling analyses. They sensed that the press had, by this time, absorbed the flow of critical reports, and had been largely persuaded by the thrust of the opponents' vast fabric of documentation and analysis.

After the August recess, Senator David Pryor of Arkansas observed that the people he encountered at home, as he shopped in his local supermarket, seemed equally divided about Bork. He'd go up one aisle, and everyone would be for Bork; he'd go down the next aisle, and everyone would be opposed to Bork. The difference, he reported, was that Bork's opponents *knew why they opposed him*. As we shall see in the next chapter, the "Book of Bork" (as well as its digests) had become a bestseller all over America.

4

THE ROOTS OF REVOLT

It permeated into the black churches of the
South. Ministers were talking about it,
choirs were singing about it.
                    SENATOR DAVID PRYOR (D-Ark.)

Bork's supporters insist that the uprising against the Bork nomination was artificially germinated by a handful of Washington
leaders manipulating passive and compliant grassroots seed-
lings. Suzanne Garment, a resident scholar at the American En-
terprise Institute and an ardent Bork partisan, explains the evolution of the grassroots opposition this way:

> First anti-Bork activists—academics, association officials, con-
> gressional staffers—decided what was wrong with Bork. Then a key
> senator, adopting their ideas, launched the anti-Bork campaign.
> Next, anti-Bork senators got together to delay the processes of con-
> firmation, so that pressure from outside organizations could be
> mobilized. Finally, word went out to the members of these organiza-
> tions that Robert Bork was a monster, and that they must add their
> voices to the pressure already being brought to bear on Senate
> deliberations.

Garment portrays the "members of these organizations" as au-
tomatons, waiting passively for Washington to tell them what
to think and do. But the uprising against Bork was sparked as

74

much by the spontaneous outrage of community activists as by the alarms of national leaders.

Activists concerned about women's and civil rights issues, environmentalists and consumerists, as well as concerned lawyers, knew about Bork—not nearly so much as they were to learn, but enough so that no external alarm bells were needed. They also knew this nomination, unlike those of Supreme Court Justices Rehnquist and Scalia, risked really tipping the balance of the Supreme Court toward the Reagan social agenda.

"Our membership," recalls Debra Ness, who oversees grassroots activities of NARAL affiliates, "had begun to focus on the courts . . . We were among the first of a number of progressive organizations which opposed the confirmation of Rehnquist as chief justice [so] NARAL had already established a ready climate for a serious grassroots mobilization."

The Washington-based leaders hardly needed to convince their members, as Garment asserts, that Bork was a "monster." National grassroots coordinator Mimi Mager insists:

> People knew what was at stake. Usually that's something you have to convince people of; we didn't have to convince people that this was something they should do. Bork's nomination touched their core values. The background work had already been laid, and as we went into different states, we found, at least in the larger states, that the coalitions had already been formed.

"Everybody wanted to get into the act!" says Althea Simmons of the NAACP:

> I had a person call me out of Connecticut. He said, "we can't have Bork, and we want to offer you our services." I said, "well, what can you do?" And he said, "I am a creative advertiser." So I expressed a packet to him, and the next thing I knew he had a guy from Madison Avenue in New York call, who said, "okay, we'll provide layout; and we're trying to get some funds together to pay for the printing."
> One guy called in from the West Coast, a Caucasian, and said, "I'm

a patent attorney. I've read this guy's writings and he would really wipe out all of the twentieth century. I plan to write a letter to the Judiciary Committee. Would you be willing to go over it to make sure I haven't missed something?"

This was not just one or two days; it happened all the time. People just came in wanting to work.

The organizing meeting for the Seattle anti-Bork coalition was held only a few days after the first organizing meeting in Washington, D.C. And, like the national coalition meeting, which left even Ralph Nader on the outskirts of the crowd, it overflowed. And in some organizations, such as Common Cause, wary national leaders were pressed to take action by the aggressive advocacy of state and local affiliates.

So Garment is simply wrong in portraying the grassroots campaign as an artificial froth whipped up by a handful of Washington-based leaders. But she is right in arguing that the campaign changed the rules of nomination politics. And what outrages her is not that the opposition to Bork conducted a "political" campaign, but that it was an *outsider's* campaign which reached beyond the legal elites who had always treated Court nominations as the lawyers' private preserve. Garment remarks:

> The anti-Bork forces would not have been able to make their anti-intellectual appeal decisive, though, were it not for the other line that they decided to cross: the line between the insider politics of judicial selection and the constituency politics of a national political campaign. No matter how fierce the politicking on the inside has been in the selection of federal judges, and it has sometimes been fierce indeed, the Bork campaign was different.

The Bork campaign *was* different. Historically, the Senate accords Supreme Court nominees great deference. The "inside" pressures on the senators are weighted toward confirmation. A very great danger existed that even those senators who were wary of a Justice Bork would be swept up in the normal momentum of the confirmation process.

The Block Bork coalition's leaders anticipated, correctly, that the well-organized conservative and fundamentalist grassroots cohorts would engage in an "outside" campaign to build massive pressure on the senators to vote for confirmation. After all, President Reagan, during the 1986 campaign, appealed to the grassroots for the election of senators who would give him conservative judges. He would certainly not hesitate to invoke the same forces to press the Senate for confirmation of Bork.

So an "outside" campaign of opposition was needed to counterbalance right-wing political pressures on the senators. Jeff Robinson, counsel to Republican Senator Specter, one of the four "swings" on the Judiciary Committee, understands the decision-making environment of the Senate:

> There has to be an atmosphere out there that lets people make up their mind . . . The fact that there is a huge [pro-Bork] grassroots effort out there, that most of your mail is anti, but that thirty percent of it is pro your position, it is encouragement. It allows you to act. If there are a hundred thousand letters all saying "we want Bork," it is more difficult for a senator to take a stand, although he may still do so.
>
> I think it had always been viewed — unless you were from a very liberal state — that voting against a president's nominee was a political minus. I think the fact that for some southerners it became a political plus to vote against him is attributable to the organizing that the coalition did.
>
> The fact that their constituents out there, and the polls show that over fifty percent of the people are opposed . . . lets a Senator [Howell] Heflin [D-Ala.] take a hard look and say, "that information frees me to make a substantive judgement," or even make a political judgment to go that way.

The Texas director of People for the American Way, Mike Hudson, described the state coalition's political goal as demonstrating to Senator Lloyd Bentsen (D-Tex.) "why it wasn't politically costly to vote against Bork—and why the votes Bentsen would lose by voting against Bork would have been lost anyway."

The Reverend Joseph Lowery of the Southern Christian Leadership Conference recalled his message to those southern senators whose elections depended on black voters: "The people who support Bork will forget how you vote, but we will never forget."

To allow the Senate to vote its collective conscience, the campaign had to assure equality of political pain. The leaders of the coalition in Washington understood that the political energy against Bork spontaneously generating at the grassroots was their most formidable political resource. Some Washington operatives "never before took the grassroots seriously," says Mimi Mager.

Ralph Neas knew that grassroots activity had to be an integrated element of a coherent, overall strategy:

> If this campaign was going to be waged on the strategic premise that this was the most important vote that senators were ever going to cast; if this was one of the most historic moments of the Reagan presidency; if this was something that would profoundly influence the law of the land well into the twenty-first century, then they would be hearing from people other than Washingtonians. If this was such a dramatic moment in American history, certainly their constituents would know about it and care about it and want to inform their senators about it.
>
> We made a commitment that the grassroots effort would be the centerpiece effort of the entire campaign and we went out and got money to finance it from member organizations. Eventually we had operations in forty-three of fifty states.

In 1985, evidence was presented to the Judiciary Committee strongly supporting charges that a nominee for the Federal District Court in Texas, Sid Fitzwater, had engaged in racially targeted political campaign intimidation. Little attention was paid to the nomination until Ann Lewis, as executive director of Americans for Democratic Action, helped mobilize a campaign against Fitzwater which fell short by only nine votes of defeating his confirmation on the Senate floor. Of the Bork nomination Lewis observes, "we had to nationalize the debate."

Nationalizing the Debate

Among the inadvertent benefits which followed from the timing of the Bork nomination was the coincidence of the regularly scheduled July annual meetings of mass membership organizations, including Planned Parenthood, the NAACP, the National Education Association, the National Organization for Women, and the National Abortion Rights Action League. These were followed by the August conventions of the Southern Christian Leadership Conference, and national board meetings of Common Cause, the AFL-CIO, and the ACLU.

It is common wisdom in Washington that organized labor is no longer a powerful political force, that union leadership has lost touch with local unions and workers, that unions no longer qualify as genuine grassroots or public interest organizations. But union leaders, union lobbyists, union organizers, and union rank and file formed the committed backbone of many state and local coalitions. Unions have always been a strong component of the Leadership Conference, and local unionists active in local coalitions were as aroused by Bork's positions on civil rights and women's issues as on issues of more direct concern to labor.

So when the AFL-CIO executive board was preparing to consider a formal position in opposition to Bork, Neas did not exaggerate when he told the Los Angeles Times, "If the AFL-CIO joins the effort against Robert Bork, it will have enormous consequences both in respect to its grassroots organization and its capabilities in Washington." While lobbying senators in

Washington is important, Neas said, "it's more important for the senators to hear from their own constituents that their constitutional rights could be overturned overnight if Bork is confirmed." And thousands of the constituents from whom senators heard were mobilized union members in their states.

Those national gatherings were quickly transformed into opportunities for strategic planning and briefings. NOW vice-president Sheri O'Dell, who speaks with the authentic voice of West Virginia's untamed corners and people, tells of their convention that summer:

> We went to our national convention loaded for bear. Our membership was ready, too, and a lot of the focus of that national conference was on Bork, because our membership was ready to go, and we used it as a rallying cry to get the spirits up, and get everybody moving. We passed a resolution; we declared a state of emergency.

Nan Aron arranged for Representative Barney Frank (D-Mass.) to speak to the large group of summer congressional student interns, challenging them to return to their campuses and organize against the nomination. Each one received a copy of a handbook, "Mobilizing the Campus."

Many of the interns returned at the end of the summer to join with others to mobilize campus activities in opposition to Bork. University of Wisconsin students organized panel discussions on the nomination. Berkeley undergraduates protested by staging readings from books that could be banned under Bork's restrictive First Amendment theories. Oberlin College in Ohio held forums and demonstrations. Many student government offices were opened as phone banks for calls of protest to senators' offices.

As thousands of activists returned home from their respective conventions in early July, aroused to organize, they found that the work had already begun. Berry Sweet of the Arizona Abortion Rights Action League discovered that an anti-Bork coalition in Phoenix had already been formed. Not one, but *two* separate coalitions were formed and working in Arizona before anyone heard from the Grassroots Task Force in Washington.

It is true, as Suzanne Garment observes, that the official decision by a national group to oppose Bork signaled state and local activists that they were free to formally participate in local coalitions. But some groups did not wait for the green light. ACLU affiliate staff and their members, for example, plunged in to many state coalition efforts without waiting for their national board's late August debate and decision to oppose confirmation.

The Washington Connection

To insist that opposition to Bork was spontaneous and widespread does not mean that local and regional coalitions automatically sprung forth, full-blown and ready for action, on July 1. Judy Lichtman was among those who early pressed for a strong support structure to help the national organizations with grassroots mobilization. "They need help," she says:

> It isn't that they don't know how to organize their grassroots; they're very good at it. But not any one of them could pick up this effort. When we worked for, and *saved* the Voting Rights Act extension, it was because of some very sophisticated grassroots organizing — both the NAACP and the League of Women Voters put resources into it. But here, we really needed to get that kind of activity, and the Leadership Conference itself didn't have that kind of capability.

Tony Podesta, the first president and spark plug of People for the American Way and a key strategic advisor to Senator Kennedy on the Bork nomination, together with Melanne Verveer, suggested that the Leadership Conference hire Mimi Mager. Aron and Lichtman were concerned that many of the groups in the Alliance for Justice Judicial Selection Project, while adept at legal action, were unaccustomed to grassroots political activity. So the Alliance contracted with a team of political consultants, Nikki Heidepriem and Carol Foreman, who had specialized in women's issues campaigns.

Still in her early thirties, Mager had devoted more than a decade to political organizing. She had worked for Senator Fred Harris in his 1976 presidential campaign and as a legislative assistant to Senator Jim Abourezk (D-S.D.). During the Carter Administration she had served in the ACTION agency as special assistant to the VISTA director and had worked with anti-poverty community organizers nationwide. In the Reagan years, Mager organized a grassroots network in support of VISTA and successfully lobbied to save the program. Every few years, when the election bells ring, she still heads off to work in the campaign of the progressive candidate of her choice. In all this, she has acquired skills and political wisdom — and one more vital resource: her personal network, hundreds of activists around the country with whom she has worked and built relationships of trust and confidence, though they may have met and worked together only by phone. As one of her co-workers in the anti-Bork campaign marvelled, "she has the hottest Rolodex in town."

That Rolodex served as the capital stock of the Grassroots Task Force, as it helped lead to battle-tested volunteers in key states who could help anchor or build bridges within local coalitions. But Mager's past congressional and lobbying roles also established a complex of friendships and working relationships with others who emerged in key roles in the Block Bork Coalition in Washington — which, in turn, helped ease potential tensions.

Kate Michelman of NARAL had early offered to hire a full-time grassroots coordinator for the coalition. She was not pleased to learn that Neas, without consultation, had seized the initiative and hired a coordinator for the Leadership Confer-

ence. But the fact that he chose Mager, who was so widely seasoned and trusted, eased the resentment.

When Nan Aron, for the Alliance, engaged Carol Foreman
and Nikki Heidepriem, in part to develop themes for guiding
the grassroots campaign, there arose potential rivalry or conflict
between the roles of the Alliance and the Leadership Conference. But that threat evaporated because Heidepriem and Mager
had worked closely and happily together on women's issues in
the Mondale/Ferraro campaign; they readily worked together
again on the anti-Bork campaign.

Annie Eberhart worked for the Alliance for Justice, "desking"
Grassroots Task Force communications with Alabama and other
southern target states under Heidepriem's general direction.
She had no difficulty working with Mager:

> I talked with Mimi every day, and even though there were a few
> tense weeks between the Alliance and the Leadership Conference,
> we had a very solid working relationship on the day to day issues
> as they were playing out in each state. Probably if she hadn't been
> in that particular position and it had been somebody else, that might
> not have happened so easily.

The "desking" operation—the assignment of a Washington-
based coordinator to serve as the designated Washington connection for a group of target state coalitions—was initially organized by the AFL-CIO's Ernie DuBester and NARAL's Debra
Ness. The assigned "desks" were to keep information flowing to
and from the field, nurture the local coalitions, and facilitate
coordinated planning. Each target state or local coalition would
be phoned at least weekly, sometimes daily, by its desk, which
meant Debra Ness of NARAL, Fritz Weicking of Citizens for Tax
Justice, Annie Eberhart of the Alliance for Justice, or Noelle
McAfee of Public Citizen.

"My work in talking with state coalitions," says Weicking,

"was in helping the state leadership reach known constituencies, and then helping them broaden and expand their base."

Karen Bosch, an organizer hired to work for two months with Arizonans for a Just Supreme Court, confirmed the importance of daily conversations with the desks: "It was motivating and it either would confirm what we were doing or help to bring another perspective to bear on what the local coalition was doing."

Each Wednesday at noon, throughout the campaign, the national Grassroots Task Force met to exchange information about activities in the field. This meeting was always enhanced by updates offered by Washington representatives of parent organizations which gathered news directly and frequently from their affiliates in the field. Thus the national coalition could draw deeply on the political intelligence gathered by local activists. According to Texas organizer Jackie Jordan-Davis, for example:

> We had different people getting information from Bentsen's local offices, his other Texas-based locations, so we could try to monitor as closely as we could not only where the senator stood, but what his feelings were about the kinds of opposition on our part to the Bork nomination, what was more acceptable versus less acceptable to him, as well as how many telephone calls, postcards and letters were coming in.

Since Ralph Neas and Nan Aron almost always attended the Grassroots Task Force meetings, and Mimi Mager attended the lobbyists' meetings, there was a continuous bridge between the central leadership in Washington and "the field."

Though the state efforts did not want for enthusiasm and intensity, certain local coalitions could not match the staff resources available at the national level. So the Leadership Conference on Civil Rights made a commitment to fund the hiring of full-time and part-time organizers to facilitate the formation of the state coalitions. With small grants (around $2500 each), the LCCR supported local coalitions in about seventeen states.

Sometimes an organizer would be hired who would shuttle among several states. In other cases, someone who worked for one of the organizations which was in a lead position coordinating the state coalition effort would receive a modest sum so that he or she could work full-time on the campaign.

Primary targets were the four states with senators on the Judiciary Committee who were "swing" votes. Besides Alabama, Arizona, Pennsylvania, and West Virginia, the national coalition devoted its resources to those states where both senators were undecided, and also focused on the "class of '86"—those five freshman southern senators whose margins of victory came from black voters.

The organizers supplied the glue, and occasionally the lubricant, for the state coalitions. One of those hired, Frank Jackalone of the Florida Consumers Federation, wrote in a letter to Mager:

> It's an exciting grassroots effort. Our joint involvement in coordinating all this spontaneous outrage against Bork's nomination will, I'm certain, provide movement enabling it to show Senators Graham and Chiles that "no" votes on Bork would be both morally and politically correct.

Sometimes the grassroots organizers functioned as neutral peace-keepers among uneasy factions. In Alabama, for example, there were existing political tensions between two groups, the New South Coalition and the Alabama Democratic Conference. Coalition-supported organizer Mary Weidler, a former ACLU staffer, enjoyed good relations with both, and helped bridge the gap between them.

In Texas, some labor unions were uneasy about coexisting in a coalition with abortion rights groups, though these groups were sensitive to this highly charged emotional issue, even to the extent of absenting themselves from meetings where their presence might prove politically awkward. The two organizers hired by the Leadership Conference had the diplomatic skills necessary to prevent fracturing of the Texas coalition, letting certain labor leaders work independently of the coalition where they were more comfortable doing so.

Unprecedented collaboration at the national level contributed to the growth of local coalitions. As the circle of national groups opposing Bork widened, the Grassroots Task Force in Washington encouraged the state leaders to reach out to the affiliates of the new coalition partners (and, reciprocally, as the task force learned of new groups spontaneously joining state coalitions, the national Block Bork Coalition was alerted to reach out to *their* national leadership).

Lists of members and supporters form the hoarded capital of volunteer organizations. Indeed, the lists form the base of financial contributors, as well as activists. No group parts with its lists lightly, especially to potential poachers. Groups with long memories of McCarthyite persecution of progressive activists maintain rigorously the secrecy of their membership. Simmons proudly points out that in 1956, the NAACP had gone to the Supreme Court to protect the confidentiality of its lists. Yet, as trust developed, the members of the Grassroots Task Force negotiated a limited exchange of key lists of activists at the state level. In practice, the state coordinators reached out freely to other state affiliates.

The state coalitions also reached out to Bar associations and the law teacher networks in each state. Some lawyers who flocked to the anti-Bork banner took a leadership role in building the state coalitions. Constitutional scholar and Democratic Party eminence John Frank, for example, who was to testify against Bork, often chaired the weekly meetings of the Arizona coalition.

Grassroots Propagation of the "Book of Bork"

The Grassroots Task Force in Washington functioned as a conduit for paper to the field. Mimi Mager was astounded at the activists' hunger for knowledge. "They were like vultures," she says, "it was, 'More paper! More paper!' That surprised me. I remember the Nation Institute came out with its report and we sent the summary. People called and wanted the 131-page report itself, and that was fine."

The Public Citizen study disputing Judge Bork's record as an impartial appellate court judge, which instead showed him as ruling in favor of corporate litigants, was seized upon by Pennsylvania activists and other coalitions, because its findings resonated with their members' concerns.

Original legal briefs and full reports on the nominee's record and judicial philosophy were also routinely distributed by the Washington operation to state and local coalition leaders. The grassroots activists were fully engaged in the intellectual struggle over Bork's views, not merely passive viaducts for slogans and distilled wisdom. And the depth of their knowledge and understanding fueled their intensity.

The information conveyor belt running between the "desks" and the state coalitions was complemented by the lines of communication between each national organization and its affiliate. Texas organizer Jackie Jordan-Davis felt that "we had a good relationship with Washington in that we had a number of organizations represented that also had a national presence. And so we were really able to share information and put the big picture together, because we had people who were directly tied into their representatives in Washington."

Judiciary Committee member Dennis DeConcini indicated to his own staff that he had been unimpressed by an initial meeting with Arizona law professors who opposed confirmation. At a second meeting several weeks later, after the law teachers had access to the Bork record and analyses supplied by the national coalition, the senator was struck by their command of the issues and by the thrust of their arguments.

A prominent Alabama lawyer in his seventies—and formerly Justice Hugo Black's first law clerk—Jerome "Buddy" A. Cooper struck up a casual conversation with Senator Howell Heflin at a fish fry, during which he expressed his concerns about Judge Bork. Cooper asked for scholarly papers and analyses from the Lawyers' Committee on Civil Rights, which in turn sent on coalition materials so that he could respond in a more informed and convincing manner to the questions Heflin, a former state supreme court justice, had raised.

This linking of local activists with the Washington-based experts was another function of the Grassroots Task Force, according to Mimi Mager:

> There were a lot of referrals. There were a lot of questions about different issues which I wasn't fully knowledgeable about. My feeling was that it'd be crazy for me to be the intermediary when they could talk directly to the expert. People were very accessible to take calls from someone in a state who needed information.

"What they needed from us," says Carol Foreman, "was more information; they needed the analysis; they needed the reports." Grassroots organizer Jackie Jordan-Davis marveled at "how the variety of information and ideas out there made the job a whole lot easier."

Each state or local coalition took the materials supplied from Washington, and recast them with an eye to the special concerns of their community. Some simplified; others provided more substance. A leaflet prepared by the Seattle coalition, for instance, outlined ten reasons to oppose the nomination, citing references which included Bork's *Indiana Law Review* article, speeches, and appellate court decisions.

All Politics is (Still) Local — and Hard Work

The real work of the state coalitions was not getting an impressive list of participating organizations on the letterhead, but activating the memberships of each group within the short time period. So the credo of local activists, says Frances Sheehan, a key strategist in the Pennsylvania Block Bork Coalition and executive director of NARAL in Pennsylvania, was "understanding the politics of the state and doing what it takes to win."

Doing what it took to win required establishing a field organization capable of generating continuous and substantial anti-Bork activities. In Pennsylvania, it took three separate coalitions to accommodate the state's geographically fragmented politics. "Whenever you're running a statewide effort, you're running three campaigns," says Sheehan:

> You're runnning a more liberal, civil rights–oriented campaign in Philadelphia where blacks and Jews, as well as labor unions, figure heavily in the political makeup of the city. It's sort of a more yuppie, socially liberal community.
>
> In Pittsburgh, you're running a very different campaign. It's a white campaign; it's very working class; it's very, very labor-oriented. You don't have as many yuppies; it's more socially conservative, but economically liberal. The third campaign you have to run is a much more rural, socially conservative campaign, in the central and northern tiers of the state.

In Louisiana, the organizing separated north from south, with the northern coalition tailored to that region's more dominant conservatism. In some states the remote location of a core of activists—say, a law school with an active faculty group opposing the nomination—would be the hub of local activity.

The anti-Bork strategists did not entertain any illusion of being able to match the letter and postcard poundage generated by the Right's massive and automated communications network, which would flood the Senate with hundreds of thousands of identical, though passionate, letters demanding confirmation.

The hope was to reduce the lopsided ratio. For example, the volume of mail to Senator Arlen Specter (R-Penn.) at the outset was overwhelmingly pro-Bork with some estimates as high as twenty-five-to-one, but the Pennsylvania coalitions were able to bring the ratio down to three-to-two by the confirmation hearings.

Much imagination went into the opposition's massive letter-writing effort, which succeeded in acting as a significant counterweight to Bork partisans. In New Orleans, for example, the Association of Community Organizations for Reform Now (ACORN) generated over 4,000 letters in a week through the network of churches in southern Louisiana. In southern Florida, the local arms of Citizen Action, the National Council of Senior Citizens, and the American Association of Retired Persons combined forces to initiate a letter-writing drive in the mammoth condominiums of Palm Beach County, with postcards urging Senators Chiles and Graham to vote against Bork. A Memphis coalition, including the AFL-CIO, NAACP, Planned Parenthood, NOW, Urban League and local churches, mounted a petition drive that delivered over twelve thousand signatures to Senators Gore and Sasser.

If the state coalitions could not match the right wing in *numbers* of letters, it could compete by the *quality* of the letters opposing Bork—the reasoned, as well as passionate, opposition—contrasted with the boilerplate communications of Bork supporters.

Texas organizer Mike MacDougall recalls: "There was no way we were going to pull even, but what we stressed was quality in the letters, not these mimeographed postcards. We tried to get people to write in hand their feelings about Bork and send [copies to us] and we got several thousand of those and I think they really made a difference."

When a group of Washington lobbyists met with Lloyd Bentsen as the confirmation hearings were in progress, the senator said he was getting tons of mail, but that he could tell the difference between "Astro turf stuff and real mail." And, according to the senator's Texas-based offices, the "real mail" was coming from Bork's opponents.

Telephone trees, rallies, meetings with senators and their staffs, both in Washington and at home during recesses, all augmented the letter-writing campaigns. Press conferences were designed by state coalition coordinators to accentuate the diversity of organizations behind the movement, assuring that the more mainstream groups were in the spotlight. Rallies would feature celebrities to ensure both a good turnout and print and electronic media coverage. Delegations flew to Washington to meet with their senators. Coalition leaders persuaded influential Democratic and Republican campaign backers to discuss the nomination with the senators they supported. Op-ed articles authored by prominent lawyers and state legislators graced even the most conservative newspapers.

Of course, every public event attended by a senator during the August recess was an occasion for bringing home the breadth and depth of opposition to Bork. Town meetings, state fairs, ribbon-cutting ceremonies, sports events, and community gatherings all provided opportunities for measured pleas for the defeat of Bork. This required a stable of informed citizens who could demonstrate to their senators how profoundly concerned they were.

When Senator DeConcini made appearances in Phoenix, according to Berry Sweet of the NARAL affiliate, "he got to the point that he rolled his eyes when certain people came to approach him because he knew what was coming . . . He was very aware of the coalition and who was involved."

The senators were hearing from respected pillars of their communities. Generating instant recognition, the names of many of the state's leading citizens (and campaign contributors) leapt off the pages of the petitions presented to Senators Byrd and Rockefeller of West Virginia. This was no coincidence.

As at the national level, the state coalitions drew heavily upon the moderate center, and put very careful thought into who played the frontline roles and who interacted with local politicians, always seeking those who could command the respect of a wide, nonpartisan spectrum of the community. In Ari-

zona, for example, the state NARAL affiliate chose not to participate in meetings with Senator DeConcini, mindful of his un-
wavering opposition to abortion.

By early September, the Austin/Dallas coalition had extended
its membership to some twenty-three groups, including the
Texas State Teachers Association as well as the rival teachers
union, the NAACP, Austin Area Urban League, several
Hispanic groups including Mexican American Democrats, the
American Association for University Women, and religious
groups. Jackie Jordan-Davis recalls her astonishment that "not a
lot of people even questioned the fact of who else was in the coalition when you contacted them about their participation, and
then in turn, did not object when they found out."

A Block Bork rally was held in Nacogdoches, a town in Texas
with a population of 12,000. When a group of Navajo Native
Americans from Flagstaff met with Senator DeConcini in the
state capitol about a bill pertaining to their reservation, they
raised their concerns about Bork. Visiting service station operators from Alabama were asked by Howell Heflin as they were
about to leave his Senate office how they felt about Bork. Without hesitation, they spoke of their fears of reopening the civil
rights wounds.

Suzanne Garment was wrong in depicting the grassroots activities as puppetry controlled from Washington. The national
Grassroots Task Force did not, and could not, control and direct
activities in the field. "Making stuff happen where the inclina-
tion was not there was something we did not do," says Debra
Ness. "If we have an inactive chapter out there, whether it is
NARAL, NAACP, or NOW, our telling them to get active doesn't
get them active."

Organizer Mike MacDougall, who roved between coalitions
in four states, adds: "The talks with Washington were mostly for
coordination purposes. There were no marching orders ever.
There couldn't have been because every state was different; but
for support services, Washington was great."

5

TIPTOEING THROUGH
THE SENATE

A lobbyist is best when the people barely
know that she exists,
Not so good, when the Congress openly
adores and obeys her,
Worst, when the Congress fears and despises
her.
Of a great lobbyist, her work done, her aim
fulfilled,
They will all say, "we did this ourselves."

LAO-TSE
Very rough paraphrase from the Way of the Tao

The relationship of the Block Bork Coalition to the Senate was
a matter of extreme delicacy. Even on the most routine bills, of
little general public concern, it is never in the interest of the lobbyist to be perceived (by anyone but his or her clients) as having
influenced the course of congressional decisions. Lawmakers
don't appreciate being looked upon as puppets, especially the
puppets of special interests. The members of Congress may not
exactly *know* why they voted as they did; and, in any event,
they always prefer to believe that they voted of their own voli-
tion, in the public interest.

In the case of the Bork nomination, these sensitivities were
magnified three-fold. While the legitimacy, or at least the nor-
mality of lobbying on legislation has become generally accepted, this is by no means true of Supreme Court nominations.
As we will see in the next chapter, the *Washington Post* editors,
as arbiters of political propriety, sternly decried the practice as
"wrong, wrong, wrong!"

Just so, the great hope and strategy of Bork's proponents was to turn the spotlight away from Bork's constitutional vision, and onto the special interest lobbies — the "mob at the gates." And, whereas on most issues before Congress the press pays only sporadic attention to the lobbying process, the Bork nomination, and all that affected it, were on center stage from beginning to end. In this case, the lobbyists had to work hard to remain unnoticed.

Moreover, the coalition's lobbyists sought to encourage an elevated sense of Senate autonomy toward the confirmation process — a sense that constitutional responsibility for the Supreme Court was shared by 101 elected officials, not concentrated in the hands of one. And they wished that each senator's deliberations would be driven — and be seen to be driven — by constitutional principle, not by competing hordes of swarming lobbyists.

Contrary to common perception, lobbyists are generally of more use in helping those who already support their positions than they are in turning votes around. The representative or senator who would lead a legislative battle commonly relies heavily upon the expertise and intelligence of the supportive lobby to augment the chronic thinness of his own, and even his staff members' knowledge. But the Senate leaders of the fight against Bork — primarily Chairman Biden (D-Del.) and Ted Kennedy (D-Mass.), Patrick Leahy (D-Vt.) and Howard Metzenbaum (D-Ohio) — together with their own expert staffs and specially assembled *ad hoc* "brain trusts," would steep themselves more deeply in the substance of Bork's record and its significance than in any matter within memory.

Some of the senators who opposed Bork did not believe that they needed help from the outside in understanding the issues; nor did they wish to be told what to do. Their pride was also at stake. They wanted to control the strategy, they wanted to win, and they wanted to harvest the appropriate credit for winning.

"From the very beginning," says Mark Gitenstein, Biden's chief counsel, "we recognized that, to the extent that members looked like they were tools of the Left (or the Right)—they would be hurt."

The standoffishness of some senators, and of Joe Biden in particular, was painfully reinforced by the embarrassment which Biden suffered following a closed meeting he held with six of the coalition's lobbyists on July 8. Biden was on the horns of several dilemmas. He was running for president, hence needed to conduct himself as "presidential," avoiding crass partisanship. As chairman of the Judiciary Committee, he had an institutional obligation to be fair to the nominee, yet politically he also needed to demonstrate to Democrats that he could lead— and what greater and more visible victory could he deliver than the defeat of Bork?

Biden was also dogged by his own volunteered statement, a year earlier, that if Reagan were to nominate Bork for the next vacancy, "I'd have to vote for him."

So the coalition's lobbyists were startled when Biden pledged to them that he would lead the fight against the nomination and resist Republican pressures to schedule hearings before the August recess. That pledge was leaked—by whom no one knows or has confessed—within hours. And the next day's headlines framed Biden as the willing puppet of the "special interests." One aide to another Democrat on the Judiciary Committee said Biden was "like a man stuck in a sleeping bag fighting bees." From that moment on, Biden sought to maintain the maximum possible distance from the coalition.

By contrast, Senator Kennedy welcomed the coalition's lobbyists openly, as trusted allies. But some of the activists were concerned that the coalition not be seen as a Kennedy apparatus —a narrow, partisan effort by the Senate's small liberal cluster.

Then why couldn't the coalition's lobbyists simply cool it? Why couldn't they let the process take its natural course, secure in the leadership of the Senate Judiciary Committee chairman, its ranking member, (Kennedy), and the handful of others who had quietly passed the word that when the time came, they would help lead the fight?

There are certainly those who believe that Kennedy and Biden and the other Senate leaders needed no help. But others—and we share this view—believe that the coalition and its lobbyists greatly helped their Senate leaders perform a series of important, and perhaps critical tasks:

- *"Freezing" the Senate*: making certain that there was no instant stampede of Senators rushing publicly to endorse Bork before his record could be examined in confirmation hearings (and before a national campaign could be mounted);
- *Countering the massive letter-writing and lobbying campaign* generated by Bork's supporters, by building and maintaining the momentum of the anti-Bork campaign;
- *Stimulating and organizing the massive outpouring* of opposition from sources which could not be dismissed as lobbyists, or the crude mob—thousands of citizen-scholars, lawyers, and law professors;
- *Serving as an intellectual resource on Bork's record* and its significance for those members of the Judiciary Committee and the Senate who did *not* have access to their own expert staffs;
- *Working in close collaboration with the staffs* of the nine anti-Bork or uncommitted Senate Judiciary Committee members, to make certain that the implications of Bork's views were fully developed at the hearings; and
- *Providing accurate and current intelligence* on the concerns and leanings of each member of the Senate—both to their Senate leaders, and to the organized opposition at large.

"Massage Distance" From the Senate

"Ralph Neas," says Carol Foreman, "has always been successful by knowing the ultimate inside approach to the Senate and was always sensitive to what might drive a senator away because he was constantly at massage distance from every staff person on the Hill."

Melody Miller, who was a staff assistant to Senator Kennedy when Neas first came to work in the Senate, recalls, "Within a week, he knew everybody. I had lunch with him just a few days after he got here, and he was calling the waitresses in the dining room, the policemen, the elevator operators — all by their first names."

To perform its sensitive lobbying tasks, the groups which made up the Block Bork Coalition had the great good fortune to be able to draw upon a richly interwoven network of lobbying relationships. In addition to Neas and Aron, the campaign drew upon a significant number of leaders and lobbyists who were, indeed, "massage distance" from large numbers of liberal and conservative, Democratic and Republican senators and their staff members. These ranged from Bob McGlotten of the AFL-CIO to Dick Warden of the United Automobile Workers; from Pat Wright of the Disability Rights Education and Defense Fund to Mario Moreno of the Mexican American Legal Defense and Educational Fund; from Bob McAlpine of the National Urban League to Faith Evans of the United Church of Christ. There were also those who had built especially strong relationships with Judiciary Committee members. Mort Halperin, Leslie Harris, and Jerry Berman of the ACLU's Washington office had each spent much of the Reagan years lobbying the Judiciary Committee — with surprising success — to stem the Reagan administration's encroachments on civil liberties. Berman, who happens also to be a neighbor of Biden's chief counsel Mark Gitenstein, notes with justifiable pride, "We've won a lot of legislative battles with the Judiciary Committee."

Elaine Jones and Eric Schnapper of the NAACP Legal Defense and Educational Fund had each served as a valued resource for Senator Biden and his staff in earlier nomination and legislative battles. "Over the years," says Jones, "we have built up a mutual respect and trust even where there is disagreement."

Of course, Leadership Conference lobbyists had long worked in close harmony with Senator Kennedy, and his highly regarded chief counsel, Carolyn Osolinik. And, though Biden sought to keep the coalition at a distance, there was no breakdown of communications with him. Gitenstein trusted, and worked in close collaboration with Neas and Verveer throughout the nomination process. Verveer and Seidman of People for the American Way were also trusted colleagues of Duke University law professor Walter Dellinger, a member of Biden's advisory group.

Some Judiciary Committee staffers enjoyed such an easy and confident relationship with Seidman and Verveer that they had come to think of PFAW as their own, on-tap research arm. "You get a call at one A.M. and it doesn't faze you," says Seidman.

Ralph Nader and Public Citizen President Joan Claybrook had worked as close allies with Senate Antitrust Subcommittee Chair Howard Metzenbaum and the subcommittee staff to challenge the Reagan administration's somnolent antitrust and consumer protection enforcement.

Though not a member of the Judiciary Committee, Alan Cranston of California, the Senate Democratic whip, was a forceful critic of the Bork nomination, and a key guide and counselor to the coalition. No one was more acutely tuned to the pulse of the Senate, or more generous with his insights. Time and again, the coalition's leaders would turn to Cranston for guidance as to the mood and drift of the Senate and for strategic counseling.

The sum of these personal networks meant the coalition had close and comfortable working relationships with the critical nine of the fourteen Judiciary Committee members.

Nor were the important network relationships limited to Judiciary Committee members. Common Cause's Fred Wertheimer and Ann McBride enjoyed a close working relationship with Senator Bennett Johnston, the Louisiana moderate who organized a series of informal discussions which led all but two of the Senate's southern Democrats to oppose Bork. Simultaneously, Neas collaborated with Michigan Congressman John Conyers and other members of the Congressional Black Caucus to meet with Johnston and other key southern Senators.

Elaine Jones, of the NAACP Legal Defense and Educational Fund, like other veteran lobbyists, had built close ties with both Democrats and moderate Republicans. The ties *stay* close because she is not inclined to talk about them. But this anecdote which escaped her gives a glimpse of her unrepressed spirit.

. Shortly after Bork had completed his testimony before the Senate Judiciary Committee, Jones found herself bound for her native Alabama on a plane also bearing a committee member, Senator Heflin. As a litigator, Jones had practiced before former state judge Heflin when he served on the Alabama Supreme Court, and she knew him well. She seized the moment to chat with Heflin, asking him what he thought of Bork's testimony that he was drawn to service on the Court because it would be "an intellectual feast." She knew that Heflin had missed that patch of testimony, and urged him to read the transcript. Then she quipped, "I wonder *who* the meal is going to be!"

Over the past decade, Oregon Republican Senator Bob Packwood had emerged as the Senate's leading advocate of women's reproductive rights, forging strong ties with women's groups in the process. So it was not surprising that Kate Michelman of NARAL, Jo Blum of Planned Parenthood, and Estelle Rogers of the Federation of Women Lawyers were each able, separately, to speak with him directly in the first days of the campaign. Nor was it surprising that Marcia Greenberger's formulations of the legal arguments against Bork's positions were welcomed by Packwood.

These "inside" networks served the campaign's fundamental needs. Most important, they enabled the Block Bork Coalition to share in the development phase of the common strategy, and to work closely and continuously with the senators who would lead the fight within the Senate to deny Bork confirmation. As veteran public interest advocates know, there is no more sacred lobbying maxim than "Follow your leaders in the Congress." But before those congressional leaders have set their courses, the lobbyists' role is to help the leaders figure out where and how they want to lead.

In early August, Senator Kennedy met with about twenty of the coalition leaders to share ideas on strategy for the coming weeks. Kennedy was optimistic. Much had been accomplished: public opinion in opposition to Bork was jelling, and the coalition was marshalling its outside forces. But, he cautioned, the coalition must be careful not to get signals crossed with Senate allies. He urged them to hold weekly meetings with the key Judiciary Committee staff members. He was right, but his admonition wasn't necessary.

From the moment Justice Powell resigned, the anti-Bork coalition lobbyists were doing just that. In daily, face-to-face office visits and phone calls, the coalition's insiders were in constant contact with the Senate staff members—and, not infrequently, with their Senate leaders, like Cranston. They worked in tandem with their supporters in the Senate—trading papers, swapping political intelligence, unearthing and analyzing Bork's record, plotting themes and strategy, and helping to plan the structure and content of the hearings—in a word, networking.

Freezing the Senate

As soon as Bork was nominated, the president and his leaders in the Senate declared Bork the perfect nominee, and a shoo-in for confirmation, calling upon Biden to eschew partisanship, to schedule hearings immediately and to begin the process for what they thought would certainly be routine hearings and confirmation. After all, as we have seen, the Standing Committee on Federal Judiciary of the American Bar Association had given

Bork its highest possible rating, "exceptionally well qualified," in unanimously recommending his earlier confirmation five years earlier to the nation's second highest court, the U.S. Court of Appeals. And the Senate had responded by unanimously confirming him.

Lurking in the minds of coalition leaders were the painful memories of the previous summer's failed effort to stop the confirmation of William Rehnquist as chief justice. Republican Senator Strom Thurmond, then Judiciary Committee chairman under a Republican majority, had confidently predicted swift confirmation of Bork — like Rehnquist, a nominee who had already once passed through the Senate's sifting process. Most worrisome, they recalled that senators from both parties had rushed to proclaim their intention to vote for Rehnquist. (It is, at least, curious that the unreflective announcement of *support* for a nominee before hearings is never considered premature, while announcement of *opposition* is treated as rash and unfair. So, while senators Biden and Kennedy were excoriated for their unseemly early opposition to Bork, the instantaneous endorsements of Bork by senators Orrin Hatch [R-Utah] and Alan Simpson [R-Wyo.] were treated as business as usual.)

The lobbyists knew well that the Senate does not welcome Supreme Court nomination battles, whatever its constitutional mandate. Such battles are bruising and time consuming; they cleave the Senate ideologically; they may be politically risky. They are unpleasant because, unlike legislative conflicts, they require the rejection of a human being, not an abstract concept. And they require standing up to the president — in this case a still popular president. So if senators are led to believe that a nomination will be popular — or, in any event, unbeatable — they are inclined to stampede, often issuing public endorsements without awaiting the outcome of the hearings.

As we shall see in the next chapter, Senator Kennedy and the Block Bork Coalition's leaders quickly mounted the rhetorical ramparts to serve public notice on the nation — and the

Senate—that there was to be a bloody battle, and that no member could assume that reflexive acquiescence to the president's choice would be without political pain.

What the coalition decided, very early, was to mount an initial lobbying campaign to "freeze the Senate"—to urge senators *not to take any position* on Bork until the hearings were complete. Simultaneously, the coalition's lobbyists were supporting Biden's determination to postpone the start of the hearings until September—giving the committee, and the anti-Bork campaign, time to fully prepare. Time was needed during the August recess to disseminate the "Book of Bork," to provide the opportunity for the senators' constituents to argue the case against Bork, and to impress upon senators the depth of their constituents' feelings of opposition to the nomination.

Ironically, some local activists were initially appalled by this strategy. In states such as Georgia and Florida, the coalition leaders sensed their senator or senators were close to announcing opposition, and sought the security of an early commitment. And they knew from past campaigns that elusive, intangible "momentum" can be generated by an opening series of announcements of opposition. But the freeze strategy was finely attuned to the sensitivities of the Senate, as well as to the needs of the anti-Bork campaign. It served several purposes simultaneously:

- *It supported the concept of a coequal constitutional role for the Senate*—not a "rubber stamp"—by treating the confirmation process as solemn and deliberative.
- *It meshed well with the parallel effort to persuade the senators* to pursue an expansive interpretation of their "advise and consent" authority, to broaden the scope of their inquiry into Judge Bork's judicial philosophy.
- *It made Bork's writings and judicial philosophy*—which would have to be examined at the hearings—rather than

Bork's credentials — which were a matter of record — the central focus of inquiry.

- *It focused attention* on the hearings and the Senate deliberation process, not on the lobbying.
- *By not asking those members* who had stood silent in 1982 as Bork was unanimously confirmed for the Court of Appeals to declare their immediate opposition, it gave them the opportunity to demonstrate care and deliberation — and to be converted, not by pressure, but by thorough review of the Bork record and the confirmation hearings.
- *Without the freeze,* it was predictable that a small group of the most liberal senators, in addition to Kennedy and Biden, would announce early opposition to Bork. By holding back their announcements, too, the freeze forestalled media characterization of the opposition as confined to left-leaning Senate liberals.
- *It served to open up dialogue* with those centrist senators who were drawn to the campaign's (flattering) emphasis on the importance of the Senate's constitutional role, but who were by no means ready to vote "no" on Bork.
- *As a limited initial goal, it also accommodated those* groups which had not yet made a formal determination to oppose Bork. Even without formally opposing confirmation, the AFL-CIO, Common Cause, and the ACLU could oppose any rush to judgment.

While the leaders of the Block Bork Coalition were taking their case for a "freeze" to the media, the lobbyists were barraging each senator's office with learned memoranda on the constitutional right and responsibility of the Senate to take a hard, independent look at each Supreme Court nominee, and on the appropriateness of inquiring into the nominee's legal philosophy.

The scholarly foundations for that position had been laid by — among others — Harvard Law School Professor Laurence

Tribe in his 1985 book, *God Save This Honorable Court*. Drawing upon that work, and the studies of Duke University's Walter Dellinger and American University's Herman Schwartz, People for the American Way delivered a memorandum on the Senate's "advise and consent" responsibilities to each senator's office within twenty-four hours of the announcement of the nomination. And by the July 4th weekend, PFAW was running newspaper ads exhorting the Senate to rise to its responsibilities. The Alliance for Justice also sent an "edit memo" on the Senate's role to editorial boards across the country.

Herman Schwartz moved with dispatch to place an op-ed column in the *New York Times* on July 3, setting forth history and precedent on the Senate's role: "If a Senator thinks a nominee will undermine his concept of the Constitution," wrote Schwartz, "the Senator has exactly the same right and duty as the President to protect that conception."

At the same time, the lobbyists called in the heavy artillery. AFL-CIO president Lane Kirkland issued a statement on July 1, insisting, "It is critical that the senators not commit themselves in advance to support or to oppose this nomination." The Washington offices of national organizations called upon their state affiliates or members to unleash phone calls and letters to their senators urging them to withhold judgment on Bork. Planned Parenthood Federation of America, which had not yet officially decided to oppose Bork, nonetheless urged its members through its national legislative hotline to seize the opportunity of their senators' home visits during the July 4th recess and request that they not take a position until more was known and understood about Bork's record. Similar alerts were transmitted by the 1.8-million-member National Education Association. And the lobbyists, singly and in groups, sought meetings with senators and staffs to deliver the same messages.

The strategy worked. The only two Democrats who voted for Bork (David Boren of Oklahoma and Ernest Hollings of South Carolina) withheld their announcements of support until after the Judiciary Committee vote. Four Democrats (Biden, Kennedy, Cranston and Quentin Burdick of North Dakota) and one Republican (Packwood) came out in opposition to Bork before the hearings. Of the seventy-eight potential Senate "no" votes, only three (John Danforth of Montana, Nancy Kassebaum of Kansas, and Dan Quayle of Indiana) announced their support before the hearings.

Winnability

Another critical task was convincing the media that the fight against Bork was "winnable," hence, serious. Neas summarizes the case made to the inherently skeptical journalists:

> I said, off the record, that it should not be dismissed out of hand; we could win. We started out with that base of thirty returning senators who had voted against Rehnquist (three retired or were defeated). Then you had the seventeen senators who had voted against Manion [an ideologically extreme and judicially inexperienced Indiana lawyer nominated by Reagan to the Seventh Circuit Court of Appeals]. Then, of course the freshman class [the eleven new Democrats elected in 1986], and then the moderate Republicans. The Senate not only had more Democrats and more *liberal* Democrats, but the Democrats were in control of the Senate. That's in contrast to [its makeup at the time of the confirmations of] Rehnquist and Scalia.

One early threat to the credibility of the "winnability" message was loose talk among Bork opponents about possibly waging a Senate filibuster. The filibuster is a potent parliamentary weapon. It would take fifty-one votes to defeat the Bork nomination outright. But if even a handful of senators vowed to exercise their Senate prerogative to speak at interminable length, it would require the votes of sixty of their colleagues to shut off debate and allow a vote on the nomination. Just so was Justice

Fortas's appointment to be chief justice frustrated by Senate conservatives, who led a filibuster and ultimately forced President Johnson to withdraw Fortas's name from consideration.

In the early weeks of the campaign, when few were confident that a majority of the Senate could be persuaded to oppose Bork, a handful of anti-Bork coalition lobbyists began talking openly about the possibility of a filibuster.

But other strategists were disturbed by such talk. "From day one, we didn't want any talk about a filibuster. We almost strangled them," says Bill Taylor, whose keen knowledge and instincts of the legislative process are well recognized. Such talk was an admission of weakness. It directly undermined the "winnability" theme. Moreover, a filibuster strategy clashed with the coalition's professed desire to seek a broad constitutional debate on the merits of Bork's candidacy, to be resolved by the Senate exercising its constitutional mandate, not by exploiting quirks in Senate procedures.

The leaders' discomfort with filibuster talk was reinforced by early intelligence gathered by the lobbyists that several supportive senators were not comfortable with a filibuster strategy. Claiborne Pell (D-R.I.) and Lloyd Bentsen (D-Tex.), for example, opposed the use of the filibuster on any nomination.

"Once you start talking about filibuster in a very public way, you have demonstrated that you can't win on the merits," says Verveer. "Cranston told us up front, 'There's no support for a filibuster . . . I think you can win this one on the merits.' "

David Cohen of the Advocacy Institute warned that a filibuster strategy would offer the White House strategists an opening wedge to those senators who were looking for a way to satisfy both sides: "The White House will take a no vote [on confirmation] from some, if they can get a pro-cloture vote [to end the filibuster]," he wrote in a memo to the coalition's leaders.

The coalition leaders debated their public posture on the filibuster issue. "My view," says the ACLU's Halperin, "was that we might need it, and to go out of our way to say we weren't going to do it was a mistake."

But the leaders contrived to have it both ways. They agreed that Senator Cranston was right to publicly disavow any intention or need to pursue a filibuster. On July 23, Cranston announced with confidence that "those who expect to wind up opposing Bork don't favor that route . . . they much favor . . . to have an up or down vote and the will of the Senate displayed."

But the coalition kept its powder dry. Neas and Verveer were convinced that if the campaign succeeded in raising strong doubts about Bork's impact on constitutional rights, but fell short of an opposing majority by a handful of votes, a number of senators who cared deeply about such rights would still feel compelled to filibuster.

Just in case, they began laying the groundwork for such a contingency plan. Verveer asked several of the legal strategists "quietly to come up with the best lines we could" to support the appropriateness of a filibuster. Fred Wertheimer of Common Cause had his staff prepare a study on the use of filibusters in past nomination struggles. Independent of the coalition, Joseph Califano, who had led the Johnson White House effort to secure the Fortas' confirmation, wrote an op-ed piece in the *Washington Post* in mid-August laying out a strong, historic case for the filibuster. He documented the Republicans' past enthusiastic embrace of the filibuster to bar Justice Fortas's confirmation as chief justice on political and ideological grounds, though the Senate Judiciary Committee had voted 11–6 to recommend confirmation by the Senate. But for the time being, the goal was a firm majority vote against confirmation. In the slippery world of perceptions and expectations, Senator Cranston wielded a potent leadership weapon: his estimated vote counts. Cranston enjoys an earned reputation for accurately predicting the outcome of closely contested Senate votes. So when he announced, in the third week of July, that the vote was dead even, the journalists paid heed. Cranston reported:

> By my count—and I've talked to every Democrat with two excep-
> tions, and I know those two are thinking about this matter, and I've
> talked to a few of the Republicans whom I thought most likely to be
> uncertain or perhaps opposed to Bork; most Republicans will be for
> him—and if the vote came today, I believe it would be forty-five who
> would vote against Bork, forty-five who would vote for him, and
> that leaves ten who are unpredictable and quite uncertain.

The coalition's leaders knew that Cranston's tally was on the optimistic side of the possibilities. Their own counts were not quite so encouraging. But Cranston's numbers certainly gave powerful impetus to the perception of winnability. Skeptical journalists, says Taylor, would simply shrug and say, "Well, we don't know, but the guy's an ace vote counter."

The success of the "freeze" and of the "winnability" message changed the perception that confirmation was assured. As early as July 10, presidential pollster Richard Wirthlin conceded that Senate confirmation of Bork was in some doubt. Five days later Senate Minority Leader Robert Dole (R-Kan.) suggested that the odds for Bork were no better than fifty-fifty. Both the public and the Senate now knew, says Neas, that this "was not a quixotic effort [and] that if we did our work we could win."

The Coalition's Central Intelligence Agency

The Lobbying Task Force was co-chaired by Jo Blum of Planned Parenthood, Mario Moreno of the Mexican American Legal Defense and Educational Fund, and Joel Packer of the National Education Association. Each was an experienced vote counter and a highly professional lobbyist. The groups who were part of the Block Bork Coalition freed their top lobbyists for this assignment.

They faced formidable lobbying resources enlisted in Bork's support, led by White House Chief of Staff Howard Baker, the former Senate Republican majority leader, a man well liked and respected by most of his former colleagues, and known as a non-ideological moderate.

When in trouble, the White House also called in Tom Korologos. Korologos, now a prosperous lobbyist, had the unenviable task of representing President Nixon to the Senate up to the darkest days of Watergate. Candid and cheery, he would disarm even the most righteous Nixon critic with a self-deprecating shrug. "Republicans," he would confess with a disarming smile, "obviously aren't fit to govern." He had worked on the campaign to secure confirmation for William Bradford Reynolds as associate attorney general, which had failed. Korologos was known for his ability to learn from defeat.

The Justice Department's forces were led by John Bolton, the assistant attorney general who had directed the department's lobbying effort to win approval of the Rehnquist and Scalia nominations the previous summer.

For their part, the coalition's lobbyists went out in force "on the Hill," and their collective networking provided the essential intelligence — where each senator stood and why — which is the bedrock of lobbying. The lobbyists learned things not only from the staffs and members of uncommitted senators, but also through the exchange of intelligence on the uncommitted with supportive senators and their staffs. And information flowed in from the lobbyists' occupational "hanging out" in the Senate lobbies and corridors. They picked up information from exchanges with journalists, and from casual conversations with senators and staff members near the Senate cloakrooms — and even with their spouses at social gatherings.

Indeed, so much intelligence came rolling in on how individual senators were feeling and questing and moving from so many roving antennae and sources that the Lobbying Task Force had difficulty managing all the data. Instead they made an effort to concentrate the intelligence-gathering and lobbying in teams of lobbyists with special relationships or insights on particular senators. "We split up the Senate," says Jo Blum. "We put together team meetings." There were teams covering each of the four Judiciary Committee members (DeConcini of Arizona, Heflin of Alabama, Byrd of West Virginia, and Republican Specter of Pennsylvania) who remained frozen and uncommitted, and the still-frozen senators from seventeen other states, especially border and southern state Democrats and moderate Republicans.

The effort certainly helped in processing information, and may have somewhat reduced the normal chaos of lobbying. Still, the division of labor was by no means orderly, and many of the lobbyists continued to lobby as they always did — whenever and with whomever the opportunity arose.

Mort Halperin, who is generally skeptical about claims of coalition effectiveness, nonetheless has words of praise for the intelligence-gathering capacity and sharing of the Block Bork Coalition's Lobbying Task Force:

> There were many more people there and many more serious lobbyists. The union people were out in full force, while usually in the Leadership Conference you have one union. That was not true, here. The lobbying meetings were very serious meetings . . . They were not the canned decision meetings. They were meetings in which we went down the lists.
>
> Someone would ask, "Bentsen?" And somebody would say, "the Texas people say he's fine. He just met with these people, and they said 'X.' " So there was a sharing of information, and I could come out of that meeting and say, "Bennett Johnston looks fine; we can put less energy into that." So those meetings were useful.

Peddling the "Book of Bork"

Lobbyists always use information as an instrument for access to the Hill, and the coalition's research and analyses of the "Book of Bork" proved a potent entree even to senators leaning in Bork's favor. Several coalition organizations parlayed the preparation of their expert papers into Senate staff briefings. Just prior to the August recess, People for the American Way arranged for Professor Paul Gewirtz to come down from Yale, to present his scholarly but urgent argument for the Senate's coequal role in Supreme Court nominations. By framing the session neutrally, as a seminar on the nominations process, PFAW was able to attract several staff members representing undecided senators. That briefing drew twenty-three staff members, including several senior members.

A few days before the hearings, the ACLU scheduled two early evening briefing sessions on Bork's civil liberties record, with sandwiches an added draw for busy, and hungry, staffers. The ACLU's Halperin describes their approach to the Senate staff members:

> We gave everybody a copy of our briefing book. What we told them was, "We think if you read, and if your boss reads what Bork said, not twenty years ago, but last month and two months before, or three months before that, you'll be against him."
>
> We gave every Senate office that we thought we had a chance with—about eighty Senate offices—copies of that book. We had about thirty-five of them at these two briefings, and we had a member of our staff in touch with every office that we thought we had a chance with, basically saying, "We're across the street. We have everything that Bork's written. We have read it all, and we're here just to tell you that if you find out what Bork said, whether it's about women, blacks, [the] First Amendment, separation of church and state, or any other issue that turns your office on, just tell us, and we'll give you more of what he said."

"People that you might not have thought would show up were there because they had a packet of material that they could at least take home and look at," suggests Jerry Berman.

In the words of one Republican Senate staff member,

Part of what a good lobbyist does is give you information when you ask for it, and they know the senator probably better than I do. They understand how he goes about making up his mind for one thing, and they understand that their best way of lobbying him is to provide the substantive legal answers to his questions which are right, number one, and which will lead him to the way they want him to go. They will select those well tailored to the interests and inclinations of each senator, drawing upon authorities that the senator would be likely to respect.

The anti-Bork coalition's lobbyists could do just that. There were enough reports, memos, and issue briefs in their possession to permit them to tailor their responses to the particular needs and inclinations of each senator, and even to those authorities likely to carry weight with that senator. Each time they were able to respond knowledgeably, the coalition's credibility as a reliable source of information about Bork was strengthened.

Jeff Robinson, Judiciary Committee aide to Senator Specter, recalls: "The most helpful thing the coalition did, from my perspective, was to make themselves available so if we had a question like 'what did Bork say about that?' they retrieved it. That was incredibly useful, the most useful thing they could have possibly done."

Structuring the Hearings

The hearings—the week Bork appeared before the Senate Judiciary Committee and the following week, when his critics and supporters examined his record and judicial philosophy—were the glorious epicenter of the struggle. And to the committee leaders—especially Chairman Biden, Senators Kennedy, Leahy, Metzenbaum, and their staffs—is due the credit for the exquisite care with which the hearings were structured: the fairness with which they were conducted, and the marshalling of intellectual force and moral probity in the opposition witnesses. With their committee colleagues, particularly Republican Senator Specter, these senators carried out an informed and probing examination of Judge Bork and the witnesses who followed him. In the process, they provided the nation with an elevated discourse on the Constitution, and on its meaning in each citizen's life, that was worthy of the drafters of the Constitution.

It was Biden and his chief counsel, Mark Gitenstein, who early on resolved to amass as imposing a list of witnesses as could be persuaded to step forward to oppose the nomination. They would be witnesses of credentialed scholarship, most nonpartisan, driven to step forward by their apprehension for the Constitution, rather than by personal vindictiveness. They would be witnesses who would speak with great force to the moderate center of the committee: Byrd, DeConcini, Heflin, Specter.

The Judiciary Committee staff lawyers—experienced, able, knowledgeable in the law, and deeply committed to the preservation of the Court's role—largely shaped the lineup of the hearings. Eddie Correia, Antitrust Subcommittee chief counsel to Senator Metzenbaum, is right when he insists: "There is a very overstated assumption of how much the coalition was involved. They had nothing to do with the fundamental decisions of how the committee operated. The Republicans would like to say that the coalition was in the back room telling us what to do; that's totally untrue."

During the August recess many of the committee members—and all their staffs—immersed themselves deeply in the Bork record, the original Bork writings as well as the volumes of study that flowed in every other day. The senators were prepared with questions for Bork and the other witnesses, which is common. They were also prepared to follow up each line of questioning with informed probes, which is *not* common.

The committee *was* in charge; but the coalition lobbyists helped. And the hearings were stronger than they might have been because the committee staffers drew upon their established networks of coalition lobbyists and experts. The lobbyists helped by sharing suggestions and offering insights on potential witnesses. They helped to persuade those witnesses who opposed Bork but shrank back from public confrontation. They helped prepare and test the witnesses before their appearances. And they helped analyze the testimony as it evolved.

Estelle Rogers of the Federation of Women Lawyers captures the nature of the relationship:

> One of the good things that happened all through the Bork campaign was that people learned to rely on each other in ways that were very efficient and smart. There were people who had contacts in a certain world that were used. The people who work on an ongoing basis with the Senate Judiciary Committee, for example, were called upon very regularly to help construct the hearings and to think about who the most effective people were in legal academia or the stars in the civil rights community, because some of us [in the coalition] have more significant ongoing contacts.

The selection of the proper witnesses is a complex task. It was not enough, for example, to find a willing witness from Phoenix, in order to appeal to Arizona's Senator DeConcini. The Senate Judiciary Committee Republicans tried, for example, by offering up as a witness Gary Born, identified as an adjunct professor of law at the University of Arizona, now a practicing attorney with Lloyd Cutler's law firm in Washington, D.C. As DeConcini pursued his questioning, it developed that Born had lived and taught in Arizona for just one year.

"This is the third time during these hearings that Arizona has been tossed up at me . . . I just don't like it, and I object to your being here as an adjunct professor, University of Arizona," DeConcini noted, with unconcealed irritation.

But John Frank was different. He was not, now or ever, a Washington lawyer, but a pillar of the Arizona Bar who heads one of Phoenix's leading law firms, as well as a teacher and the author of many books on constitutional law. As a moderate constitutional scholar—who had actually testified, at the invitation of the Judiciary Committee, in *support* of Judge Haynsworth—Frank's authority—and his Arizona roots—were unimpeachable. Senator DeConcini knew Frank well and regarded him highly. Frank had also taught constitutional law at Yale to Pennsylvania's Arlen Specter. The coalition lobbyists had suggested that Frank be among the scholars invited to testify. DeConcini treated Frank's testimony with great respect.

Sometimes, there was vigorous give-and-take between the staff and the lobbyists over the composition of such expert panels as that on equal protection. Committee staff director Diana Huffman remembers how one coalition lobbyist guided the staff to substitute a lawyer with more conservative credentials for one prospective witness whose partisanship might have put off the undecided senators.

The lobbyists were also able to take soundings with the staffs of uncommitted senators on the potential impact of proposed witnesses. Jeff Robinson, Senator Specter's Court specialist, remembers:

> Through the coalition or through the committee staff, people would ask me informally what I thought about a particular witness. When people were talking about getting [William] Coleman, I said "excellent, Senator Specter respects him. Yes, he'll make a wonderful witness as long as he talks substance"—which is what he did.

Persuading those who had close ties to the legal or Republican establishment—or who feared retribution from right-wing Senators, or even judges—to testify was not always easy, despite their strong feelings about Bork. The first response was, more often then not, "maybe," or "I'll have to think about it." Verveer recalls, "It was rare that a single straightforward call was all it took." It might also require a formal request from the chairman or other committee member, so that the witness would appear less an eager volunteer. When the response was "maybe" or "I'll have to think about it," more discreet talk ensued.

Former President Gerald Ford could not venture beyond his prepared testimony in support of Bork to respond to substantive questions raised by committee members. When DeConcini asked Ford if he had read *any* of Bork's law review articles, he answered that while he had read "synopses of some of those articles, . . . I have not read individual law review articles."

By contrast, coalition lawyers actually staged mock hearings, acting the roles of an insinuating Orrin Hatch and an apoplectically indignant Alan Simpson. How extensive was this "prepping" of witnesses? The answers are shrouded in the reluctance of the coalition lawyers to detract in any way from the performance and independence of the witnesses.

It is noteworthy not only that the opposition witnesses were eloquent, but that none of them slipped, or was unprepared.

6

FRAMING THE DEBATE:
Seizing the Symbols

> From the beginning, the administration was
> trying to make this a partisan battle and a
> liberal/conservative battle. They wanted it in
> its most political terms. Our approach was
> to say, "No, no, no! By anyone's
> standards—liberal, moderate, conserva-
> tive—this fellow is *outside*."
>
> FRED WERTHEIMER, Common Cause

The leaders of the coalition were committed to making the "Book of Bork"—Bork's academic and judicial record, his legal philosophy—frame the debate over his confirmation. The White House had other plans.

Alexander Cockburn, the *Nation* magazine's resident scourge of hypocrisy, captured the essence of the Reagan White House's famed communications genius (with a little help from a compliant press):

In stage one, the President announces that white is black. The media is skeptical, but dutifully reports the claim. In stage two, the stage of reluctant admission, the media responds to the White House's vigorous repetition of the claim by reporting black can be gray and gray can be white.

In stage three, willing submission, the press reports that the President appears to have prevailed on the issue, and cites polls showing that 53 per cent of Americans now believe that white is black, an increase from the 37 per cent who held that view last month. Finally there comes the stage of complete prostration, when criticism of the idea that white is somehow not black is relegated first to the op-ed

117

pages, then to the letters columns, and finally is eliminated from the public dialogue altogether.

Herman Schwartz, in *Packing the Court*, quotes an anonymous White House aide's reference to Bork as a "right-wing zealot." And he cites those voices among Bork enthusiasts who greeted the nomination with un–self-conscious fervor. The Heritage Foundation's Bruce Fein promised that Bork on "the fighting issues — abortion, affirmative action, free speech, church-state — will make a difference." Christian Voice, an evangelical organization, called Bork's nomination "our last chance . . . to ensure future decades will bring morality, godliness and justice back into focus."

But, for the benefit of the White House press corps, the president did not openly label Bork as the Republican guided missile he had promised, in the 1980, 1982, 1984, and 1986 elections, to blast away the constitutional detritus of the last three decades. Instead, he canonized Bork only as a "brilliant legal scholar, a fair-minded jurist [and] a respected teacher," dedicated to "judicial restraint."

A chorus of Bork proponents available to the media anointed him "a deep thinker," "exceptionally well-qualified," "intellectually powerful," "an impressive legal mind," "a premier constitutional authority." Anticipating a ground of attack, they also sought to portray an avuncular Bork: "open-minded," "seasoned," "tested by a full career," and "appealing," "genial," "a ready wit."

In a report published on July 20, the *Legal Times* of Washington concluded:

> The selling of Robert Bork has begun, and in an unusual display of accessibility, Bork himself has been out front, trying to obliterate claims that he is a dogmatic conservative.
>
> Launching a public relations offensive with a series of newspaper interviews, including one with *Legal Times* last week, the U.S. Su-

preme Court nominee has tried to depict himself as an open-minded, flexible student of the law who neither pre-judges cases or issues nor possesses a set ideology.

Bork had conducted a not too subtle campaign for nomination to the Court, appealing in speeches to conservative audiences for the conservative vision of the Constitution embodied in his own conservative jurisprudence. But, "I don't consider myself a conservative," Bork told the *Legal Times* during a forty-five-minute interview.

This assertion troubled more than liberals. Bruce Fein of the Heritage Foundation was deeply troubled by Bork's reincarnation. "He is trying to fold his views into the mainstream," Fein told the *Boston Globe*'s Ethan Bronner. "He is trying to say, 'In some respects, yeah, I am a Justice Powell clone,' where he is not."

Melanne Verveer of People for the American Way recalls:

> Bork campaigned in the media like no other Supreme Court nominee. He promoted himself in interviews with *USA Today*, and other newspapers. He was saying something like, "I can't talk about my nomination, but look, I'm Mr. Nice Guy, I'm a moderate, I'm not an extremist." We knew we had to counteract his PR campaign by discussing his record.

Bork's media-wooing was sometimes subtle. It was an intermediary who suggested to the *New York Times* editorial board that Bork might be available. He evidently considered it unseemly to appear to beseech the *Times*' for support directly by presenting himself at their editorial offices. So a discreet luncheon was arranged with the *Times*'s editors at a restaurant within the shadow of the *Times* building.

The White House and Justice Department media spokespersons were also seeking to frame the appropriate role of the Senate as narrow and limited. They insisted that the Senate was limited to assuring itself of the competence of the nominee —

legal training, judicial experience, intellectual capacity — and
the absence of scandal. Any attempt to inquire into Bork's judicial philosophy or the potential impact of his philosophy on the
law was out of bounds. The New York Times's Tom Wicker summarized the White House position as requiring Senate confirmation of any nominee "with a law degree and no jail record."

But the Justice Department well knew, if the president didn't,
that the Senate frequently asserted its constitutional role in the
nomination process to reject nominees precisely on ideological
grounds. As the ACLU reported, past nominees had been rejected solely for their views on "federal supremacy, civil service, slavery, immigrants, unions, business, and civil rights."
At the close of the Constitutional Convention in 1787, framer
Governor Morris paraphrased the constitutional provisions on
judicial appointments as leaving to the Senate the power "to ap-
point judges nominated to them by the President."

In challenging Lyndon Johnson's nomination of liberal Justice
Abe Fortas as chief justice, the Judiciary Committee's ranking
Republican member, Strom Thurmond, passionately maintained that the Senate had the responsibility of probing into "his
philosophy," along with his other qualifications.

With the election campaigns of 1986 tucked away and forgotten, President Reagan now pleaded, in a radio commentary to
the nation, that "to maintain the independence of the judiciary,
I hope we can keep politics out of the confirmation process."

But it was Reagan who had injected politics into the Court as
recently as the 1986 congressional election campaign, when he
pleaded with the electorate for Republican senators who would
help him transform the Court. In that campaign, he complained
to the Los Angeles Times that "Congress has been unwilling to
deal with these problems that we brought up." And he speci-
fically endorsed the campaign goal articulated by one of his senior aides, Patrick Buchanan: "If you got two appointments to the
Supreme Court it could make more difference on your social
agenda in achieving it than twenty years in Congress."

That Bork now resisted the label "conservative" did not make him any less a conservative. That the White House was attempting to achieve its highly *political* goals through the media by evoking the *apolitical* imagery of the judicial appointment process did not make the nomination any less political.

The Bork nomination was a political fight from the beginning; it was initiated by the president as a political fight, it was hailed by his right-wing cohorts as a political fight, and it was responded to by the Block Bork Coalition as a political fight.

"[W]e have never had a political 'candidate' marketed . . . for the nation's highest court before," wrote Renata Adler—a self-labeled Republican—in the *New Republic* shortly before the hearings. "It is astonishing how far the 'defactualization' has already gone."

Stoning the Opposition

Just in case any senator might be inclined to oppose Bork, the White House and its allies sought to delegitimize the opposition to Bork as "partisan," "ideological," and "captive of special interests." Bork himself dismissed his opponents as "ultraliberals, radicals, and leftists." Yet those who testified against Bork spanned a broad spectrum of political thought, from liberal and progressive to moderate and conservative. His record deeply troubled great numbers of otherwise apolitical lawyers and legal scholars.

Reagan defined the "choices" faced by the country with what *Washington Post* columnist Colman McCarthy called "spray-paint simplicities":

> Three choices are what this battle is all about: The choice between liberal judges who make up the law or sound judges who interpret the law. The choice between liberal judges whose decisions protect criminals or firm judges whose decisions protect the victims. The

choice between liberal judges selected by the liberal special interests or distinguished judges selected to serve the people.

The Reagan White House was doing what it did best: media
advocacy. It clasped to Bork's bosom all the affirmative symbols
and themes it could muster, however falsely, while dumping on
its opponents a grab bag of negative, wounding, and false
symbols.

Out of the Gate

The initial White House portrayal of Bork, and its characterization of the confirmation process, posed a series of strategic problems for the Block Bork campaign. The first danger was that the
media would accept the administration's characterizations, and
that this would fix the terms of the debate. As Jack Nelson of the
Los Angeles Times commented to Mark Hertzgaard, author of
On Bended Knee: The Press and the Reagan Presidency, "They
[the White House communications staff] realize that first impressions are lasting impressions, that's part of their public relations genius."

There is an old story about a farmer who had come to his wit's
end with his mythically stubborn mule. In desperation, he had
summoned the local mule tamer, who calmly proceeded to beat
the mule within an inch of its life with a baseball bat. To the
farmer's anguished protests, the mule tamer replied, tersely,
"The first thing you do with a mule is, you got to get his attention."

Ann Lewis, the progressive political consultant and "mule
tamer" who counseled the coalition, frames the challenge posed
by the White House media initiative:

> This had to be fought beyond the walls of the Senate. If this were
> carried out as an internal Senate battle, we would have deep and

thoughtful discussions about the Constitution, and then we would lose. The way to achieve this was to move it beyond the Senate, to nationalize the debate.

If the Bork nomination was to be challenged in the Senate, it would first have to be challenged in the media *to get the Senate's attention*. And if it were to be challenged in the media, it would not be sufficient merely to supply the press with the massive "Book of Bork." The coalition would have to wrest the symbols of the debate from Bork's White House handlers with a media advocacy strategy as sophisticated and compelling as that of the White House.

But first, those who would oppose Bork understood that they had forcefully to gain their own constituents' attention, so that aroused constituencies could arrest any tendency on the part of the Senate to stampede toward confirmation.

As we have seen, the Block Bork Coalition's lobbyists knew they had to "freeze" the Senate—to hold back members who would normally be inclined to fall into line with the president and commit themselves publicly and irrevocably to Bork. Yet the administration's rhetoric was artfully calibrated to lull moderate senators into believing that no serious challenge to Bork would be made.

So the rhetoric of the groups who would oppose Bork, those first days, was not muted. The *National Journal's* Kirk Victor described Bork opponents as zooming "into scathing, rhetorical overdrive."

The president was not prepared to draw out the concrete consequences of a Supreme Court in which the balance was tipped by Bork. But Senator Kennedy was: Within an hour of Reagan's announcement of the nomination, he was on the Senate floor, warning of "a land in which women would be forced into back alley abortions, blacks would sit at segregated lunch counters, rogue police could break down citizens' doors in midnight raids . . . "

"The statement had to be stark and direct," Kennedy told Ethan Bronner of the *Boston Globe*, "so as to sound the alarm and hold people in their places until we could get material together."

As David Cohen of the Advocacy Institute observed: "We learned from the Rehnquist fight that if you're going to oppose somebody you've got to be clear and definitive in your opposition. You've got to get the nomination perceived as an immediate, salient, *political* question." Cohen cites Kennedy's Senate floor speech as the essential "Paul Revere's ride" of the anti-Bork campaign.

Uppermost in the minds of those crafting the initial response to the news of the nomination was the need to convey to both their constituents and the members of the Senate that the stakes in this Supreme Court nomination dwarfed those in all previous Reagan nominations, and that this nomination would therefore be resisted with all the resources that the coalition could command. Why was this nomination so uniquely threatening? Because the confirmation of Bork would destroy the balance between moderate and conservative judges.

Even before the White House announced that Bork would be the nominee, Kate Michelman of NARAL vowed "to wage an all-out frontal assault like you've never seen before."

Within hours of the nomination, NOW President Molly Yard had labeled Bork "a neanderthal." The Alliance for Justice's Aron served notice on the Senate that a vote for Bork would be politically costly, vowing "mass mobilization" against the nomination.

The Chairman of the Leadership Conference, Benjamin Hooks, charged that Bork's confirmation "would dramatically alter the balance of the Supreme Court, jeopardizing the civil rights achievements of the past three decades. Just a few days later at the national convention of the NAACP, Hooks used more emphatic language: "We will fight it all the way—until hell freezes over, and then we'll skate across the ice."

On the evening of July 1, John Buchanan, chairman of PFAW, appeared on the MacNeil/Lehrer Newshour, warning, "This is a critical decision for the U.S. Senate. It could influence the course of judicial history into the next century."

Kennedy and the coalition members effectively alerted activists to take up arms against the nomination. But the heightened rhetoric had its costs. A Supreme Court nomination was not, after all, an election campaign. Though it was the president who initially politicized the nomination, the opponents risked being labelled desecrators of the Court and of the process.

They were. To Aron's July 1st pledge, "there will be a mass mobilization," the *Washington Post* editorial page the very next day scolded "wrong, wrong, wrong!" Later the newspaper deplored the opponents' "knee jerk" responses, "distortions," and "self indulgent overkill."

There were those among the coalition's leaders who believed that, while it was critical to sound the alarm, it was a mistake to engage in extreme rhetoric or to threaten political reprisal. The use of words like "neanderthal" to characterize Bork tended to mark the speaker, not Bork, as the extremist. And threats of political retaliation needlessly invited a harsh response.

As Bill Taylor puts it, "Civil rights groups can't go around threatening political reprisals. The way you get your message across is to say how deeply you feel, and that you're ready to make your case. But the people who were unsophisticated and harmful were those who were saying, 'I'm telling my senator, if he doesn't go my way, I'm going to get him.' "

A painful lesson in the dangers of flexing political muscle came from the NAACP's board member and Democratic National Committee–woman from New York Hazel Dukes, who introduced Daniel Patrick Moynihan to the NAACP national convention as a senator who certainly would vote against Bork. When she later learned of Moynihan's reluctance to declare how he would vote, Dukes responded: "I have the votes in New York, I'll get what I want. It's strictly politics."

Dukes's rhetoric not only ran counter to the coalition's "freeze strategy," which asked only that Moynihan and his colleagues remain uncommitted until the hearings were concluded, but also placed Moynihan in a compromised position: even if he arrived at a vote against Bork through reasoned scrutiny of the Bork record, he risked *appearing* to have been intimidated by political pressure. "If the pressure becomes too blatant," warned political analyst William Schneider in the *National Journal*, "the Senators may try to score points with the voters by openly defying the threats."

Senator Cranston, who has a deep understanding of the motivations and sensitivities of the Senate, confronted the coalition's leaders and warned them not to allow any repetition of the Moynihan incident.

Ralph Neas drove home this very point when he spoke in early August to the annual convention of Citizen Action, a two-million-member, multi-state network of activists: "Don't be heavy-handed. Do everything you have to do, but in a low-keyed way."

Within two weeks of the nomination, David Cohen and Mike Pertschuk circulated to key coalition strategists a memorandum discussing the importance both of seizing the affirmative symbols of the debate, and of avoiding the negatively charged. The memo suggested:

> Extreme rhetoric is likely to characterize the opponent, not Bork, as the extremist. There's a fine line to be drawn here. Bork is an extremist and must be labeled as such . . . Symbols won't take unless they are grounded in the facts; there is no substitute for the painstaking task of building the case against Bork which arises foursquare from his record. . . . While abortion and gay rights are issues with strong constituencies, Bork supporters will work tirelessly to portray the Bork opposition as limited to narrow constituencies or special interests. The constitutional risks Bork's nomination poses need to resonate with universal concerns of the broadest possible public.

Judy Lichtman of the Women's Legal Defense Fund recalled meetings with various public interest groups around the country where the memo served as a vehicle for discussions. Another objective was to focus the media's attention on the battle of symbols, especially the White House effort to frame the debate, and an op-ed based on the eight-page memo appeared in the *Washington Post* nine days prior to the start of the Senate confirmation hearings.

The Message Emerges

The more experienced and sophisticated groups needed no prompting. They had already begun to refine their messages within the first weeks of the campaign. Indeed, to a very large extent the basic themes of the campaign emerged during the first week. It was at the first mass coalition meeting that Bill Taylor, Court and constitutional scholar Herman Schwartz, and Joe Rauh, among others, suggested that the central issue should be framed in terms of Bork's assault on the fundamental role of the courts in defending individual rights.

At that July 2nd meeting, Bill Taylor distributed an eight-page "Talking Points" memorandum for the Block Bork Coalition which spelled out the central themes of the campaign, arising directly out of the "Book of Bork." It is, in a sense, one of the earliest artifacts of the campaign. While "focus group" tests and later polls may have helped the campaign relate Bork's legal views to broad public concerns, the "Talking Points" memo contains the bedrock of issues on which the ensuing campaign was to be constructed: "The primary reason for opposing nominee Bork is that he has aligned himself against most of the landmark decisions protecting civil rights and individual liberties that the Supreme Court has rendered over the past four decades."

The memo proceeded to summarize Bork's record of opposition to Supreme Court decisions attacking "Race Discrimination," "Other Invidious Forms of Discrimination," "Restrictions on the Right to Vote," "Restrictions on the Right to Privacy," and "Restrictions on Free Speech."

But not all groups were then speaking with a uniform voice, and there was a danger that divisive or discordant issues raised by some groups would drown out the campaign's more global messages.

Thus, Althea Simmons's initial resistance to the appointment of NARAL's Kate Michelman as co-chair of the Grassroots Task Force did not reflect her personal feelings about abortion, but her strategic concerns: "I was concerned about this not turning into an abortion fight which would kill our efforts; I thought that we ought to do everything possible to keep it as neutral as possible."

That required persuasion, but the prospect of actually defeating Bork encouraged reason and restraint. "It took some cajoling and some real careful conversations," recalls Estelle Rogers of the Federation of Women Lawyers, "to convince some people that although this was their issue, that there were very big stakes here and that sometimes somebody's issue has to take the back seat. And I think that happened fairly successfully—although with some pain."

Michelman, after long talks with Lichtman and Neas, among others, came to perceive the necessary strategy to defeat Bork just as Simmons did:

> The Coalition was very concerned about this not turning into a referendum on abortion. I recognized and agreed that this was a wise strategy. I said to them, 'Look, I've already discussed abortion in the context of women's rights, self-determination and privacy.' We decided that the right to privacy was the way to address this important threat to women's reproductive freedom.

This was not a strategy of convenience, an artificial masking of the *real* issue, abortion. The broad concerns about Bork's record on privacy and equal protection rose up, uninvited, out of the Bork record. As Marcia Greenberger of the National Women's Law Center relates:

> Many of us had known that the Supreme Court was closely divided on specific issues such as abortion rights and affirmative action, and that Bork could provide the decisive vote in overturning past precedents in those key areas. But what surprised us when we looked at his record was how fundamental his opposition was to privacy rights in general, not just as they applied to abortion, but as they applied to a broad range of family issues.
>
> We discovered that he had repeatedly stated his opposition to the Supreme Court's now well-established practice of interpreting the Fourteenth Amendment's equal protection clause to strike down discrimination suffered by women. After we pieced Bork's positions together, we explained to the groups in the Coalition how devastating their implications were for virtually all of the rights women had secured under the Constitution. The only right Bork hadn't criticized was the right to vote. We urged that these broad-based privacy and equal protection issues be emphasized and were gratified to see how central they became in the debate.

Greenberger and her colleagues argued, successfully, that "as important as the issue of abortion was, it would have been *inaccurate* to highlight the right of abortion as the only key women's right at stake."

The leadership of the coalition breathed a collective sigh of relief. As Planned Parenthood lobbyist Jo Blum emphasized, the decision to subordinate the abortion issue "kept everybody on an even keel and did not alienate the labor unions."

Other groups dedicated to specific, narrowly focused, divisive issues — such as gay and lesbian rights — also came to understand early that the effort would be doomed if the opposition to Bork could be tarred with the administration's broad-sweeping "special interest" brush. The political wounds remained fresh from the 1984 presidential race, when Walter

Mondale's image was tainted with the "special interest" curse. As Neas says,

> We had to demonstrate that across the board on constitutional issues, Robert Bork was terrible. During the first week it meant working with pro-choice groups and minority groups and making sure that no one was advancing a specific agenda. With several minor exceptions, [in] the first ten days, every part of the civil rights community adhered to that strategy.

Refining the Message

The campaign did not need to craft "defactualized" themes with which to discredit Bork. What the campaign did need was to keep the themes that flowed from the "Book of Bork" front and center, to keep the White House from reframing the issues or deflecting the media's attention onto diversionary issues.

The opposition also needed to frame its basic themes in ways which resonated with the concerns of the larger public—those who do not follow closely the Court or the Constitution, but who nonetheless harbor strong, if sometimes inchoate feelings about the significance of constitutional rights in their daily lives.

The Block Bork Coalition's leaders did not turn over the task of "message formation" or "spin control" to communications specialists removed from the substance of the campaign. But they did reach out for those political professionals within the progressive community who had demonstrated special skill and insight in framing media messages. Among them were Nikki Heidepriem, Kathy Bonk, Phil Sparks, and Ann Lewis.

Heidepriem had handled women's issues for the Mondale/Ferraro campaign, and would later play the same role in the Dukakis/Bentsen campaign. Bonk had masterminded a skillfully crafted media campaign in a losing cause, NOW's campaign for the Equal Rights Amendment; now she had dedicated herself to strengthening the public interest community's media skills and presence. And Sparks, as communications vice-president of the American Federation of State, County, and Municipal Employees (AFSCME), sought to keep public interest advocacy on the leading edge of media advocacy technologies.

Lewis had been political director of the Democratic National Committee and was to be an informal advisor to presidential contender Jesse Jackson. She was herself a leading media spokesperson for the party's liberal wing, appearing with regularity as a commentator on the MacNeil/Lehrer Newshour—to which roughly *half* of political Washington, including most of the journalists on the Bork beat, were tuned. While a consultant to the Alliance for Justice, Lewis was not constrained by any organizational inhibitions from speaking forcefully, with both wit and appropriate acerbity.

As Heidepriem recalls, the challenge to the media specialists was complicated:

> We had to craft and bring together the elements of polling, our understanding of political message making, and the political and cultural climate in which we were operating. You had to understand the Senate, and the various senators; you had to understand the media, and how they would play this; you had to understand the special interest rap with which the Democrats were tarred in 1984, of which we were the living embodiment. You had to understand that this would be viewed as a partisan issue, and that the White House would try to paint us as the epitome of the special interests. The American public and the U.S. Senate do not think that anyone is entitled to have a justice on the Supreme Court who agrees with him or her. I'm not entitled because I'm pro-choice to have a pro-choice justice. I may be entitled to have a justice whose judicial philosophy is consonant with the twentieth century. This makes it more complicated than a political campaign: in a political campaign, nobody thinks issues aren't legitimate. But here, your issue agenda has to be a demonstration of why his philosophy is unacceptable.

But, as complicated as the challenge to the coalition was, its *message* had to be clear and simple. Ann Lewis explains:

> There's been an evolution in the way you reach public opinion. Public attention is a limited finite resource: you get less and less attention, and more and more you need to use the media. People who are very successful in reaching public opinion do it by learning to use a few themes and repeat them. You need to do that particularly in coalition campaigns because you're much more likely to be picked off by your disparate parts.
>
> You take a couple of issues and you hammer at them, and you keep repeating them. The issue is repetition, and if an issue is working for you, say it ten times more. So if you keep saying the same thing every time, the few times they tune in, it will reinforce.

Lewis suggested to Michelman of NARAL that a series of "focus group" sessions would be very useful in helping the campaign to narrow and refine its messages. Working with pollster Harrison Hickman, they designed and conducted focus group sessions on the nomination. Two were held in late July in Philadelphia, and two in late August in Birmingham, Alabama. Lewis recalls the rationale:

> The message we sent out should not be developed in Washington. *We needed to try it out among real people.* We did the focus groups two ways. One, we did them with white collar and blue collar, on the theory that the new neighborhood is the workplace. In Alabama, we also had to do it by race because as we found in making the arrangements, there is no such thing as an integrated focus group in Alabama . . . so we did blue and white collar white. Outside Philadelphia, they were mixed. We did Alabama and Pennsylvania for several reasons: we knew that they would be heard by people on the Judiciary Committee, and we wanted swing areas where we could test what about Bob Bork they would react to.
>
> Even in the heart of Alabama, people did not get emotionally aroused by the thought of the Supreme Court. There was no stomach anywhere in this country for recapturing the Court; those battles are over. Working-class people in Alabama don't want to refight them.

They think, if anything, their own economic progress was retarded by the number of years they spent fighting those battles. They are not prepared to join up for the next brigade to take large giant steps, but they want to leave well enough alone.

So you could not get them angry, even with a southern-talking moderator trying to egg them on about the Court. Done. Over. Done deal. You could arouse them about a couple of issues, and again, the issue that worked best was the idea of choice, expressed very differently by women and men. Men: "no government has got the right to come into my house." But women: "every woman has got to make her own choice for herself". Very different.

Most people don't spend their time counting who's on each side of the Court, but the idea [was] that society had achieved a balance on issues of racial justice, and they didn't want to reopen it. We could go from there, understanding that balance was important, and talk about it in terms of the Court, but it was real and believable to them that in society we had reached a kind of balance, and they didn't want to go backward.

The things that worked were "not going backward." The things that worked were "not tipping a balance that had been achieved," and the things that worked were "choice."

Interestingly, the "balance" Lewis talked about was not the same "balance" some Bork opponents had raised as an issue early in the nomination battle. To alert and alarm their activist constituents to the stakes in the Bork battle, the leaders had focused on Bork as a potential fifth and deciding vote on critical civil and human rights issues. They expressed the specific concern that the replacement of Justice Lewis Powell—who had been a moderate "swing" vote on critical decisions—with the extremist Bork would "tip the balance" of the Court. That worked to mobilize activists, and, initially, to signal to the Senate, the media, and the public how high the stakes were for the country and the Constitution if the nominee became the swing vote.

But, as Lewis observed, most people do not follow the ideological makeup of the Supreme Court. That "balance" which the participants in the focus groups wanted to preserve was the social balance which had been painfully struck by the Court and by society, over several decades, between black and white, the government and the citizen—between majoritarian and minority values and life styles.

The results of the first focus groups were presented to a meeting of the coalition's Steering Committee one month into the campaign, in early August. They contained other useful insights into the public mind, particularly the fact that many Americans were well aware that Reagan's choice of Bork was ideologically motivated, and that they accepted the legitimacy of the Senate challenging a candidate who harbors an "extreme" ideology. While suggesting that Bork's willingness to uphold state action restricting abortion rights was a strong motivating force for many women opposing Bork, the focus group report concluded:

> The overall sense that he is an extremist is a more powerful argument against him than his stand on any single issue. People want a nominee who reflects the general values and consensus views of the majority of Americans and not someone who represents the opinions of those at either end of the political spectrum.

The focus groups also confirmed what the coalition's leaders had reluctantly concluded: that Bork's role as solicitor general during the Watergate crisis, his association with the darkest days of the Nixon fall, did not move people. Bork's willingness to carry out the president's orders to fire Watergate special prosecutor Archibald Cox after Attorney General Elliot Richardson and Deputy Attorney General William Ruckelshaus resigned in outrage, was a focus of media attention in July. Some anti-Bork activists remained convinced that Bork's performance in the "Saturday Night Massacre" should remain on the agenda of issues to be raised. But, as Lewis reported, "We were told clearly that they didn't give a damn about Watergate. You try that out in a focus group and you have people say, 'That's the way people in Washington behave.' "

People for the American Way also arranged with pollster Peter Hart for a focus group in Atlanta in August, whose results they also shared with the coalition. That survey strongly confirmed that even white conservative southerners were troubled by government intrusion into the privacy of the home.

At about the same time, Phil Sparks of AFSCME was bringing his and the union's political communications expertise to bear on the anti-Bork campaign. With the support of the Leadership Conference, Sparks convinced AFSCME's President, Gerald McEntee, to commit $40,000 for a national public opinion poll. A small group of coalition leaders was convened together with pollster Tom Kiley (whose firm, Marttila & Kiley, had also been conducting polling for Senator Biden in his presidential bid) to identify the kinds of questions that needed to be answered. This core group, in turn, was able to draw upon the Bork research and issue-framing efforts so that the poll could guide the campaign's issue priorities. It also posed specific questions about the decisions Bork had rendered and reactions to views expressed in Bork's own writings.

In addition, Sparks says,

We wanted to get some idea as to the extent of knowledge and information that people had about the Supreme Court. How did people see their stake in this nomination? Do people feel, 'Well, it's Reagan off on an ideological binge, but it won't make any difference in my life?" Or did they understand that this was a bad judge who was a swing vote, who could reverse the progress they cared about? In August, when we were polling, people didn't yet have much information about Bork. So we were, in effect, previewing the kind of public education campaign that was to run two months later, trying to find out in advance what the best themes and strategies would be. We would throw the kitchen sink at them in terms of background on the Judge and find out what worked and didn't work.

The poll, which surveyed about 1,000 voters, contained few surprises, but it strongly confirmed the evolving collective judgement.

First, the poll helped solidify the growing perception within the coalition that Reagan had failed to convince the public that the Bork appointment was non-ideological. As for the role of the Senate, the poll showed that, by a margin of eighty-two percent to fifteen percent, people believed that it was appropriate for the Senate to examine Bork's "background, his beliefs about the Constitution and his past decisions as a judge, and should approve him if they conclude that he would be good for the country."

Next, the poll confirmed the groups' judgement about which issues and themes would not work, such as reviving the sins of Watergate. And it offered help in fine-tuning the messages; pollster Kiley wrote:

> We believe opponents must do two things. First, they must focus attention on Bork himself—his record and his positions—as being at the center of the controversy. The White House, with some success, has portrayed the tactics as divisive and controversial, shifting attention away from the nominee's own record. Second, opponents must develop themes that inform people about Bork, rather than merely reinforcing anti-Reagan sentiment. For better or worse, voters have already made their fundamental judgements about Ronald Reagan, and they also think they know why he selected Bork . . . The question we want to focus American attention on is not 'why did Ronald Reagan select Robert Bork,' but rather, 'what is it about Robert Bork and his background that has caused such a swirl of controversy.'

Kiley's findings suggested that, while evidence (and rhetoric) about Bork's extremism inflamed liberal opposition, only a quarter of those polled felt that the Senate would be justified in rejecting a nominee whose "legal views and philosophy are so sharply different from the majority that it would clearly upset the Court's balance."

Kiley concluded:

> Those who form the moderate center will move toward a rejection of Bork only if they find in his background and record a pattern of insensitivity that suggests he may harbor a predetermined attitude against certain causes and issues, if not classes of people . . . [We] found that the two most salient themes—Bork's "insensitivity to minorities and women" and his predisposition to "favor the wealthy and big business over the interests of the less powerful"—both bear directly on the criterion of fairmindedness.

Curiously, in the light of the Harrison Hickman focus group results, the Kiley survey found that "the privacy theme appears from our results to be somewhat obtuse and limited in its potential for broad based communication." But he did note that the respondents exhibited resentment at "attempts by the government to interfere with their freedom to choose how to conduct their lives"—especially the government's authority, which Bork supported in criticizing the *Griswold* case, to deny adults access to birth control devices. Above all, Kiley argued that the opponents must keep their messages "clear, simple, and direct."

The focus groups, the poll, and the memos were designed to—and did—help the coalition's leadership confirm, discard, fine tune, and concentrate on a limited number of "direct and simple" press lines. The overall strategic objective was simplicity, clarity, and focus on a small number of basic themes.

With the Taylor "Talking Points" memo as one starting point, and the Kiley poll as another, the coalition lawyers and media specialists hammered out a three-page "Themes" memo. Phil Sparks wrote a first draft; Kathy Bonk edited. They asked Public Citizen's Joan Claybrook and others for a critique.

This process was not without its tensions. Some of the lawyers were dubious about the wisdom of reducing the Bork record to three pages. "They kept trying to come in and make it 'ver-baggy' again," says Bonk. "Finally, we got everyone to agree."

"Five central themes emerge as the best arguments against Bork," the memo summarized:

a. *The Stakes* — The nomination of Robert Bork raises the "stakes" in this nomination battle. He is not simply a replacement for the moderate to conservative Associate Justice Lewis Powell. He will provide the decisive vote to turn back the clock for a number of decisions regarding civil rights, women's rights, consumer rights, etc., which might force the Court to *repeal* and *reverse* many landmark decisions made over the past two decades which are now accepted as the rule of law.
    Frankly, the polling data suggests that the Americans accept and want to put behind them rulings on issues like abortion, birth control and school prayer.

b. *Civil Rights* — Bork opposed one-person, one-vote principles (he has said that this principle "runs counter to the Fourteenth Amendment"). In addition he has opposed the Supreme Court decisions eliminating the poll tax and statutes eliminating literacy tests. Both were used to limit voting by minorities in many states. Finally, when the Civil Rights Acts of the 1960s were being considered, he opposed provisions which desegregated restaurants and hotels. *The NAACP is a forceful opponent of Bork because of his anti-civil rights stands.*

c. *Consumer Rights/Workers' Rights* — Bork has supported big business and big government in many of his judicial decisions. In *OCAW v. American Cyanamid* he ruled in favor of a corporate policy requiring female workers in a hazardous area to be sterilized or be fired. In addition, in a case involving *Jersey Central Power* he allowed the electric utility to pass on to consumers $400 million in costs the company accumulated when it suspended construction of a power plant *and* to charge ratepayers a rate of return on the losses incurred when the project was cancelled. Finally, *analysis by Ralph Nader* of his record as an Appeals Court Judge shows him to be anti-consumer and pro-business, siding with big government.

d. *Women's Rights* — Bork has said that the historic *Roe v. Wade* abortion decision is "unconstitutional." He has labeled as "unprincipled" the Court decision in *Griswold v. Connecticut* over-turning state law which made it a crime to advise married couples about birth control devices. He believes that women are not protected from sex discrimination under the Constitution (he does not believe that the equal protection clause of the 14th Amendment protects women), and has argued in his judicial opinions that the 1964 Civil Rights Act does not protect women from on-the-job sexual harassment.

e. *The First Amendment* — Bork does not believe that the First Amendment covers artistic or scientific expression and says that even political speech can "be cut off when it reaches the outer limits" of convention. In addition he is opposed to political speech which advocates violations of laws, however unjust. For example, Dr. King's sit-ins would not have been protected by the Constitution, in Bork's view.

The themes memo concluded:

The polling data suggests that the battle for public opinion is winnable. The arguments listed above *do* move a majority of the American people into opposition to the Bork nomination. Further, our arguments in opposition to Bork are much more credible than the White House's attempt to paint Bork as a moderate also favoring law-and-order solutions to many of our problems.

Heidepriem, separately working with Lewis, drew upon the focus groups and the Kiley poll to refine an earlier "message" memo developed for the guidance of "grassroots leadership." Her memo was widely circulated to members of the coalition for review and comment, so that by the time it was disseminated to state coalition leaders, on August 27, it had been absorbed into the media strategies of most national groups.

Though that memorandum contained thirty pages of detailed documentation, including the Alliance for Justice's "Fact Sheet on Robert Bork," its "general message" was summarized in two sentences:

- *Judge Bork is not a fair-minded person. . . . [and]*
- *Judge Bork is a judicial activist whose record reveals a lack of sensitivity to civil rights and equal justice for women and minorities.*

"If all of us use the . . . framework consistently," Heidepriem urged, "it will help focus our message about Judge Bork and improve the chance of penetrating the din around the confirmation."

Fritz Weicking, who "desked" several of the target states, believes that persuading grassroots activists to adopt this unified message was one of Washington's most important contributions to the state efforts:

> People in the field generally know how to organize and we lubricated and supplemented their work. But our unique contribution, unlike many other coordinated grassroots campaigns, was to point them to and persuade them to adopt a common series of tested messages and lines so that key senators not only heard that people didn't want Bork, but also so that they believed that the opposition was motivated by reasons that they [the Senators] found persuasive.
>
> The most common problem in coalition organizing is that each group wants to use its own message—which reflects their own issues and intended organizational needs. This effort avoided that. Groups in the field showed remarkable, astounding self-discipline in swallowing their own preferred messages and instead adopting the commonly agreed national message.

Heidepriem testifies to the importance of the poll results, in particular its guidance in abandoning, for a broad public audience, the theme that the precarious balance of votes on the Court was at stake—a theme which was very powerful with activists, and an effective means of energizing them:

> The polling was absolutely critical to our compass. Earlier, I did a message piece based on public opinion polling done over a year before, and it was wrong. The old polling said the notion of balance

would be a powerful message. We thought we should go to the American public, and say, "The Court will no longer be in balance; you need a moderate." That's a very tricky argument to make, because no one on our side was credible in saying that what they wanted was a balanced Court. When we tested that, people didn't care at all about that; didn't even know what we were talking about. We also now knew that the American public didn't think it was inappropriate to campaign about judges. With Kiley's polling, I was able to write a message piece.

Durwood Zaelke of the Sierra Club Legal Defense Fund was one who appreciated the guidance:

> A great thing the coalition did was the polling and then the advice based on the polling surveys and how they were able to focus on certain themes. The coalition kept the themes constant; there was no flip-flopping, no unseemly opportunistic switches . . . When we were doing our analysis, we were mindful of the polls so we would not omit investigating the things that the citizens in general seemed concerned about. In our press releases, we tried to keep the same theme to the extent it fit with environmental concerns. The theme was designed so that every individual concern could fit . . . a very sophisticated approach.

Again, both national and local groups felt free to develop their own "spins" and local touchstones in shaping their messages. "We did shape the tone to some degree, but we didn't police it the way that we all originally thought we could," concedes NARAL's Ness. In Atlanta, for example, the Southern Christian Leadership Conference invoked the Reverend Martin Luther King: "Bork is anti-King" read their flyers.

But one ground rule which the national coalition pressed, usually with success, was the avoidance of aspersions on Bork's personal integrity or character. From time to time, overzealous efforts by enthusiasts to raise issues about Bork's occasional hard drinking, or his minor tax dispute with New Haven authorities, were restrained. One unfortunate exception was the theme

of Bork's reputed religious agnosticism, which some Alabama
Bork opponents raised, taking their cue from their own Alabama Senator, Howell Heflin, who raised this issue in the
hearings.

The focus groups and the Kiley poll also eased the anxieties
of supportive, but politically wary senators, especially southern
senators, by demonstrating as much public support for their
broad themes in the South as elsewhere. The poll results became an effective tool of persuasion for Senate leaders of the
campaign, such as Majority Whip Alan Cranston, who took
Kiley and pollster Patrick Caddell around with him to reassure
the uneasy. Ann Lewis confirms this utility:

> It was the largest scale independent public opinion poll that
> could say that the majority of the people don't like this guy, and it
> did well in the Senate because of its sponsorship, because it was in-
> dependent, because it had names [leading pollsters] they had heard
> of. So, it was effective in talking to senators. It was a useful compo-
> nent. They were already hearing from their constituents, but this
> confirmed the message they were getting from their constituents.

The senators were not just comforted by the poll data; many
went on use it themselves. Sparks comments:

> Senators actually picked up this poll data. Many of their state-
> ments and questions emphasized the issues which the polling data
> emphasized. So the way the senators questioned Bork, they did it
> in terms that were understandable to the American public.

The Kiley poll also guided the paid advertising campaigns,
especially those designed by PFAW and NARAL. David Kusnet
of PFAW reflects on the usefulness of this survey:

> The poll confounded both the assumptions of the Left and the
> Right, because I think both the Left and the Right in America are an-
> gry. They think that the status quo in America is bad, and that if you

only gave an uncompromising left-wing message, or an uncompromising right-wing message, the great silent majority would fall
in line behind them. The poll showed us that, basically, people
were pleased with the Supreme Court; it got favorable ratings. People did not believe what Bork was saying—that the Court was this
unelected tyranny over American life that was destroying our society. One thing that Kiley is very good at is framing questions that
give different arguments to different players that a debate will present, and he gave pretty good summaries of right-wing arguments
and people did not accept them. On the other hand, the poll also
showed that people didn't take an overwhelmingly negative view of
where the Court stood after four years of Reagan appointees. So
there wasn't really this free-floating anger out there either to be
mobilized by the Right against the Supreme Court and its decisions,
or to be mobilized by the Left against what was now a Rehnquist
Court, with Scalia and O'Connor on it. What we learned from that
was that emotively, you couldn't do a spot with sixty seconds of fear
and anger. That was not the emotional pitch people were operating
on. It also assured us that if the Right ever went in, they wouldn't
win with a spot that was sixty seconds of fear and anger against the
Supreme Court.

There are differing views on the significance of the focus
groups and poll—indeed, on the relative contribution of the media specialists to the framing of the debate. The veteran lawyers
and lobbyists see the framing of the issues as arising from the
experience of the half-dozen campaigns of the 1980s, from the
Voting Rights Act extension to the campaign against Rehnquist.
Seizing the symbols of the debate, for these veterans, was the
product of experience and judgement, not the wizardry of the
media mavens. It was grounded in the political realities of the
campaign.

"A key to winning the battle was the civil rights issue," says
Common Cause's Wertheimer.

It was simply a question of who won the battle for the southerners,
and it would be won by blacks in the South, and those working with
them . . . Key was the capacity of blacks in the South, Hispanics

in certain parts of the country, to convince senators how important this was to them . . . [One southern senator] said something along the lines of, "If I vote against Bork, my constituents will remember it for a week, and forget about it. If I vote for Bork, they'll remember it for a lifetime."

Again, the salience of the "privacy" theme was not highlighted by the polling data, nor by the themes memo, yet it, too, was politically crucial. Wertheimer explains:

The privacy issue was very important for two reasons: it meant abortion wouldn't be a principal public focus in this battle which was important in terms of the key senators who would be deciding the issue. Secondarily, the privacy issue was a broad issue and a cross-cutting issue. Privacy is not, and did not turn out to be, a philosophical, ideological issue. Liberals have their own views of why privacy is important and conservatives have their views of why privacy is important and they feel just as strongly about it, even though the views aren't the same.

There is a persistent underlying tension between the vision of the traditional civil rights leaders and that of the apostles of contemporary media skills and strategies. It is not that the leaders are any less aware or concerned about the framing of the issues in the media; it is more that they rely upon deep experience rather than the tools of opinion analysis, which they view as overrated. They want it understood that the leaders of the coalition did not delegate the framing of the message to detached media wizards, and that the message itself was never detached from the Bork record. They shudder at the suggestion that the campaign's media strategy was an artificial construct, as "defactualized" as the White House effort to pretend that the nomination of Bork was not "political." Yet even they acknowledge that the media professionals, and the focus groups and poll, helped highlight the issues to be stressed, helped relate the Bork record to the public's concerns, and helped reassure anxious senators, who are addicted to polls.

Bill Taylor helps to resolve the tension. "One had to use the techniques of modern communications," he says, "because that's the arena within which we work. But it was not to generate something that was not there. It was to make sure that the basic message was a substantive message about what Bork's views were, his judicial philosophy."

7

COURTING THE MEDIA:
An All-Court Press

> We were working the editorial pages; we
> were working the feature writers in
> Washington; we were working the op-ed
> pages; we were working radio news through
> radio actualities. We were working radio
> commentary through radio talk shows; we
> were working TV news — locally through the
> satellite news feed. We were working net-
> work news through the inside. Then we
> had, of course, paid advertising on top of
> the whole thing. So we had all these differ-
> ent strategies going at the same time.
>
> PHIL SPARKS, AFSCME

In the campaign to defeat Bork, the coalition sought access for
its spokespeople and its messages to the news, or "free media."
It made comparatively limited use of print and electronic issue
advertising, or "paid media." It dedicated as many resources and
as much intensity of effort to media strategy and implementation as to lobbying, research, and grassroots activism.

The threshold problem for most public interest issue campaigns is gaining the media's attention — putting their issue on
the media's agenda, and, hence, on the nation's. That was not
a problem for those opposing Bork. For much of its four-month
run, the Bork nomination led the news each night and morning.
The media clamored after the advocates, competing for quotes
and "sound bites" from its principal spokespersons. Indeed, the
media not only paid heed to the opposition's views about Bork,
but also paid uncomfortable attention to the coalition itself. "I

would get calls," remembers Emily Tynes, who helped coordinate press relations for the coalition, "saying, 'O.K., Emily, where's that meeting? We want to get a shot of all you coming out of there.' " *That* kind of coverage the media strategists did all they could to deflect, as they sought to refocus attention onto the issues swirling about Bork, and away from their own lobbying.

The challenge, then, was not simply to gain attention, but to gain the attention of the right journalists for the right stories to reach the right audiences. First, the coalition needed to make certain that the news and commentary read by the senators and their staffs accurately reflected the seriousness and extent of the opposition to Bork. They needed to reach their own members and activists, to motivate and sustain their campaign energies—and to stimulate contributions to sustain the campaign. They needed to reach the "attentive public": community leaders who read editorials and op-ed pieces and whose judgement about Bork would have a disproportionate impact on the senators who heeded their voices. And they needed to reach the broad public, whose evolving views on Bork and the opposition's campaign would be charted by each succeeding poll, and carefully noted by the Senate.

For the most part, the nation learned about Bork from about 150 print and broadcast journalists based in Washington. At various points in the nomination process, they would be drawn from three traditional beats: the Court (legal reporters), Congress (especially those assigned to the Judiciary Committees), and the White House.

Between these journalists and the leaders, lobbyists, and media specialists of the major groups within the coalition there were relationships cultivated during earlier battles. Coalition members' ties with the White House press corps, on the other hand, were not quite as close, generally, as with the Capitol Hill reporters. Worse, the White House reporters were receiving a steady stream of news and press "lines" from the White House media apparatus.

NARAL's familiarity with the Supreme Court reporters was built upon that organization's active involvement and readiness to comment on Court decisions affecting abortion rights. This not only gave NARAL a preexisting set of relationships, but also enabled NARAL's communications staff to fathom and take advantage of the particular needs of the journalists on the Court beat. Says Richard Mintz, NARAL's communications director,

> For the reporters who cover the Court, the Bork story was unusual. You don't cultivate sources at the Court; there is just nobody who is willing to talk to you. They, themselves, were put into a different situation in which they had to become much more entrepreneurial in terms of their reporting.

There were, of course, politically attuned Supreme Court reporters who needed no introduction to issue politics, such as National Public Radio's Nina Totenberg, the *Washington Post's* Al Kamen, the *Los Angeles Times's* David Lauter, and *USA Today's* Tony Mauro — who packed remarkable substance into *USA Today's* chronically thin diet of two-hundred-word stories. But for others who covered the courts, Mintz and his colleagues were there to help guide them through the less familiar territory of a political campaign.

No segment of the press corps was neglected. "We — LCCR, the Alliance, PFAW, NARAL, others — inundated the Hill, the White House, and also those on the Court and Justice Department beats," says Neas, "constantly staying on their case. From the beginning there was a focus on all three. In addition we spent a lot of time and effort on regional reporters and editorial boards."

With the Court's summer recess beginning the very day before the nomination, and the scene not shifting fully to the Judiciary Committee until the hearings began in mid-September, the Court reporters would have a voracious, and not easily satisfied, appetite for story material throughout July and August. So the

Photographs

This is not a book about Robert Bork; it is a book
about the campaign to defeat the appointment
of Robert Bork to the Supreme Court. It is the
story of citizens rising in defense of their vision
of the Constitution and the Court....

1. President Reagan announces to reporters in Washington on July 1, 1987, that he is nominating Judge Bork to fill the vacancy on the Supreme Court. (PHOTO: *UPI/Bettmann Newsphotos*)
2. Nan Aron, Executive Director of the Alliance for Justice. (PHOTO: *Carl Clark*)
3. Mimi Mager, Grassroots Coordinator of the Leadership Conference on Civil Rights.
4. Ralph Neas, Executive Director of the Leadership Conference on Civil Rights.
5. Althea Simmons, Director and Chief Lobbyist of the Washington Bureau of the NAACP.
6. Kate Michelman, Executive Director of the National Abortion Rights Action League.
7. Bill Taylor, Ricki Seidman, and Melanne Verveer of People for the American Way. (PHOTO: *Jim Marks*)
8. Kathy Bonk of AFSCME, Emily Tynes of the Communications Consortium, and Phil Sparks of the NOW Legal Defense Fund. (PHOTO: *Junior Bridge*)
9. Joan Claybrook, President of Public Citizen (PHOTO: *Beverly A. Orr*)
10. Molly Yard, President of the National Organization for Women.
11. Anti-Bork campaign leaders from the AFL-CIO: Kenneth Young, Jane O'Grady, Ernie DuBester, Lane Kirkland, Bob McGlotten, and Janet Kohn.
12. Dr. Joseph E. Lowery, National President of the Southern Christian Leadership Conference, presents a petition with 20,000 signatures to U.S. Senator Sam Nunn.
13. At the Funeral for Justice in Philadelphia on September 14, 1987, Councilman Angel Ortiz helps another protester up the aisle of the Bright Hope Baptist Church. (PHOTO: *The Philadelphia Inquirer*)
14. A group of anti-Bork activists enters the Federal Building in Philadelphia on September 15 to meet with a representative of Senator Arlen Specter. (PHOTO: *The Philadelphia Inquirer*)
15. Bork testifies on September 19, 1987, the fifth day of the confirmation hearings. (PHOTO: *UPI/Bettmann Newsphotos*)

1

2

3

4

5

6

7

8

9

10

11

12

13

14

15

Block Bork Coalition kept up a steady summer flow to the Supreme Court reporters.

The reporters who covered the Senate Judiciary Committee were quite attuned to the pull and haul of political conflict, accustomed to the easy exchange of information tidbits and banter with the lobbyists on both sides. The ACLU's Jerry Berman, a ten-year veteran of a dozen or more Judiciary Committee battles, and hence a familiar and comfortable source for the journalist on the beat, recalls:

> I went down the list and stayed with the major outlets. The wires were also important; I would call them five times a day. I will also go up to the press gallery in the recesses . . . just chitchatting it up. I enjoy talking to them . . . to get the flow of the story . . . find out where they think it's going, suggest an idea, whether it's the [Bork] flip-flop, or 'Have you noticed that forty-two senators seem to be talking about privacy, isn't that an interesting line'?

After Labor Day, as the hearings approached and the central story shifted to the Senate, Berman and the other experienced lobbyists were already in close and continuing communication with the reporters on the Hill beat.

There was, however, no neat and tidy allocation of media initiatives. It was more a media free-for-all, with each national organization putting itself and its spokespersons forward. For example, Mintz chronicles some of NARAL's initiatives:

> In July and August, we arranged one-on-one meetings and lunches with just about every one of the key reporters; sat down with each one of them individually — Linda Greenhouse of the *New York Times*, Ed Walsh of the *Washington Post*, Tony Mauro of *USA Today*, Anne Constable at *Time*, Ann McDaniel at *Newsweek*, Tim O'Brien at ABC . . . telling them where we were going to be coming from, what our strategy was, what our people were going to be doing in the field — and those personal contacts were very important.
>
> We did a press breakfast on the [Harrison Hickman] focus group in the doldrums of August when there wasn't much going on. We

got some very good press; we got page five of the [Washington] Post, major wire stories, so that was successful. And then, of course, this is something which probably nobody talked about much in terms of cultivating reporters, but that everybody did, which was backgrounders on what happened at the coalition meetings. Also backgrounders of the meetings with senators. Obviously, the background discussions were very sensitive.

We also came up with some good lines that kept us in the news. The "one Justice away from injustice" line, I think, we rightfully take credit for.

By August, and into September, the steady flow of reports analyzing and critiquing Bork's record provided much of the substance for coalition media calls — and helped keep the stories focused on Bork's ideas, and not so much on the "horse race" aspects of the campaign or on the coalition itself.

While the coalition's Media Task Force theoretically was charged with coordinating media strategy, much was loose and informal coordination — hours on the phone — among the media specialists and those experienced lobbyists who had naturally been drawn, over time, to the role of media sources to the principal journalists. Mintz comments:

> [The Bork campaign] was unusual in the degree to which we had to work with so many other groups, and it was also unusual in that people [in the coalition] always returned your phone calls. In terms of the state-of-the-art campaign, the model is the way the coalition was able to allocate responsibility, and the reporting and accountability mechanisms that were built into it.

The Paper Place

People for the American Way, through its role as a central information resource center for any journalist seeking guidance through the Bork record, had built a special set of media relationships. "They were the paper place for everybody," says Nikki Heidepriem.

Bill Taylor salutes Melanne Verveer and Ricki Seidman as PFAW's "dynamic duo." Both have deep political issues experience; both have directed substantive legal research. But it was their personal qualities that drew journalists seeking knowledge to them: each radiated energy, an inexhaustable willingness to be helpful, constantly recharging spirit, and a scrupulous fastidiousness with facts. And they seemed able to radiate these qualities to the enthusiastic researchers and volunteers who helped give PFAW its unique depth.

"One of the reasons that we spent so much time with the reporters," Seidman explained, "was that they looked at us as a repository of information. So many of the calls had to do with, 'What do you have on this? Do you know if there's anything on this issue? Now, this is how I see it; is this right? Or was there something else that went on?' "

Seidman, in particular, would serve as a clearinghouse for the answers to technical questions from the media. Often, she knew the answer, but if not, she knew which legal scholar to turn to for the answer. As Bill Taylor remembers, "Ricki became indispensable to a lot of people in the press . . . A columnist would call Ricki, and say, 'By two o'clock I want to know two or three things that I want to put in my column.' "

PFAW's so-called Information Central was a powerful complement to the coalition's organized press operation, managed by Kathy Bonk and Phil Sparks. This was precisely because Seidman and her colleagues sought to establish their credibility with the press as an information resource, rather than a promoter of comment and viewpoint. Yet many reporters who came or called for information stayed to seek guidance. As Melanne Verveer explained,

> We rarely went to spin a story a certain way. Sometimes we had information that we thought would be interesting, and we would

explain why we thought it was interesting. But you can't have any ongoing relationship with reporters if you steer them wrong. Our effectiveness came from the fact that we spent an inordinate amount of time reading and learning about Bork's voluminous record. There were only a small number of reporters doing that. There were a larger number who could only do limited research — and these issues are complex issues, and they couldn't be dealt with in a simplistic way.

Many people who work on the Hill or in the media didn't have the luxury of dealing solely with judicial issues, and they all had to be brought to a level of sophistication on these issues very quickly. This constant stream of information and analyses they could get from us was helpful to them. There weren't many people they could go to and talk to about Bork's writings, so they would come to us, and ask, "Did you read this? Did you read that? What did you think?" As time went on, we developed good working relationships with many reporters, so that later, when the journalists were covering the hearings or other Bork related events rather than analyzing his record, they would still ask, "What do you think of that? What does that mean?" And that can involve a more subjective perspective than just providing information.

They didn't always agree with our judgement, but they knew they could get an informed point of view.

PFAW would caution journalists against overstating the flaws in Bork's record. "I can think of at least one reporter," recalls Seidman, "who was ready to go with a more extreme characterization than we had documentation for. We restrained him."

"I remember talking to reporters about Bork's views on free speech," says Verveer, "and making sure they had his later views, and didn't just go with his earlier statements, because his earlier views were so much more restrictive."

Bork Central

Kathy Bonk of the NOW Legal Defense Fund, Nancy Stella of PFAW and Richard Mintz of NARAL were the designated co-

chairs of the Media Task Force. The choices were doubly logical: NOW, PFAW and NARAL were among the few organizations that had dedicated substantial, discrete staff resources to
media; they were also part of an emerging core group of public
interest leaders committed—indeed, missionary in their
commitment—to the critical importance of media advocacy.
Also among this core group was Phil Sparks of AFSCME.

As we have seen, the larger groups, such as the Alliance for
Justice, the Leadership Conference, PFAW, AFSCME, NARAL,
and NOW each launched broad, sophisticated press initiatives
from the first day of the campaign, and continued them throughout, loosely and informally coordinating themes and messages
through the Media Task Force.

But the media specialists who served the campaign generally,
especially the Leadership Conference, were Bonk and Sparks,
and their colleagues, Emily Tynes and Henry Griggs. In a sense,
this Supreme Court campaign was the first opportunity for
Bonk, who was in the process of developing an informal communications network, to deliver an object lesson to the laggards
among the more traditional public interest groups and lobbyists
in the virtues of media professionalism. As Ann Lewis
comments,

> Bonk's communications network did the literal interfacing with
> the press, which they do extremely well. They ran the lists; they did
> the press releases. The way they work is to say to the groups, "You
> arrive at a consensus on what you want, and we will put it out."
> They're terrific in doing that. In fact, it's a model on which the Com-
> munications Consortium has now grown.

Early in July, Bonk and Sparks recognized that the campaign
would need at least as much intelligence about the journalists
on the Bork beat as the journalists would gather about the campaign, and that the energy expended by the campaign in attend-

ing to the journalists had to match that directed by the lobbyists at the Congress.

First, the Block Bork Coalition had to know what was happening in the media. The task of comprehensive tracking was taken up by the communications network—"even if we didn't have money for it." A handful of staff members and interns, including interns, devoted the pre-dawn hours of each morning to monitoring the media coverage, clipping, and pasting. The staff would begin their reading at 6:00 A.M., not only clipping the papers available in D.C., but also receiving faxes of key articles from volunteers among the network of activists in target states, such as Pennsylvania and Alabama. Each night, and each morning, the staff would monitor and record the principal television reports.

In early August, the communications network began sending out a weekly packet of clips, with a menu of suggestions for stimulating media attention, to all the organizations opposing the nomination. Especially for the smaller organizations, those for whom the Bork campaign was not a central issue, and those for whom media work had always taken a relatively low priority, the packet helped stimulate media awareness and initiative.

By early September, each daily 8:30 A.M. strategy session of the coalition's Steering Committee would begin with a summary of the coverage by the media specialists, the distribution of a sheaf of key clips, and videotaped highlights from the TV stories.

While the coalition's old hands had strong relations with veteran journalists on the beat, the prominence of the Bork story continued to draw new waves of journalists less familiar with the players and the issues. Bonk and Sparks coordinated the "mapping" of the expanded Bork beat. Bonk explains:

> I was starting to get calls from reporters, saying, "I'm on the Bork beat; I've just been assigned to the Bork beat, and do you have anything I can write about?" So when enough reporters called me to say,

"I'm on the Bork beat, give me a line," I decided what's going to
emerge is a Bork beat and we had better identify what this Bork beat
is. We phoned every bureau to find out who was going to be covering Bork. What we decided to do was put together an "inside the
Beltway" press list that was clearly the Bork beat.

The larger news organizations assigned reporters on all three
beats—the Court, Congress, and White House—to cover the
Bork story. PFAW and LCCR, among others, shared their precious media data banks with the communications network. The
combined Bork reporter database grew until, by Labor Day, it
could spit out labels for 2,000 journalists in minutes. A separate
list of editorial writers numbered 1,700.

In the days leading up to the hearings, as the Bork nomination
was becoming the daily lead news story, Phil Sparks and Kathy
Bonk concluded that the Leadership Conference had to central-
ize and coordinate its media relations. So they each delegated
a media specialist to serve as a media coordinator: Emily Tynes,
active in the communications group, and Henry Griggs, from
AFSCME. As the hearings began, Griggs set up a media post in
a cramped corner of the LCCR's basement offices. Tynes was to
be on the Hill, at the Senate hearings, at Neas's side every day.
Sparks recalls:

> Right after Labor Day, we've got the big list together, the 150
> [reporters], and we sent them this packet. We were announcing that
> the Leadership Conference had its own press operation and here
> were the two people to contact and, as you begin to get on the beat,
> here are the six or eight people in the various organizations to con-
> tact for specific information; here are their telephone numbers and
> their press contacts. That first page was, in effect, the Rolodex for
> nine out of ten reporters.

Reconstructing a day in the media life of the Block Bork Coalition, Griggs rummaged through the sheaf of phone messages for
a typical day in September:

Saul Levine, CNN, wanted to set up an interview . . . Channel 32, here in Washington, wanted info on the Bork hearings. . . . Here's someone from the United States Student Association. They wanted to hold a press conference blasting Bork.

Business and Professional Women — call as soon as possible, their council is meeting at 4:00 P.M. today, they want to know about press strategy . . . Let's see, SANE/FREEZE is going to decide on a Bork press conference Monday—that was a change in schedule . . . Here's someone from the Sierra Club, waiting for me on hold. I was calling them to pull together a radio actuality that could be fed to Western states: "Bork on the environment." . . . Storer Broadcasting wants to do an interview . . .

Most of them were calling to do an interview with Ralph Neas and I was pre-screening his calls. This person is from the *New York Times* and wants an interview today. We were going to contact Emily [Tynes], who will know where Ralph is and get him to a phone to talk to Ruth Marcus of the *Washington Post* . . . *Christian Science Monitor*—they were lucky enough to call at the same time, so I think we knocked out two or three interviews . . .

Here's someone from one of the PR firms that was working with us, regarding setting up talk show interviews . . . KRNU in Lincoln, Nebraska, called. They said, "we are being bombarded with radio propaganda from the other side." This was somebody from Lincoln looking for a little balance. "Do you guys have anything?" . . . Mutual Broadcasting system wanted to do some kind of interview tomorrow afternoon. Rather than giving everything to Ralph, we tried to spread it around.

The volume of media demands upon the coalition's leaders was formidable. It forced the Leadership Conference and the other groups to systematize their media relations in new ways. Mintz recalls NARAL's "media triage":

We try to decide what the hierarchy should be, what interviews you do first, particularly when you're faced with a situation in which you literally have dozens of reporters calling you at the same moment. How do you go about handling that? The most effective tool that I've found is immediately, even before you have a definite idea of what the situation is, what the circumstances are, have a comment on the wire, running comments from people, and if you are among the first people that the assignment desks see, also the edit desks see, they will come to you. After that we do the assignments, that's to the TV assignment desks, and while we're waiting for the TV crews to show up, we do radio because radio is obviously the most immediate of the media and you do all seven major radio networks, and then you do TV. Then you do daily newspapers, the back of the wires, and then last you do the news magazines, at the time, that usually fell on Friday.

Fortunately, Griggs and Tynes displayed the tact of Balkan diplomats; they were not cowed or diverted by strong egos. They needed to be fair and evenhanded in directing media coverage, ever sensitive to the institutional needs of the groups that made up the coalition. They also needed to structure interviews so as to reinforce the major themes of the anti-Bork campaign. They knew that not all the available spokespersons were equally effective — and not all the organizations equally embodied the most broadly appealing symbols of the campaign.

The messengers were also the message. Just as key witnesses — such as William Coleman, Shirley Hufstedler, and Barbara Jordan — embodied in their styles and effects and public identities the qualities of judiciousness, moderation, and temperateness, so the media managers sought to put forward those leaders who equally embodied these qualities. Neas was among the most effective spokespersons, and that effectiveness — and Neas's visibility as executive director of the Leadership Conference — was reflected in the constant demand by the media for Neas above all others. There was a conscious effort to focus attention on the Leadership Conference's central role, as Sparks explained, "because the best hook we had was going to be civil rights." Moreover, Neas seemed gifted with the ability to speak forcefully about Bork without appearing inflammatory or radical.

Neas's media prominence troubled a few of the coalition members. Part of their concern came from the natural competi-

tiveness of the campaign's diverse leadership, apart from what
David Cohen slyly attributes to "column inches envy"—
competition for newspaper coverage. Ann Lewis dismisses
most of the tension as simple "human nature," but she adds that
there were also substantive and institutional causes:

> I should say there was a little tension because it was perceived
> that Ralph was less willing to talk about privacy and choice issues,
> and therefore, there was particular concern by the women's commu-
> nity, who felt that they were playing a much larger role than was
> sometimes acknowledged in Washington. They were central in the
> grassroots effort, and that was an issue. The other was that people
> simply have institutional imperatives. Everybody in that meeting
> came with a board, and was, in effect, representing an organization
> and organizations that knew that they were devoting resources and
> people to this and wanted some affirmation of their roles.

Within each of the organizations that made up the coalition,
there were competing goals and agendas. As Mintz illustrates,

> There was what it meant for the country, what it meant for
> progressive causes, what it meant for reproductive rights, what it
> meant for NARAL, and what it meant for each of us personally. You
> needed constantly to balance all those interests against one another.
> For example, on reproductive rights, there was Planned Parenthood
> and there was us, and there were the other reproductive rights
> groups, and the progressive cause. We needed to be careful about
> how we dealt with the rest of the coalition—and for the country, we
> were always cautious about how we would proceed.

For connoisseurs of coalition politics, this chronic tension
produced one of the campaign's more amusing tableaux. Griggs
tells the tale:

> One Friday, towards the very end of this, I walked into the Leader-
> ship Conference office, and there's Ralph sort of sitting on this

couch, where we kept all the newspapers, nodding his head, going, "Oh, this is perverse! This is really perverse!"

I said, "Ralph, what's wrong? What's gone wrong, here?" I thought some senator had made the wrong decision, or something. "No, ABC wants me to be their "Person of the Week" and I just don't want to do it. Can we stop this?" I looked at him and said, "Ralph, from a public relations standpoint, this is worth maybe a quarter-million dollars. This is what Michael Deaver would want for his folks."

Neas knew that Griggs was right. Indeed, when the feature aired on ABC, the producers had prepared a warm and sympathetic background portrait of Neas, including his moving struggle with Guillain-Barre Syndrome. That profile brought the contrasting portrait of a coolly intellectual Bork into sharp relief.

But before Neas would agree to accept the honor, he needed to assure that his appearance would not disrupt the coalition's harmony. He got on the phone, and called perhaps a dozen of the coalition's leaders, earnestly seeking their counsel and guidance. Judy Lichtman of the Women's Legal Defense Fund, among others, cites his call of consultation as a vintage example of Neas's ability to disarm with earnestness — yet to gain the freedom to do what he intended to do anyway.

Richard Mintz recalls:

I remember the day that Ralph became ABC person of the week. I called Henry [Griggs], who is a personal friend, right after watching it and said, 'Great piece!' Ralph overheard, and said, 'Give me the phone.' So Ralph gets on the phone and said, 'Richard, I want to explain; I didn't want to be person of the week, etc.,' and he went into his usual apology for being center stage. I said, 'Ralph, I don't have to hear it. Congratulations; I'm happy for you.'

Getting Outside Washington

The national campaign's media strategists and technicians were not content to leave the delivery of their messages to the

Washington press corps. From Washington they initiated a full range of "unpaid" media initiatives designed to gain direct access to media outlets throughout the country: editorial writers, op-ed page editors, local broadcast news, and radio talk shows. The Washington media operations of the larger organizations and the Grassroots Task Force, as we've seen, also kept feeding out concepts and materials which state coalitions could adapt for local media initiatives.

Each state coalition assigned members to concentrate on media advocacy. In Texas, for example, a separate committee was established to keep the growing opposition to Bork in the local news and, especially, to reach out to editorial boards.

Supreme Court nominations are the ideal matter for editorial writers. Great constitutional principles are at stake; the clash of ideas and ideologies invites thoughtful analysis (even if it also tempts windy pontification). Legislators pay attention to editorial pages.

Certain advocacy groups, especially Common Cause and PFAW, have raised the "editorial memo" to an art form. The best editorial memos engage the editorial writers with efficiently packaged information not easily available elsewhere, soft-sell persuasion, a balanced and temperate tone, a sense of genteel urgency (not, says AFSCME's Henry Griggs, "a scream").

The effective editorial memo walks a fine line: paying dutiful respects to the nonpartisanship and fierce independence of the editorial writer, while conveying forcefully the impression that the momentum of informed, respectable opinion is leaving the station, and it's time to jump aboard.

Within twenty-four hours of the Bork nomination, PFAW mailed to its list of 1700 editorial writers and other press contacts a six-page edit memo crafting the constitutional arguments for a coequal role by the Senate in the confirmation process. The memo also raised questions concerning Bork's fitness for the Court. More memos were to follow throughout the nomination process, from the Alliance for Justice, the Leadership Conference, NARAL and other individual organizations. These were only loosely coordinated, but were insistent in their physical — and substantive—bulk. Though the conservative Coalition for America and the American Conservative Union counterattacked with their own editorial packets within the week, there was, in general, no comparable flow of tailored editorial memos from Bork's supporters.

Coalition members supplemented the barrage of paper with follow-up editorial board visits, especially to key papers, both national and regional. Bill Taylor, Ralph Neas, Judy Lichtman, and John Buchanan visited the *Washington Post* editors in an effort to ameliorate the *Post*'s disdain for the campaign, and to strengthen its faint substantive misgivings about Bork. The *Post* editorial board was evidently deeply divided. As with many Washington insiders, some of the *Post* editors knew Bork socially, and liked him. Informal feedback from the meeting suggested that the editors had found the substantive case made by the delegation useful, and it may have contributed to the *Post*'s ultimate decision to oppose confirmation.

Bork's allies, such as Washington lawyers Lloyd Cutler and Leonard Garment, were actively promoting the case for confirmation with the editorial writers of the major national newspapers. Bork himself had lunch with the *New York Times* editors, who also met with Elaine Jones, Marcia Greenberger and several others from the coalition. The *Times* opposed Bork vigorously. It's evident that Bork was not persuasive; it is less evident whether the coalition made a difference, since the *Times*'s editorial writer on the judiciary, Jack Mackenzie, had closely followed the Court and Bork's record for years.

NARAL's Mintz recalls an incipient effort to orchestrate coordinated coalition editorial board visits to papers in all the key states. Scheduling logistics defeated the scheme but representatives of both national groups and their local affiliates did target both editorial writers and journalists in the key states. For example, sensitive to Senator Specter's uncommitted status,

NARAL's Michelman, together with local NARAL members, met with the *Philadelphia Inquirer* editorial board. Judith Lichtman met with the *Atlanta Constitution*. And Georgia state coalition leaders had early and continuing contact with editorial boards throughout the state.

The informal communications network monitored editorials, according to Bonk, "as closely as we monitored vote counts," paying special heed to editorials from the swing vote states. Singly, and in packets tailored to each office, the editorials were distributed to every corner of the Senate.

To supplement the flow of editorial memos, Henry Griggs provided a steady stream of selected materials, including provocative editorials, to editorial page editors. Griggs explains their intended effect:

> I made a point of finding good things in the editorials in the Flint, Michigan *Journal*, for example, and if I thought that was good, I'd send it out to the rest of the country: "This is what the Topekas, and the Flints, and the Sunnyvales across the country are doing." That helped take this out of the elite category and make it more national. Every Friday, I'd send something from that week, whatever was best. For example, what Barbara Jordan said in her testimony was just fantastic. We thought, "People can write editorials on this, so let's just give them ten pages of raw testimony out of the congressional transcript."

Nor did the coalition neglect the page facing the editorial page, the "op-ed" page, with its opinion columns, letters to the editor, and "guest" opinion pieces. On September 15, the *New York Times* ran a long op-ed article by William T. Coleman, Jr., titled "Why Judge Bork Is Unacceptable." The piece presaged Coleman's later potent testimony before the Judiciary Committee, and helped to frame the issues for Bork's testimony, which would begin hours later.

In the field, grassroots activists kept up a steady flow of their own op-ed columns and letters to local editors. Several of the

larger national groups crafted op-ed articles, both under the by-
lines of their national spokespersons and as generic pieces, to
be submitted under the names of local leaders. The Rev. John
Buchanan, chair of PFAW and a former eight-term Republican
congressman who suffered the crude vengeance of the fundamentalist right at the ballot box for his deep convictions about
civil liberties, authored an op-ed piece that was featured in at
least a dozen papers, ranging from Utah's *Deseret News* to the
Columbian Missourian — broad exposure for one 200-word
column.

Sparks supervised the preparation and distribution of op-ed
opinion pieces for local AFSCME leaders:

> We prepared, for distribution by a network that AFSCME has de-
> veloped, a generic op-ed piece in Ralph's [Neas] name condemning
> the nomination, following exactly the lines suggested by the poll
> results, that we sent out to every paper in the country the week be-
> fore the hearings started. Then we encouraged and helped prepare
> state-specific op-ed pieces for in-state authors: the dean of a law
> school in Florida [and] a prominent civil rights lawyer in Alabama,
> for example.

State coalitions were simultaneously preparing and promoting their own op-ed articles. "We had a few op-ed pieces that we
shared," says grassroots coordinator Mimi Mager, "but for the
most part, they really came from the state, and were targeted toward the state."

A well placed op-ed piece can also perform — at no cost — one
of the functions of a paid ad: it can help secure credibility for
leaders in the campaign. Kate Michelman, for example, was determined to place an op-ed piece on Bork in the *New York
Times*. "I was going to send it elsewhere if the *Times* didn't take
it, but I wanted it in the *Times*. It was very important to me that
they published that piece for lots of reasons, especially our organizational credibility." Richard Mintz adds:

We took Kate's op-ed for example, and recycled that for our affiliates. Each editorial board has a different policy about whether they take national people or local people, and we basically did a little bit of both. We were very careful about, for instance, the *Times* op-ed. We knew the *Times* would syndicate it. We tried to think about ways we could leverage more media.

Broadcast

No contemporary issue advocate can afford to ignore or to be inept on television. The most sophisticated recognize that the morning or evening network news shows are a prime arena in which national stories are shaped and framed. So it is not surprising that the coalition's national leaders were camera ready. Many were experienced and comfortable with television journalism. They knew when and how to make themselves available to the network news and MacNeil/Lehrer, and to regional and small chain Washington TV news bureaus. They knew how to compress their messages into fifteen, or even seven-second sound bites. And, as we shall see in chapter 11, during the hearings they continuously challenged Bork and his supporters for center stage.

What is perhaps more noteworthy is that many of the activists in the field proved equally adept at gaining access to local TV news, and making good use of the opportunity. They knew how to draw TV attention with a press conference featuring prominent community leaders from an unlikely—and hence newsworthy—breadth of organizations. In Pittsburgh, for example, anti-abortion groups staged a rally to demonstrate support for Bork on the same day that the Pittsburgh Block Bork Coalition staged its own rally. The pro-Bork rally actually drew larger numbers, but the Pittsburgh media, TV and print, gave top billing to the anti-Bork rally, emphasizing its broad reach, while treating the anti-abortionist event as a right-to-life march rather than a pro-Bork event.

The local coalitions knew how to stage photo opportunities. At a news conference in Seattle, thousands of letters opposing confirmation were collected and piled high, before being delivered to the senators' offices.

The Georgia coalition took advantage of a meeting Senator Nunn had scheduled to discuss farm issues. They alerted the local broadcast and print journalists, who faithfully recorded the coalition's decorous delivery to Nunn of 12,000 signatures on petitions urging him to oppose Bork.

In Minnesota, Peck Scott of AFSCME, working with the Abortion Rights Council of Minnesota, planned and executed a lively ambush of their Republican senator, David Durenburger. NARAL's communications director, Richard Mintz, who helped contact the national media, recalls the events with evident pleasure:

> This happened on Labor Day weekend. [Senate Minority Leader] Bob Dole was going to be doing an event with Durenberger at the Independent Republican booth at the Minnesota State Fair in St. Paul.
>
> We sent a lot of news crews up there. They wanted a place where they could get a sense of where the grassroots was. So I got on the phone to ABC, Barry Sarafin, and pushed Sarafin to go up there, and alerted MacNeil/Lehrer and all the network crews that this was going to happen.
>
> So Dole was thinking that all these crews are there covering him and Durenberger, and the crews wanted this piece so they weren't going to tip anybody off. And Durenberger and Dole walk out of the tent and there's this bunch of people milling around and out come these bright orange signs saying "Stop Bork," and the people start chanting and completely surround Dole and Durenberger, and the camera crews were right there. You can see it on the ABC tape. They only showed about seven seconds of it, but you can see it.
>
> It was very humorous. They didn't get a good shot at Dole's face, but people who were there say it was kind of like, "where am I?" They followed him. Dole and Durenberger walked around the State

Fair shaking hands and these people followed him the entire two hours he was at the State Fair, never relenting. They were handing out Bork brochures as they followed him around.

There is a tendency to dismiss radio as among the more primitive of media. But, though much of the campaign's energies were focused on serving the needs of television producers and reporters, the imaginative and aggressive exploitation of radio opportunities demonstrated the campaign's attention to the details of media advocacy.

As Kusnet observes, talking about the persuasive powers of radio as a medium, "People driving to and from work; people in offices who get to listen to radio, people who go home and make dinner and have the radio going . . . You get to enter people's lives with radio. It almost becomes like the background of your life, and you can have this authority figure voice giving information and points of view, and it sort of seeps into your consciousness."

Booking radio talk shows by telephone (AFSCME has a radio talk show booking service) is not precisely high-tech. But AFSCME also pioneered in the development of the radio "feed", or "actuality": an audio package, prepared in Washington, which introduces and presents the voice of a leading advocate in a 60, 90, or 120-second news format, delivered by mail or (more timely) phone banks to radio stations for easy, "no-hands" insertion into hourly newscasts.

Ann Lewis persuaded Jesse Jackson to take time out from his presidential campaign during the first week of the hearings. Jackson taped five different radio feeds for use by black stations around the South. Henry Griggs describes the process:

Basically, what I'd do is take the taped interview, select out several sound bites, and for each one, write an "intro" and an "outro"—and I used Jackson's sound bites as sort of the filling for a jelly doughnut. I try to keep the whole tape down to about forty-five

COURTING THE MEDIA 167

seconds. We would convert each completed feed into a cartridge tape, which eliminates the need for rewinding, and then feed each report to several states over the course of a week or two. In this way, I was able to feed something different every single workday for five weeks. We didn't use the mail to notify stations that the feeds would be coming.

The transcript of one Jesse Jackson radio feed reads as follows:

As Senate hearings on the nomination of Robert Bork to the Supreme Court continued into their second week, a number of civil rights leaders raised opposition to Bork, saying his stands on constitutional rights of minorities are critical. The Reverend Jesse Jackson had these comments:

"Judge Bork is a threat to the future of civil rights, workers rights, and women's rights. The achievements of the last thirty years are threatened by Judge Bork not only because he disagreed with those decisions—the Civil Rights Act of 1964 or the Voting Rights Act. He also would have the power on the Supreme Court to overrule or undercut those decisions; he is backwards and he is activist in his intent to undercut our progress."

For such key states as Alabama, in addition to Jackson, Griggs recruited Ben Hooks and Althea Simmons of the NAACP. In Pennsylvania, concerns about Bork's position on consumer protection and the restraint of big business played well, so Joan Claybrook of Public Citizen blocked out a day to conduct radio talk show interviews booked by AFSCME. Griggs estimates that Claybrook did as many as twenty-seven separate interviews that day. For Arizona, Antonia Hernandez, president of the Mexican American Legal Defense and Educational Fund, signed up to do about a dozen interviews. Griggs recalls that she was not only very effective, but doubly welcome as bilingual. "The Spanish language stations were just thrilled that they had somebody who could speak Spanish as well."

AFSCME also produced some television actualities. For example, while Joan Claybrook was on the air with radio interviews, AFSCME was using its broadcast studio to produce satellite (TV) feeds of Ralph Nader actualities to TV stations throughout Pennsylvania.

Larger coalition groups also helped book prominent state and community leaders on local radio talk shows. They proved welcome guests for shows chronically hungering for new voices and lively subjects. From past progressive political and issue campaigns, as well as the coordination of the coalition's field operation, Mimi Mager drew on her vast network of activists in virtually every state.

"Mimi was great," says Griggs, "I've never met anyone in an organization that could find good people in every state in the Union, somehow. I could say to her 'I need a black woman, young, maybe a state legislator, in Alabama. Who have you got?' And she could crosshatch the whole field; it was amazing the way she could do that. I've never seen anything like it."

As we have seen, much original and creative media advocacy originated at the grassroots level, only indirectly stimulated by the flow of materials from Washington. But the informal communication network also constantly sought to stimulate and support media initiatives at the state and local level (and to make certain that their affiliates got their share of media attention). Mintz, for example, catalogues what he and national NARAL headquarters did:

I think of myself as a political operative who does media relations, as opposed to a public relations person who happens to do politics. For most of our activists that's generally the case. Media is something that they're generally very uncomfortable with.

There's a general reluctance to do aggressive media. One of the things you can do is to give them something that is eminently newsworthy, so that they can have confidence that, when they call a newspaper, they won't be rejected. Whenever I spoke to a reporter in Washington who was from a regional paper, I would give them

the NARAL situation, and [tell them] "you must call Jo Ellen Pass-
man in California," or, "you must call so and so in Minnesota and
talk to them about what's going on." The fact that they had reporters
calling them from D.C. for comment built their confidence level,
which allowed them to then approach people at their metro desks
when they would do local coalition activities.

The coalition activities were covered from the metro desk, wherever the city was, but the broader stuff was covered out of D.C. So
they were dealing with their reporters and I was dealing with ours.
I would give the reporters in D.C. the grand picture, but they needed
to speak to people about what was going on at the grassroots.

The Devil and Abraham Lincoln:
The Role of Paid Advertising

Procter & Gamble needs to spend millions for advertising to sell
soap, because if they don't the "great unwashed" will never learn
of the virtues of Ivory. But with 150 Washington reporters
clamoring to transmit to the public the sage words of the Block
Bork Coalition's leadership, why on earth should the coalition
pay a cent for advertising?

We might begin to answer that question by examining the pre-
cise role that media advocacy professionals assign to "issue advertising" or "paid media" in the media advocacy process. Of
course, one role for paid media is as a last resort when the news
media ("unpaid media") simply won't pay attention to the issue,
or the advocacy group's view of the issue. If that were really all
there was to paid issue advertising, then it would hardly seem
appropriate for the Bork campaign.

But issue advocates have discovered that paid media can do
more—much more. With paid media, advocates have the control to frame and present a concentrated advocacy message
without static or dilution. The paying advertiser shapes and
controls the message, the medium, and the time it is aired. By
contrast, brilliant words offered up in a press release (even a ra-

dio or TV actuality) can be ignored, garbled, superficially demolished by an even more brilliant quote from an adversary, distorted by journalist or editor bias, diminished by the journalist's search for "balance", cut to accommodate space limitations, or blown off the air by a fast-breaking tornado disaster.

Usually, the most time allocated in a TV news show to the most eloquent of spokespersons will be a fifteen, or even eight-second sound-bite. Experienced advocates learn to talk to the camera in "bites," but when the entire story, bites and all, is compressed into ninety seconds, even such compact bites will often be left in the editing room. Yet most Americans get their news from TV or radio, give only a few minutes' attention to most issues, and form their judgements accordingly. So a sixty-second advocacy commercial forces the advocates to compress their arguments and present them precisely as it wishes. As PFAW's Verveer observes,

> As much as we did to cooperate with the professional news, we thought a necessary element of making our case was to present the themes of the case against Bork as we understood them, directly, without the media's interpretation.

Even low budgets can allow for strategically critical paid radio advertising. Radio commercial production costs and radio time are relatively low-priced, and advocacy radio ads can be effectively "narrowcast" to reach a key population segment.

"Paid media can help structure unpaid media." That observation comes from Tony Schwartz, the creative media genius who pioneered and has perfected the art of deploying paid advertising in issue advocacy campaigns. In an election campaign, attacks on a candidate's position on certain issues raise the salience of those issues for the news media. Likewise, in an issue campaign, paid ads can influence the way in which the news media cover the issue.

Paid ads can themselves create news which ripples far beyond their media "buys," and, in so doing, frame the debate in the news media. "In order to make an impact on public debate," says PFAW's Kusnet, "you don't have to make a multi-million-dollar buy of radio and TV and print. You can get ideas and concepts and themes into public debate with a much more minimal buy, if you have something compelling to say, and if you say it in a compelling way."

A news conference to announce the "premiere" of an anti-Bork commercial starring Gregory Peck, for example, is certain to attract more press coverage, especially TV, than the release of a scholarly report on Bork's record (though the quality of the coverage may be inferior). The scene of a tourist family standing awestruck on the steps of the Supreme Court, while Peck's "voice-over" extols the glories of the Court and the dark shadow cast by Bork, is certain to capture the theatrical sense of the TV news producer. "Anything that is more entertaining than the single-spaced printed word of the 'talking head,' " says Kusnet, "gets attention":

> Try to put yourself in the mindset of someone making up a network news show. Much of their available footage for the news every day must consist of talking heads saying the same kinds of things, over and over. So if someone's done a video or radio spot, its different. It's different from all those generic authority figures talking into a camera. It's different from all the talking heads. If you have a media product, it gives you an enormous advantage in getting free media.

In a society that takes money seriously—so seriously that we are sometimes accused of letting the bottom line determine the hierarchy of all values for us—spending money, or the willingness to spend money, becomes a symbol of the spender's seriousness in pursuing the goal. Buying time or space, observes Kusnet, "establishes that your group is a real player and that a serious fight is being made on that issue."

The very act of producing and launching a paid media campaign on a public policy issue serves notice on both the media and policy-makers that the campaign is serious. Journalists and editors also read ads in their own publications, and those ads may tell them that there is a story evolving that ought to be better covered.

Kate Michelman claims that paid ads were the least effective of the media strategies employed by NARAL in "getting the message out." An op-ed piece does the same thing, "but NARAL's ads well served its institutional goal of establishing NARAL's 'presence.' " She observes,

> The ad did serve the visibility of the organization. For NARAL, the ads were targeted at policy-makers and the press; we believe it was beneficial for NARAL. It's getting yourself out there. We said some important things in our ad and I'm very glad we did it. Phones rang off the hook the day we ran the ads. But, really, it established NARAL's presence again, because an ad makes a statement. A full-page ad in the *New York Times* ran on a Sunday in the "Week in Review" section. I was doing an event that night in New York, and so many who attended brought the ad with them. They were impressed. These were a select group of people, high-dollar donors who pay attention to these issues, so for a certain level of presence and recognition, the ad was very important.

Paid ads "rally the troops." When a member of NARAL opens her morning paper and finds *her* organization in print, proclaiming its role in the battle, the fight becomes more real, more tangible. For many Americans, TV confers legitimacy: "You really don't exist in this country," says Kusnet, "unless you're on TV."

The Ads

The most famous, or notorious, of the paid ads used against the Bork confirmation was "The Last Word," which came to be known as the "Gregory Peck ad." It ran during the first ten days of the hearings. Wise media observers praised the subliminal skill of PFAW's famed communicators in craftily invoking the deeply imprinted image of Peck as the noble defender of civil rights in the film *To Kill a Mockingbird*, and as that embodiment of all that is just in American public values — Abraham Lincoln.

Suzanne Garment, an impassioned Bork supporter who loathed the ad, describes its salient features in a January 1988 article published in *Commentary* magazine:

> The spot was narrated by Gregory Peck, whose screen image is one of rectitude and whose voice we all trust. "There's a special feeling of awe people get," intones Peck in the commercial, "when they visit the Supreme Court of the United States, the ultimate guardian of our liberties." As Peck speaks, a traditional four-person nuclear family, with faces we have rarely seen since "Leave It to Beaver," is walking up the Court steps. Father points the building out to the children. Peck goes on. Bork should not be on the Court, he says, "He defended poll taxes and literacy tests, which kept many Americans from voting. He opposed the civil rights law that ended "whites only" signs at lunch counters. He doesn't believe the Constitution protects your right to privacy. And he thinks freedom of speech does not apply to literature and art and music." The commercial ends with the family in profile, gazing reverently at the Court. A gentle wind blows through their hair. The camera focuses lovingly on the cherubic face of the youngest. The end.

PFAW's David Kusnet, widely recognized as the creative force behind many progressive media initiatives, played a major role in the development of the Peck ad, which he describes:

> At PFAW, the technical, substantive issue people had generated and discovered an enormous amount of material about what was wrong with Bork's record. Then, the challenge became, "How do you convey this material through a medium that will reach people in terms they can understand. We figured you can't just go on TV saying, "Did you know that Robert Bork did this, this, and this," like a coffee auctioneer for sixty seconds, and have words trailing on the

screen. The question was, what is a motivating approach that can attract people's attention and hold it for sixty seconds while you talk about the record?

I think the contribution I made was a matter of tone. In my view you needed an upbeat tone to get people's attention, and make them listen respectfully to what you were saying. The Kiley poll had shown that, for all the attacks from the Right and Left, people like the Supreme Court. Basically, Americans like America. And, all things being equal, people respond better to a positive tone than a negative tone.

What we hit upon was the notion that thousands of tourists come on their pilgrimage to the nation's capital to see the basic institutions of our society. People go to the White House, people go to see Congress, and people go to the Supreme Court. There's not a day that goes by that you don't see people with cameras and maps going to the Supreme Court building. It's not an overstatement to say you can detect a kind of awe when they go to these shrines of our democracy.

So the concept was to have a family go to the steps of the Supreme Court building, and to have the narrator first speak in very positive terms about the feeling of awe that people get from going to the Supreme Court, because it's the ultimate guardian of their constitutional rights, and that's why it's so important who sits on the Supreme Court. Then the "bridge" was, "That's why we're so concerned that Robert Bork has been nominated to the Supreme Court." That "setup" took up somewhere between fifteen and twenty seconds.

Then, allowing for a ten-second conclusion, we had no more than thirty seconds to make the salient points of the case against him. What we did was select a few highlights or low points of his public record that hit the basic notion that he was against fairness and equal justice, and the narrator recites these. Then, there is a final pitch, "He would have the final word on your rights. Fortunately, the Senate has the last word on him."

That setup [worked] much better, because you had two opposite symbols interacting with each other: this nice American family and this great American institution; then you have Bork looming as a threat to the people and the institution, rather than just having a negative tone from the beginning.

The funny thing is, that made it less of a nasty attack on Bork than it would have been, had it been just sixty seconds of what's wrong

with Bork. Instead, it was twenty seconds about what's important
about the Supreme Court, thirty seconds of what's wrong with Bork,
and ten seconds of sum up.

Peck turns out to have been an afterthought, not part of a
Machiavellian scheme—the happy inspiration of PFAW
founder Norman Lear only after the ad had been written. Indeed
Kusnet shudders to think about how the ad would have fared
had it been written with Peck in mind. "We might have
choked—Jackie Blumenthal and Joe Rothstein and I, and everyone involved with the project. We might have thought, 'My
God, we're writing for Gregory Peck.' The fact that we were
loose and able to do the ad under pressure and deadlines may
have been because we didn't know we were doing it for Gregory
Peck."

"The irony," says Kusnet, "is that a lot of the coverage, pro and
con, has suggested that here was a slick, polished production
using a celebrated Hollywood movie star that sunk a Supreme
Court nominee. But, in point of fact, it was closer to a home
movie."

The Gregory Peck ad is the one most often cited in denuncia-
tions of the use of paid advertising to defeat Bork. Bork himself
denounced the "blitzkrieg" of negative advertising deployed to
defeat him. Actually, "the buy for the Gregory Peck ad was in
the neighborhood of $170,000," says Henry Griggs, "which
doesn't sell Kal Kan in Detroit."

It wasn't money but the Reagan White House itself that assured immortality to the Peck commercial. White House spokes-
man Marlin Fitzwater saw the network news stories on the ad
and blasted it in his following morning press conference. That
assured that the ad would remain in the news—and served the
White House strategy of deflecting attention from Bork's legal
philosophy to the campaign to defeat Bork.

Perhaps it is fitting that Gregory Peck himself should have the
last word, (though we explore the criticism of paid advertising

in chapter 12.) The December, 1988 *Parade* magazine carried an interview with Gregory Peck. The interviewer asked Peck, "was it not true that your voice-overs on the anti–Judge Bork spots were primarily responsible for the flood of letters that stopped Bork's confirmation to the Supreme Court?" The author recorded Peck's response:

> "No," he said, "I don't think my spots did it or that they alone would have done it. What gave them so much importance was when Marlin Fitzwater [the President's press spokesman] said publicly that Reagan regarded me as a "former friend." He paused again. "Before I agreed to do them, I read everything I could lay my hands on about Bork. After that I didn't consult anybody. I came to the conclusion that having that guy on the Supreme Court would be the beginning of turning back civil rights—and I felt it was time to step up to bat."

8

BUILDING MOMENTUM

The campaign succeeded by mid-July in establishing credible "winnability." As the summer passed, and the culmination—the hearings—loomed near, the campaign had now to establish that it was gaining momentum—that it was, in fact, *winning*.

Momentum was needed to sustain enthusiasm and energy. It would push over the line wary groups and wavering individuals, who still held back. It would reassure litigating lawyers who were troubled by Bork's views but might fear subtle reprisal from a Bork-dominated Court. And even the staunchest senatorial conscience is not immune from the prospect of being on the winning side—the majority. The bandwagon of history offers comfort and security.

So the Block Bork Coalition polished and burnished each small piece of evidence that the momentum was with them. If they succeeded in persuading a journalist that there were signs of movement in their direction, they would then take care to circulate the article generated, as yet another sign of movement. Others would pick up the refrain. Perception and reality advanced in sync.

A mailing from the Grassroots Task Force to state coordinators in mid-August highlighted an article from the *Los Angeles Times*, under the headline, "Bork: Opponents of Nominee Seen as Gaining Ground." That article quoted Bork supporters as confessing weakness, and was strongly bolstered by the professed optimism of his opponents.

"[H]is liberal opponents," wrote the *Times*'s David Lauter, "say the odds on his eventual confirmation by the Senate have slipped — from being 'a tough fight, but he'll win' to 'He may win but it will be tough' . . . 'The fight is eminently winnable,' a key liberal activist remarked this week."

Good news from any quarter — whether it was Senator Cranston's generous vote counts, another anti-Bork newspaper editorial, or a new poll showing growing opposition — was recycled to the grassroots, to members of the press, to the Hill. Ricki Seidman of People for the American Way describes the flow of paper to Senate offices:

> We decided very early on that we were going to send a packet up to the Hill every week . . . most of the time we had written something new . . . [We] also included the best editorials, the best op-eds, letters from people who were important. Something new all the time, to show the staff that things were moving, that things were progressing.

On October 1, a few days before the Judiciary Committee vote, the *Atlanta Constitution*, a moderate, highly regarded newspaper, published a poll of twelve southern states showing that not even a majority of those southerners who described themselves as conservative favored Bork's confirmation. "We got the results late the night before," says Seidman. "I got on the phone with my parents who live in Atlanta, and arranged through my father who works for a women's clothing company to have their shipper get to the airport at 8:00 A.M. the next morning and put fifty copies of the paper on the plane. By noon, [we] had them deliv-

ered to target offices—not xerox copies, but the actual newspaper."

An Army of Bork Scholars

Many of the grassroots activists were not content with brief
summaries of Bork's record, but avidly sought and studied the
scholarly, analytical reports which minutely documented the
Bork legal mind. And the more these concerned citizens—civil
rights advocates, constitutional law professors, leaders of
women's groups, consumer advocates, environmentalists, and
others—actually read Bork's writings, the more impassioned
they became in their opposition. As the coalition members read
the "Book of Bork," the reading fueled their passion,and added
to the weight of their opposition to his appointment to the Supreme Court.

In the typical public interest lobbying campaign, expertise—
scientific, technical, or legal—is usually lodged in only a handful of experts. The activists learn from the experts just enough
to deliver a coherent set of talking points, but their substantive
knowledge remains relatively shallow. By contrast, in the Bork
campaign, the coalition's numerous books on Bork—the research and analyses—enabled activists to engage in a massive
constitutional law seminar on the Borkian threat to constitutional liberties, thereby empowering through knowledge an
army of citizen advocates.

Pro-Bork critics portray the opposition as a liberal variety of
know-nothing politics—a campaign dictated by a core of elitists
to an inflamed mass of ignorant interest group followers. Yet
literally hundreds of those involved in the campaign studied
the "Book of Bork" on their own initiatives. These included lawyers and non-lawyers, those in Washington and those in the
field. This hunger for knowledge in depth came as a surprise to
many. Jenny Pfizer, legal director for the National Abortion

Rights Action League, confesses her astonishment: "People on our side were honestly reading the stuff."

James Brosnahan, a former U.S. attorney for the city of Phoenix and a prominent figure in the Bar, volunteered to work with the Judicial Selection Project in opposing Bork. He spoke at a coalition-sponsored forum in California designed to involve American Bar Association (ABA) conventioneers in the campaign to oppose Bork. Estelle Rogers remembered Brosnahan's comments:

> I ended up reading every one of Bork's opinions because I was talking to so many people in the Bar over that period who said, "Well I haven't read everything but" . . . and I said to them, "Well I have and I know." I've never been so glad to have spent a weekend reading opinions in my whole life, because I really gained some credibility that I never would have had.

As each new group entered the campaign or contemplated entering the Block Bork Coalition, it set about performing its own independent analysis of the Bork record. The Sierra Club Legal Defense Fund, the Lawyers' Committee on Civil Rights, and others did not rely upon the reports of other groups, but dedicated hundreds of hours of staff time to the direct study of Bork's writings, with special attention to how his judicial views impacted on their specific concerns.

The coalition Research and Drafting Task Force made certain that all the coalition members and potential coalition members received all the secondary reports and analyses. But such key primary sources as Bork's *Indiana Law Review* article and his recent Worldnet interview were widely and rapidly disseminated in their entirety. In this process, the leaders of each group built their own competence, credibility and confidence. Their mastery of the material would prove persuasive with senators and their staffs. Mario Moreno of the Mexican American Legal Defense and Educational Fund cites this phenomenon as a source of the coalition's moral and intellectual strength:

> If you had just one central group do the research, it would conceivably take longer to get that information disseminated. By having these organizations do their own homework and prepare their own position papers, an in-house expertise was developed which proves important in gauging the nomination's impact on various groups. The other way you would have had to convince them that first, your material was accurate, and then you'd have to get them to analyze it in terms of their own perspective. The organization wouldn't have gained by developing an in-house expertise. This was quite important because as the campaign went on the need for Bork experts became crucial. The more people were well versed on Bork, the better; the information dissemination aspect of the campaign became easier. Central dissemination would have been time consuming and cumbersome. Although there's a downside to duplication, in this case it was like everyone in the class doing their homework.

Reaching Out

When Senator Robert Byrd of West Virginia, who seemed to be leaning toward Bork, told a coalition lobbyist, "I'm not getting very much mail from home opposing Bork," he might have wanted to convince himself that a vote to confirm would not be politically painful. The campaign needed to convince him that a vote to confirm was no more cost-free than a vote to oppose.

And when a liberal New England senator like Claiborne Pell characterized the opposition to Bork, in an early and disturbing meeting with Washington lobbyists, as a "bunch of radicals," he needed to know that non-radicals, lots of them, opposed Bork in Rhode Island, and that a vote for confirmation was a vote against the center. "Nothing impresses a member of Congress more," says Carol Foreman, "than the most disparate elements possible walking in together."

The Coalition's annotated editions of the "Book of Bork"

served as a mammoth recruiting poster. And the Alliance for Justice's Aron proved a gifted recruiter.

Leonard Rubenstein of the Mental Health Law Project didn't see, at first, how the Bork nomination affected his constituency. Aron convinced him, both by argument and documentation. He became convinced that Bork posed a severe threat to the rights of the disabled, and drafted a strong report in opposition to the nomination which, in turn, recruited the support of almost thirty other disability-related organizations, including the National Mental Health Association and the Epilepsy Foundation. These groups, as Rubenstein emphasized at a press conference in Washington, are "mainstream groups which cannot be characterized as liberal interest groups by anyone's definition."

James A. Autry is a business executive with the Meredith Corporation in Des Moines, Iowa. His lawyer son has epilepsy, and his preschool son is autistic. He has been active in the Epilepsy Foundation. He wrote a moving op-ed article in the *Des Moines Register* decrying Bork's view that applying the Fourteenth Amendment's promise of "equal protection" to such groups as the handicapped is nothing more than judicial "adventurism." Autry wrote:

> There is nothing adventurous in the courts protecting the human dignity of United States citizens . . . Pardon my righteous indignation, but my sons have a right to be protected from discrimination and bigotry even if it upsets Bork's academic/intellectual apple cart.
>
> Bork's confirmation could be particularly devastating for the cause of handicapped rights because, unlike many of the Court's decisions on women's rights and civil rights that Bork promised to "accept," much of the case law on disability rights is yet to be developed . . .
>
> Bork's views, if they held sway, could have a profoundly negative effect on my life and on the lives of many of my friends and associates.

Brock Evans of the National Audubon Society is surely one of the most experienced and reflective of environmental lobbyists.

He recalled his initial concern, both as a citizen and as a lawyer, about Judge Bork's "general assaults on progressive values." But, at first, Evans and most of his colleagues did not believe that the Audubon Society and the environmental movement should join the campaign, for fear that such participation would mar their success in keeping environmental issues free of partisan politics.

Evans recalls a critical meeting, in which Nan Aron, Ralph Nader, and other coalition leaders made the case that the Bork fight was the environmentalist's fight, too. Bill Schultz and his colleagues at Nader's Public Citizen Litigation Group, who had analyzed Bork's record as an appellate judge, made a convincing case that Bork was a specific threat to environmental interests. "Bork seemed to come up four-square for business, polluting, or anti-environmental interests every time he had a chance," concluded Evans. "No impartial judge, this person."

And Evans remembers Nader's "pitch":

> In his intense way, he said something like, "We in the progressive community can get the votes on the East and West Coasts; but we have trouble in the center, the heart of the nation . . . you have great strength there and we need your help . . . This is, should be, your fight, too . . . Bork will be the ruination of what you care about."

Evans was convinced, and inspired:

> I left that meeting . . . convinced that we as a movement had to do something and soon. I was on my way to see Senator Durenberger's staff on another big issue — protection of the Arctic National Wildlife Refuge. Durenberger is just the kind of moderate Republican whom we have ties with and should reach on such a vote . . .
>
> Well, I burst into his office, saying something like, "Forget about the Arctic National Wildlife Refuge — let me tell you about the environmental issue we really want you work on . . . " And as I told him about Bork and his disastrous environmental record, he groaned, "Oh, God, no! Don't ask this of us, please — we thought at

least this would be neutral environmentally." He also knew that I was the political chairman of the League of Conservation Voters, responsible for endorsements, and Durenberger badly wanted our endorsement.

The Sierra Club, with its 416,000 members (many of whom vote Republican), as well as the Sierra Club Legal Defense Fund (SCLDF), were persuaded to put aside other priorities and conduct their own independent study of Bork's record. After a guided tour through the "Book of Bork," the SCLDF took the lead for environmental groups in issuing a report urging Senate rejection.

The Executive Committee of the Audubon Society did not reach a consensus on whether to oppose the nomination, but Evans says, "We were all certainly there in spirit and talked it up wherever we went."

Hope Babcock, Audubon's general counsel and a former law student of Bork's, sent a memorandum to all fourteen Judiciary Committee members documenting how Bork's rulings on "standing to sue" threatened to deny access to the courts for citizens who seek to challenge such government malfeasance as "the weakening of national surface mining regulations," or seeking to compel the government "to issue regulations protecting visibility in our national parks to protect some unique and threatened resource like Mono Lake, the Alaskan Coastal Plain or whooping cranes in Central Nebraska."

The building momentum swept along with it organizations whose members overwhelmingly opposed Bork, but were constrained by competing institutional guidelines or traditions. The ACLU is a frequent litigator in the Supreme Court, and had scrupulously maintained a non-partisan position on Court nominations. In its seventy-year history, it had only opposed one judicial nominee, William Rehnquist. But, though the ACLU had opposed Rehnquist's confirmation as an associate Supreme Court justice in 1971, it did not oppose his elevation

to chief justice in 1986. It was not until August 31, after strenuous internal debate over whether Judge Bork was so far out of
the mainstream on civil liberties, that the ACLU board officially
voiced its opposition to confirmation.

Jonathan Cuneo, an advocate for strengthened antitrust laws
and enforcement took the lead in organizing the "Pocketbook
Coalition." In addition to consumer groups, this mini-coalition
drew together the attorneys general of New York and West Virginia and small businesses, such as Burlington Coat Factory,
Service Station Dealers of America, and Melart Jewelers, a
nineteen-store retail company operating in Washington, D.C.
(whose President, Burt Foer, just happened to have been a
former federal antitrust enforcement official). Each saw Bork as
the ideological ally of big business.

On October 1, the Council of Aging Organizations, a con-
federation of some twenty-five national groups which represent
senior citizens, sent to all members of the Senate a joint statement of opposition, accompanied by a critical legal analysis
prepared by senior advocate David Marlin on "Judge Bork and
the Elderly."

So successful was the coalition in building bridges to disparate constituencies that some of the women's leaders—
especially Kathy Bonk of the NOW Legal Defense Fund, Estelle
Rogers of the Federation of Women Lawyers, and Irene
Natividad of the National Women's Political Caucus—became
concerned that women's issues were getting lost in the din.
Representatives of twenty-two national women's groups held a
joint press conference to announce their common cause in opposing the nomination four days before the hearings began. Particularly newsworthy was that nearly half of the membership organizations, such as the National Federation of Business and
Professional Women and the American Association of University Women, had never before opposed a Supreme Court
nominee.

The Block Bork Coalition had achieved the goal of co-chair

Nan Aron: "to keep up a steady drumbeat of opposition to confirmation." Just before the start of the televised hearings, the national coalition, in a press release, claimed, "Organizations With
More Than 20 Million Members Mount Opposition to Bork."

Momentum at the Grassroots

In mid-September, after the first rush of energy had peaked, the
Grassroots Task Force, and especially the "desks," helped keep
the state activists' spirits and energy from flagging. The task
force diffused tactics which had proved useful for one state or
local coalition to the others. "We could find out what was going
on around the country," says Berry Sweet of the Arizona Abortion Rights Action League, "and get some ideas."

NARAL circulated to state affiliates its weekly "Bork Beat,"
which highlighted events around the country. NARAL's Debra
Ness says, "This homespun weekly update on grassroots activities not only facilitated the transfer of creative ideas and tactics,
but also inspired healthy competition between states as to who
could generate the most grassroots action." The national Media
Task Force's calendar of grassroots activities had the same
effect.

A profusion of initiatives flourished as state and local coalitions stepped up the pace of their activity. The following is just
a sampling:

- *NOW held a "Burma Shavathon" in Florida.* Like the old
  Burma Shave signs strung out on every highway, NOW's human billboards stood at intervals along the road, each holding a sign with a brief pithy phrase; strung together, they delivered the anti-Bork message.
- *A coalition-sponsored mock hearing was staged* in the House
  chambers at the state capitol in West Virginia to dramatize
  opposition to Bork in an appropriate setting.

- A *newspaper titled the "Bork Blocker"* was distributed to 48,000 West Virginians.
- The *League of Women Voters sponsored a debate* on the nomination in Dade County, Florida, and after both sides made their case, the audience voted by a two-to-one margin against confirmation.
- *"Bork Sunday" was celebrated* in black churches throughout Georgia, at which the collection plates were piled high with masses of handwritten letters to senators protesting the Bork nomination.
- The *Northern California Coalition Against Bork demonstrated* outside the annual meeting of the American Bar Association, chanting, "We Want Justice, Not Bork."
- The *Southern California coalition held a press conference* to announce a "search party for Wilson," to dramatize the Republican senator's elusiveness in failing to meet with constituents opposed to Bork.
- A *"lunchtime letters" campaign by Providence lawyers* spurred the flow of handwritten letters opposing Bork to the two Rhode Island senators.
- At *the behest of the local coalition,* the City Council of Pittsburgh, Bork's hometown, passed a resolution opposing the confirmation.
- The *Georgia Abortion Rights Action League* held a "we won't go back" party/fundraiser, where a disc jockey spun records from 1973 (the year of *Roe v. Wade*), and members dressed up in clothes from the ancient 1970s.
- An *"information picket" was conducted by NOW* outside Specter's Philadelphia office. They let it be known that they were not protesting against Specter, but simply wished him to know where the citizens stood.
- *Oregon activists attached anti-Bork banners* to bridges over the airport access road, so that Senators Packwood and Hatfield would not miss them as they returned to Portland for the August recess.

- In Connecticut, the coalition organized a "Bork watch" during the Senate hearings, designating spokespersons all over the state who would be monitoring the hearings and available for minute-by-minute commentary.
- One strategy drawn from the sixties was "adopt-a-senator" campaigns in which by activists whose own senators were certain to vote for Bork wrote to uncommitted senators in neighboring states.

Initiative, innovation, humor, keen instincts for local concerns and themes — all contributed to the growing public awareness of people rising in defense of their liberties. For some, these activities awakened echoes of earlier citizen uprisings, notably the civil rights movement.

The Citizen-Scholars

Even momentum has its risks. The more the groups piled on to the anti-Bork campaign, the greater was the risk that Bork's proponents would be seen as justified in their complaint that the judicial selection process was being submerged in unseemly politicization. And some senators who looked upon their constitutional responsibilities as quasi-judicial might well recoil from the exuberant campaigning.

But there was one group of citizen-scholars who could claim both special knowledge and understanding about the law and a legitimate interest in the nomination, beyond any claim of "special interest": the nation's lawyers, and most especially, its teachers and scholars of the law. Lawyers are, formally, "officers of the court." And no senator could consider it inappropriate for lawyers and law teachers to communicate their concerns about the dangers to the law and to the courts of Bork's judicial and constitutional philosophy. And, as members of a generally conservative profession, the lawyers were perhaps the single most credible constituency for conveying to the Senate the extremism of Bork's legal convictions. Indeed, most uncommitted members of the Senate, in the course of their deliberations, actively sought out the guidance and counsel of legal scholars, especially from "back home."

Yet, at the outset, leaders of the coalition feared that few mainstream lawyers would openly oppose the nomination. Many, they believed, would be inhibited by Bork's reputation as a great constitutional scholar. Litigators would think twice before risking the alienation of a future justice. "We knew that lawyers are the last ones, the last people on earth, to get involved in a judgeship battle," says Nan Aron. "They're intimidated; they don't want to have to speak out against a judge and then have to appear before him or her the next month. So our record at getting lawyers was absolutely horrendous."

These fears were compounded by the strong endorsement of Judge Bork by Lloyd Cutler, a leading Washington lawyer with strong civil rights and Democratic credentials. His *New York Times* op-ed column ("Judge Bork: Well Within the Mainstream") in mid-July was seen by chagrined coalition lawyers as a preemptive strike, well timed and placed to chill broad lawyer mobilization against Bork. Cutler's unexpected endorsement was followed by an unusual outspoken endorsement from Supreme Court Justice John Paul Stevens, one of the Court's respected moderates. It appeared as if the legal establishment, the moderate center, was about to coalesce in support of its friend and colleague.

But it soon became apparent that the Cutler and Stevens endorsements could not stem a spontaneous outpouring of resentment from the nation's lawyers. "We got more calls into this office from people wanting to help than on any issue we've worked on, and a lot of the people who called were lawyers and law professors," says PFAW's Ricki Seidman.

Within twenty-four hours of the nomination, civil rights veteran Bill Taylor received an unsolicited phone call from Ted

Kennedy. Would Taylor go to work enlisting and coordinating the efforts of constitutional law scholars and law school deans opposed to Bork? Both Kennedy and Taylor had been involved in and impressed by the uprising of the law teachers in the previous year's nearly successful fight to deny confirmation to poorly qualified Indiana lawyer Daniel Manion in his appointment to the Seventh Circuit Court of Appeals. And Aron, with her colleagues in the Alliance, had gathered the signatures of about a hundred law deans and professors in opposition to the elevation of Rehnquist to chief justice.

Taylor, and American University law professor Herman Schwartz, together with Ricki Seidman and John Haber of People for the American Way, set up an informal coordination center for civil rights lawyers, deans, and law professors seeking to lend their names and knowledge to the anti-Bork campaign. Massive packets of the coalition's "Book of Bork" were shipped out to faculty members at law schools everywhere.

Simultaneously, committee staff were working on a parallel track. Senator Metzenbaum's Antitrust subcommittee counsel Bill Rothbard recalls:

> Over a period of several weeks in July and August I spent a good deal of time calling Bork's former colleagues and students at Yale and law professors around the country and prominent Bar leaders like [William] Coleman to see how they felt about him.

The expansion of the network of lawyers opposing Bork needed no stimulation. Through the summer, lawyers and law professors undertook to organize each other. Law deans called their counterparts at other law schools. One or more of the law faculty members undertook to recruit and organize the opposition at each law school. Half of the lawyers in Philadelphia's large firms — including former colleagues of former prosecutor Senator Arlen Specter — added their names to the lists of those who feared the consequences of a Bork appointment. The prestigious 17,000-member Association of the Bar of the City of New York took an unprecedented formal position in opposition to confirmation.

Seattle attorney Frank Shoichet, a leader of the local Block Bork Alliance, first drafted a one-page letter of opposition, then secured the signatures of three retired state judges, including a former chief justice of the Washington state Supreme Court. He then sent this letter to the 13,000 members of the Washington Bar, urging them to write and express their concerns about Bork to Senator Dan Evans.

While the University of Chicago Law School faculty was rallying in support of Bork as the the most distinguished member of the "Chicago School" of legal analysis, John Clay of Mayer, Brown & Platt in Chicago began organizing "Lawyers for the Judiciary," which ultimately claimed more than 700 names. The group conducted "fly-ins" — it chartered planes and flew to hold press conferences in key locations throughout Illinois.

While the nation's lawyers and teachers were joining the anti-Bork movement, coalition lawyers Nan Aron, Herman Schwartz, Estelle Rogers, Elaine Jones, Judith Lichtman, and others set their sights on the established leaders of the Bar — Lloyd Cutler's counterparts. If they were able to persuade a critical mass of such leaders to make their opposition public, their stand would be sure to send a strong message to the Senate and stiffen the resolve of their lesser colleagues at the Bar. Aron explains:

> We knew that if we could get former judges, legislators, former governors, all of whom are lawyers and pillars of the Bar, that would send a very mighty message to the Senate: "We are not intimidated; we will speak out; this is an issue of such great moment that we will sign up and register our outrage." This was the first attempt that we had ever made to do this, and it wasn't easy.
>
> We knew we could get hundreds of lawyers in Washington, D.C., to sign a letter, but what we were striving for was to get lawyers across the country, and across the political spectrum, to sign on.

They persuaded five "pillars of the Bar" to form a committee to circulate a letter which gathered signatures from other "pillars" in more than thirty states. The committee was composed of Marvin Frankel, a former federal judge; Oscar Ruebhausen, former president of the Bar Association of the City of New York (and a former federal judge and former counsel to Republican Nelson Rockefeller); Jay Topkis, a prominent constitutional lawyer; David Isbell, former president of the D.C. Bar (and a law school classmate of Senator Specter); and Robert Kapp, former co-chair of the Lawyers' Committee for Civil Rights Under Law (whose law partner was Frank Fahrenkopf, chairman of the Republican National Committee).

The five names were magical door openers, says Aron:

> Those names allowed us to buttonhole people at the ABA [American Bar Association], people in Utah, people in California, people in thirty or forty states, and get them to give us names and work with us. We spoke with retired judges, many of whom on their off hours called up lawyers and got them to sign up. Some of our lawyers signed on and then sent us op-ed pieces they had written. As in any organizing campaign, you get people to sign up first, and once they sign their name on the dotted line, they're willing to lend their name and their efforts to other things—and so what we looked for was their signature, and then we went back to them, time and time again, to make calls to senators.

Armed with the letter and the growing list of prominent signers, Nan Aron and Estelle Rogers laid siege to the more than 13,000 delegates to the American Bar Association annual convention in late August in San Francisco. They arranged for such speakers as constitutional scholar Walter Dellinger to participate in a forum on the nomination held at a nearby hotel— which was an event entirely separate from the ABA, but drew dozens of conventioners. The *Washington Post*'s Ruth Marcus noted that "The most talked-about lawyer at the largest gathering of lawyers in history has been one who didn't even make it

to the American Bar Association annual meeting here." Aron
reminisces:

> After the campaign was over, a lawyer in town called me up and
> said, "I just have to let you know that when I read these articles about
> multi-million-dollar lobbying campaigns being waged on either
> side, I have a distinct memory of you standing in the lobby of the
> Hilton Hotel in San Francisco with your two shopping bags, hand-
> ing out leaflets left and right." That was the reality of organizing.
>
> One of the things that struck me was the way I could get to a lot
> of the lawyers, most of whom are male, at the ABA was to talk to
> their wives . . . In terms of mass mobilization, any opportunity to
> get a captive audience of a couple hundred or a couple thousand
> people, was good.

Hundreds of the nation's most able lawyers wrote letters full
of learning and passion; they did not send postcards. They
wrote op-ed articles and letters to the editor. As leading
citizens, they had little difficulty arranging to meet with their
senators during the congressional recesses.

Bork's supporters in the White House and Justice Department
and in the legal community, some of them his former teaching
colleagues, were simultaneously seeking to recruit support
from members of the Bar. Their efforts bore sparse fruit.

Senator Orrin Hatch released a list of "100 Selected Law
Professors" supporting confirmation. (The number shrank to 99
when Senator DeConcini received word from a former dean of
the University of Arizona who had not authorized the use of his
name.) The outreach effort coordinated by Nan Aron and Leslie
Proll of the Alliance for Justice attracted the signatures of 102
"Pillars of the Bar."

The coalition also registered the opposition of 32 law school
deans, 71 constitutional law professors and 1,925 law
teachers — 40 percent of the full-time law faculty members at
ABA accredited law schools. Their impact was felt, not so much
from the gross numbers, but from the state-by-state breakdown

of letters to each "swing" senator from lawyers and teachers and judges who taught or practiced or enforced the law, and occupied a position of community leadership, in that state. "You couldn't have manufactured it if it wasn't there," says Bill Taylor, "and those thousands was an absolutely extraordinary turnout of people."

Neas believes, "Cutler turned out in the end to be as much a positive as a negative. If his endorsement hadn't happened when it did, I'm not sure we would have gotten so galvanized."

And galvanized they got.

9

BURY BORK—OR THE CAMPAIGN?

Block Bork Coalition stalwarts in Washington flinched when they heard that Maggie Kuhn, the mischievously resourceful founder of the Gray Panthers, proposed holding a mock funeral for the Constitution in Philadelphia just one day before the Senate hearings. At first other leaders of the Philadelphia coalition were doubtful, too, about the seemliness of such a spectacle, as they visualized scenes of exuberant mourning over the death of civil rights at the murderous hands of a Borkian Court. Let us stick to more sober, less aggressive activities, they argued.

But the concept took on life. This was, after all, Philadelphia, birthplace of the Constitution, in the very year of its bicentennial. And this was a coalition which had boldly called itself the "Philadelphia Ad Hoc Coalition to Save the Constitution."

The more the state coalition leaders talked, the more they liked the idea. The black churches and their ministers were at the heart of the Philadelphia coalition; their churches would be an apt setting for the "Funeral for Justice," especially the Bright Hope Baptist Church of William Gray III, minister and respected black congressman, chairman of the House Budget Committee.

Why not include lamentations over a casket symbolizing a post-Bork Constitution, bearing the ashes of civil rights, and borne by a rich diversity of pallbearers in a mass funeral procession through the streets of Philadelphia to Senator Specter's office?

And why limit participation to Philadelphia? Why not a "Train for Justice," originating in Pittsburgh, and stopping to take on mourners as it passed across the state to Philadelphia? So the plan grew. A special committee was established and assignments were made: organizing the program, the speakers, the props, the funeral and procession ceremonies. The "Train for Justice" required the joint planning of the two coalitions in Pittsburgh and Philadelphia, and all their constituent organizations. Energy poured forth.

Kate Michelman, co-chair of the Grassroots Task Force, says she "was absolutely panic stricken about it, and our affiliate was working on this. So I got on the phone with them, and said, 'What is this coffin garbage?' I really felt that the coffin idea was just too hokey and I told her how worried I was about it because I had made a commitment to the national coalition to keep things on a dignified level."

Frances Sheehan, the Pennsylvania NARAL executive director, tried to reassure Linda Schwartz, the organizer hired by the Leadership Conference to work with several state coalitions including those in Pennsylvania. "I don't think this event *could* have boomeranged," says Sheehan. "It was a good event from the beginning of the concept, and they just didn't know the community well enough to know that. They didn't know the players; they didn't have the vision of the event that we did, and they didn't trust. I understand that. I think the thing about being in Washington is that you also hear all the nightmares."

The Washington worriers were not mollified. Nikki Heidepriem, who helped develop the campaign's themes, cringed at the concept: "Message has to do both with what you say, and how you say it. A 'Funeral for Justice'—now this was not consistent with our view of the line of the campaign; it was heart-stopping."

And all the "signals" from Specter's office were grim. The senator would be offended; might be alienated; would be angered by intemperate attacks. The worst nightmare: Arlen Specter, one of four swing votes on the Senate Judiciary Committee might even be goaded into voting for Bork to avoid any suggestion that he would succumb to intimidation! "We kept telling them it was stupid," says Jeff Robinson, Specter's subcommittee counsel. "You've gotta do what you've gotta do; but if what you're interested in doing is convincing him one way or another, that sort of thing has a zero impact, or a negative impact!"

In near desperation, key strategists of the national coalition pleaded with Kennedy's staff to get him to call the Pennsylvania organizers and urge them to call off the event.

He didn't—and their fears proved exaggerated. Some 1,200 people attended the funeral. It was a model of tact and decorum, and profoundly moving in the depth of feeling—conveyed by speaker after speaker, and by an overflow audience—for the Constitution as a living shield against racism and injustice. Press coverage was excellent, and sympathetic, including national coverage by CBS, NBC and ABC's "Nightline."

(In fairness, the funeral did provide a chilling glimpse of just the attacks the Washington insiders feared: one speaker departed from the prevailing respectful attitude toward Specter's careful deliberations. He denounced Specter and threatened to unseat Specter's wife from her long-held seat on the Philadelphia City Council. Such tirades, had they otherwise characterized the funeral, might well have infuriated Specter. And perhaps the alarms sent out from Washington at least reinforced the funeral organizers' insistence upon restraint, so that such bully rhetoric was confined to the one speaker.)

Mimi Mager, the national grassroots coordinator, cheerfully admits being flat wrong:

If there's one place where we should say a *mea culpa*, it was that event. In fact, it was a terrific event. It got wonderful coverage and it was an example of where the event was done by the black community, primarily by the ministers. They knew what needed to be done, and they knew what was going to work. It really was the right event for that community and it did the job of energizing the people it was intended to.

There were few events by state coalitions which provoked as much "creative tension" between "Washington" and the "the field." Those shorthand labels themselves reveal the germ of the problem; they are "we-they" terms. The professional public interest lobbyists, media strategists, and organizers based in Washington tend to view their local members and activists in the field as a resource to be cultivated, then controlled. They are reluctant to leave any part of a national grassroots campaign untended; surely there must be a coordination process controlled by a central authority if there is to be unity of themes and strategies.

Grassroots activists, on the other hand, tend to view even their own colleagues and leaders in Washington as tainted by their surroundings, by the arrogance of the centrality of power. They feel they are closer to "the people," while Washington, and all who work within it, are isolated from the real country. They feel Washington appreciates neither their knowledge and learning, nor their strategic skills, nor their prudence and judgement.

There is some truth to both perceptions; but they can be exaggerated. And exaggeration does lead to tension, both in strategy and relationships.

A campaign characterized by tempered decorum may suit senatorial notions of the judicial confirmation process, but activists, once alerted and engaged, may well have different notions of propriety. And all Americans, progressive political activists no less than libertarians, resent and resist dictation from Washington.

There was a consensus among most of the Washington-based

strategists that the Bork campaign had to be far more decorous than a typical legislative campaign. Althea Simmons, the NAACP's veteran field general, was clear as to the winning strategy: "A low profile. Don't tip your hand. No statements. No inkling of thrust." She recalls:

> My gut feeling [was] that if we had the coffins, the caskets, and all that kind of crazy stuff we were going to turn off even our friends. The Supreme Court nomination has a status that is higher than other pieces of legislation. Those tactics would be perceived as a "no-no." In the NAACP literature I sent out, on page one of my cover letter, I said, "Do not engage in demonstrations."

Kate Michelman agreed:

> We had to be careful not to get lumped in with the crazies out there; we had to raise issues that had substantive research behind them, so our reason for not supporting massive rallies was that they can easily get out of control. We were worried that rallies would draw out the kooks, the anti-abortion groups.

Their convictions were widely shared among the members of the national coalition, but not unanimously. The National Organization of Women, in particular, demurred. Sheri O'Dell spelled out NOW's view plainly:

> We looked at what role we could play here that was beyond just our members writing and calling and making constituent visits. We were well aware that some of the people working on the grassroots component didn't like the rally idea. They thought it was going to backfire. Our position was, "That's bunk." It's absolutely critical that there be constant awareness through the press and the public, getting people riled up sitting in their living rooms. By the time they got ready to take that vote, the public had spoken, and they said, "You'd better not put this guy on the Court!" And I don't think that public opinion would have hardened against him without that level of activity, and without the very visible actions and the pickets and the rallies.

NOW and its members sought to draw media attention to the intensity of the opposition. Others, like Simmons and Michelman, feared that the *medium* for gaining press coverage — boisterous rallies and events — would become the *message* that Bork's opposition was what President Reagan enjoyed labeling as the "loonie Left."

But, once roused, would grassroots activists be led? Would this widely diverse, activated citizenry follow the carefully calibrated themes and campaign design emanating from Washington? And should they? The answer, as the "Funeral for Justice" illustrates is: "Yes, and no!"

Washington could provide support, it could suggest, it could cajole, but it couldn't control. The field people believed they understood, better than distant Washington, the political culture of their own states, the salient issues, the local leadership structure, and the local media. Bill Robinson of the Lawyers' Committee on Civil Rights, believes they were right:

> Out in the country, this thing acquired a life of its own. You couldn't direct everything because there had been a snowball effect. Organizations in major centers had prepared information and gotten it out, but once it got out there, another level of leadership in the country took over and it assumed a life of its own.
>
> These local people should not be underestimated. The point person in Alabama is . . . a very experienced lawyer, member of the state Senate — a grassroots type of guy in no way lacking in sophistication. The people in Washington were no more sophisticated either intellectually or in oral persuasion ability.

While the national Coalition, through its "desks," attempted to monitor the universe of grassroots activities, the coalition's Grassroots Task Force sometimes did not hear about planned events until after the fact. Unlike the "Funeral for Justice," there was a boisterous, unruly anti-Bork demonstration in Texas, which drew network coverage — conveying an image of unreasoning zeal, not reasoned opposition.

The Alabama coalition chose to appeal to churchgoers by

making an issue of Bork's reputed religious agnosticism — an issue first raised by Senator Heflin. The raising of such an issue — personal and far afield from Bork's legal philosophy — was deeply troubling to coalition leaders in Washington.

Such episodes led the coalition's national leaders, at times, to seek to discourage or restrain events enthusiastically planned by grassroots organizers.

Thus, the campaign faced a series of inherent conflicts: "inside" vs. "outside" politics (and Washington-based "insiders" vs. activist "outsiders"); central direction and control vs. the blooming of a thousand diverse expressions of opposition; decorum vs. intensity.

NOW President Molly Yard wears her Washington outsiders hat as a badge of honor. A great and courageous political organizer for unpopular causes of principle, there is, as the *Washington Post*'s Jacqueline Trescott put it, "nothing subtle about her, just an abiding attachment to unreconstructed liberalism." Yard expressed her concerns about the insider-outsider conflicts:

> Our organization is on the cutting edge stating the problem. We recognize that other people are back here doing what is possible. They're doing what's possible because we're out there pushing, and both roles are perfectly legitimate . . . My real distress is that I find a lot of our colleagues either not understanding how we operate or not willing to accept that it's a legitimate way of operating. I accept what they're doing as totally legitimate, and I think you have to have both. I don't think you get very far without both.

Mid-course Corrections

It took prodding by a key Senate leader to get national coalition strategists to consider turning up the heat. Nearly two months into the campaign, around the third week of August, Ralph Neas received a call from Senator Howard Metzenbaum, who

has a keen sense of the ebb and flow of the Senate tides. Neas
paraphrases Metzenbaum's warning:

> I think you're underestimating what it will take to win this battle.
> In my opinion, senators have got to understand how controversial
> this nomination is, and I think you've got to raise the temperature.
> I think that you've got to make them feel the heat. All the national
> leadership in the world won't make a difference. You've got to get
> the women and blacks in the states involved. I think that if you can
> get rallies that reflect the diversity of the coalition — and in the South
> you certainly want a lot of NAACP and the other national organiza-
> tions, but you want to bring in the churches and the ACLU and the
> unions, but [Senators] Heflin, Johnston and the others have got to
> hear it. Even though it could provoke counter-demonstrations,
> that's not going to hurt you. It's going to underscore the controver-
> sial nature of this nomination.

"We were going to have to create some storms," realized Neas.
"This was one of the few times that there really was a fairly sig-
nificant alteration in the strategy."
As Mimi Mager reflects:

> We changed our philosophy as we went along. Initially, when
> someone said, "We want to do an event outside the senator's office,"
> we would say, "No, you can't do that; we don't want anything that's
> confrontational." That was probably the right judgement, but it was
> a little too rigid. We needed to look at it case by case. But knowing
> when you had crossed that line was the more difficult part. A num-
> ber of the groups had done so much, they had laid the groundwork,
> that to energize them, to keep them going, you had to give them
> something else, and to say that they couldn't do it really was defeat-
> ing our larger purpose and agenda.

Georgia furnishes a good example of "stepping up the heat."
The state coalition had become increasingly frustrated at the
lack of a firm response from their junior senator, Wyche Fowler,
whom many of them had supported. "People were just so outraged [at Bork], that we wanted to know something before the

hearings," says the Rev. Tim McDonald of the Southern Christian Leadership Conference. "We were afraid Bork was going to be Ollie North; he almost persuaded some of those folks. We weren't going to be duped by that. We wanted him to know what the grassroots thought about Bork. We thought it was more important for him to hear it from the people than from Bork."

As the hearings concluded, despite countless meetings with Fowler and his staff, letters, and calls, the coalition had received no clear signal of a Fowler decision to oppose the nomination. They decided to hold a prayer vigil at Fowler's Atlanta office. Rev. McDonald remembers:

> We got a press release out, and we were getting ready. I received a call: "Listen to your radio tomorrow, at four o'clock, and you'll hear something very important. And take that under consideration as you consider your prayer vigil." That was all they said. The announcement was that Fowler was going to oppose Bork, and it came on . . . the news station here. At that point we called off the prayer vigil.

For a short campaign, much learning took place. And that was so largely because the principals, both in Washington and the field, were open to learning. The learning had to flow both ways. As Mager observes:

> Many of the outsiders probably didn't know there were two games being played. Unless you were able to play in both of those fields, it never would have worked. A number of groups outside Washington didn't start off with a good taste for what Washington lobbyists do, and equally, the people in Washington think, "What could those people back home do that's going to make any real difference." I think that all turned around.

The first lesson for those in Washington less practiced in grassroots campaigning was a dose of humility. Even experienced coalition-builders and networkers remarked on the level of knowledge and sophistication displayed in the Bork campaign by local activists. Mager speaks of the national coalition providing local activists with "the framework, and then they would build in the important issues for their state. I was surprised at the level of expertise and sophistication of the people who were part of the coalitions in the states, it was incredibly high."

Again, it is Mager (who was among those least needing to be taught) who acknowledges the lesson:

> We certainly did learn about the capability of the grassroots groups, what the potential is, and what the relationship should be and could be between Washington and the grassroots. Many Washington-based people started with the view, "Fine, we'll tell them what to do, and as long as they do that, we'll support them."

But, as Bill Hamilton, a wise and experienced Planned Parenthood lobbyist, observed, "The train had left the station." State activists would respect and be guided by the coalition's determination not to let the nomination struggle be turned into a debate over abortion or affirmative action. But within the large framework shaped by the national coalition, the local coalitions demanded respect and autonomy.

Arizona grassroots organizer Karen Bosch makes it clear why day-to-day decisions had to be made by those who knew the community:

> Washington gave us very concrete ideas as to what might be helpful, particularly if we asked. They might make a recommendation and then the Arizona coalition would consider it, but wouldn't necessarily always take that advice. By the same token, Washington did listen to us also. All the final decisions, however, were made in the field as to what we would do or not do, because we were closer to the situation there and knew what was needed. The people who were implementing the action really had to be the ones making the final decisions about what was needed and what had to be done.

In the case of the "Funeral for Justice", the Philadelphia coalition understood explicitly what the Grassroots Task Force knew in the abstract: the key to the politics of the Bork campaign in the home of the Constitution, Philadelphia, was strong community-wide support for civil rights, and the key to mobilizing for civil rights was the strength of the black ministry. Without the uniting role of the black ministers, and the focal point of the black churches, Philadelphia would prove hard to organize. The funeral in a black church also provided a singular mechanism for uniting blacks and whites in a city where racial tensions run deep and would otherwise be hard to bridge.

There was a generic lesson to be learned: A tightly controlled campaign which attempts to blanket excessive displays of passion can end up smothering energy and enthusiasm. (Ironically, conservative critics of the White House contend that the president's team leached the energy out of *their* campaign for Bork, dampening activism by promoting Judge Bork as a "moderate.")

The "Funeral for Justice" and the "Train for Justice" illustrate the creative energy available to a national coalition that leaves its grassroots activists room for local initiative. In such a situation, the Washington-based Grassroots Task Force worked best as resource, not as a hierarchy.

Though the coalition eased its rigid opposition to rallies, and acknowledged the force of the "Funeral for Justice," the flow of admonitions from Washington did serve to dampen the more exuberant tendencies of grassroots advocates.

Largely, throughout the country, a balance was fairly struck between decorum and intensity, restraint and passion. With the exception of the irrepressible NOW, there were relatively few rallies. Most state coalitions concentrated on leafletting, organizing phone banks, getting letters and postcards out, circulating signed petitions, securing op-ed columns, holding press conferences, and quietly engaging the involvement of those prominent community leaders whom the combined coalition networks recruited for the massive anti-Bork campaign.

Debra Ness of NARAL sums up:

Once we had done a good job of conveying the importance of tone and message, and the kind of impact we judged necessary in Washington, D.C., we often needed to take that leap of faith and trust—the common sense, organizing skill and political savvy of our local people. Of course, this is always easier in places where you have a trusting relationship and a proven track record of effective political work and community organizing. But you can't just say to folks out there, "We need you to turn on the juice"—and then keep censoring the energy and creativity that pours forth. This is always a sensitive aspect of the relationship between national organizations and their local counterparts. At best, this inherent tension can be a creative force.

10

"LYNCH MOBS" AND OTHER DISTRACTIONS

Two days before the confirmation hearings began, Kathy Bonk sat watching the Sunday news commentary show "This Week with David Brinkley" from her home in Annapolis, Maryland. ABC White House correspondent Sam Donaldson had refocused the central story on the "interest groups," their lobbying, and especially their use of paid advertising. The story reflected her worst fears: that the White House press corps had come increasingly under the influence of the White House spin masters. Bonk recounts what happened next:

> I called Ralph at home, and (because we get the show forty-five minutes earlier than in Washington), I said, "Turn on the Brinkley show, because it's a disaster for us." I said, "It's the White House's press line." We were in a battle of symbols, and the Brinkley show was what we were going to be up against for the next two weeks. Well, he turned on the Brinkley show, and the next thing I knew there was a meeting being called at the Leadership Conference.

Through August, and into September, the basic themes of the Block Bork Coalition had remained fixed upon the Bork record and its strong antipathy to the concerns of the nation's majority. But a political campaign is not static. The White House had lagged and stumbled through the summer in developing its thematic thrust—torn between those in the White House who sought to portray Bork as a moderate to allay the fears of moderates, and those true believers in the Justice Department who were ready to launch an open conservative crusade for Bork. By early September, however, the White House had hit upon certain themes which had begun to find a response in the media.

As the hearings approached, the White House and the Justice Department stepped up their efforts to redirect the focus of media attention and public disapproval to the coalition itself, and to its lobbying tactics. A choice inventory of the inflammatory rhetoric amassed for this purpose can be gleaned from an interview given by Attorney General Meese to the editors of *U.S. News and World Report*, summarizing the anti-Bork campaign. Meese railed at "the distortion of the process . . . in a highly organized, well financed political campaign outside the normal processes . . . gutter politics . . . political circus . . . character assassination . . . down in the gutter." He characterized the opposition as "this small band of special interest lobbyists . . . left-wing groups."

Meese was predictable. But the *Washington Post*'s senior political writer, David Broder—wise and balanced, and no toady for the Reagan administration—reflected the deep inroads made by Bork's supporters when he decried a process in which "judges are lynched to appease the public."

"It was an inappropriate phrase, but it wasn't just Broder," says Common Cause's Wertheimer. "There was a growing sentiment out there. The problem with the 'lynch mob' issue was that there was developing in the media a sense that some of these activities had gone too far. You had a wide spectrum within the media who were starting to say, "Well, even if he shouldn't be confirmed, this is not the way these kinds of fights should be handled."

There were dangers on a second front, too: shifting perceptions of the political momentum. One week before the hearings,
Ann Lewis sent members of the Media Task Force a memo in
which she voiced her concerns:

> We have spent too much of our time reacting—especially to White
> House orchestrated arguments. As a result, *we are on the defensive
> not on the substance but on the politics of the issue*. Specifically, the
> perception:
>
>   That the fight is all over and Bork will be confirmed;
>
>   That Democratic Senators (especially from southern and border
> states) who vote against Bork are taking a big political risk; and
>
>   That the opposition to Bork is a problem for the Democratic party,
> bringing echoes of 1984.

What were needed were not new themes; the facts and the
poll data challenged the White House assertions. What the coalition needed, advised Lewis, was better coordination of its media advocacy effort—a stepped-up capacity for fast response to
White House statements and the evolving media environment.
Creative opportunism, not always a social good, was essential.
"Above all," urged Lewis, "we want to be sure we can move
quickly to point up the good news when it happens and to react
coherently and positively to all breaking news."

Message Control Central

Just before the hearings opened, the Block Bork Coalition began
meeting daily, at 8:30 A.M. at the ACLU's Capitol Hill office,
two blocks from the Senate. Each day's meeting would begin
with a press briefing by Emily Tynes and Henry Griggs of
AFSCME, media specialists on loan to the Leadership Conference to support Neas and other coalition members in getting out
their message. Most of the leaders and lobbyists would have

caught some network evening and late night news shows, and MacNeil-Lehrer, and have read the *Washington Post*, *New York Times*, and *Wall Street Journal* before arriving. Bonk, Sparks, Tynes, Griggs, with the help of a handful of early-rising interns and media watchers in cities around the country, systematically monitored the evolving Bork story and passed on to the daily meetings their analyses of how the messages were playing, what wasn't working, which themes needed "fine tuning."

There followed briefings and discussions of events unfolding in Washington and around the country, a preview of the day's events, and the allocation of tasks and assignments. Along with lobbying assignments, there were media assignments. Kathy Bonk marks it as a sign of the coalition's media sophistication that they took their media assignments as faithfully as they were accustomed to taking lobbying assignments.

There was a collective effort to frame the salient issues that had been the focal point of the day before, or promised to be the central focus of the upcoming day's events. Recalls Lewis, "The last part of each day was always devoted to 'what's our message for today, what's the song, what is the point we want to make today?' At that point, once we had a consensus on that, everybody could go out and make it in their own way."

Among the most skillful message crafters was Lewis herself. "She could come up with the 'one-liner' that would contain the message," says Tynes. "It's not just what she said; she knows when to say it; her timing was excellent. Her ability to put a spin on something, and to be powerful, was perfect."

On the last day of Bork's testimony, for example, the coalition was confronted with a series of stories arising from the so-called "attack video" in which Senator Biden was shown to have spoken "from the heart" in a series of presidential campaign appearances in words which were manifestly lifted from the eloquent campaign speeches of British Labor Party leader Neil Kinnock. These stories, in turn, led to alleged revelations of plagiarism by Biden as a law student.

How should the coalition respond? Rally around Biden, who was their Senate leader by the lottery of seniority, and not by choice? Or should they distance themselves from Biden for fear that the campaign would be discredited by too close an association with him? Reporters were pressing for comment: "What will be the impact?" "How is Biden going to be able politically to survive this?"

The consensus reached that morning was that the coalition members would reaffirm their support for Biden, *as Chairman of the Judiciary Committee*, taking care to avoid comments on the implications for his plummeting presidential campaign. "We wanted to make sure," says Neas, "that no one said anything that was going to hurt Biden and hurt the Bork effort and hurt the coalition."

Henry Griggs recalls Ann Lewis's singular contribution:

> She would sit there and almost go into a sort of Greek monologue—"What we say is this: 'Chairman Biden has run a great hearing; he's been fair you can even ask Senator Thurmond, blah, blah, blah . . . ' And it was in quotes. It was not as sketchy as this, it was the map; it was what they give you at AAA; it was a Triptik, and you just can't make a mistake if you follow the lines.

More often, says Verveer, "we were simply talking out loud, not so much crafting press lines as fixing our own minds on the nature of the issues." Griggs adds:

> What was more important than looking good, or sounding good, was that, where there were possible points of disagreement, we did not disagree publicly. For example, the issue of should we testify or not. That could have ripped us to pieces. That could have been the beginning of the end of the coalition, but that did not happen. And that's more important than having somebody with the right makeup or a red tie.
>
> More than actually saying, "This is exactly what you're going out and do today," it was more, "Don't say this," and "Don't say that",

and, "Remember that the reporters are going to sit down and pretend they're off the record and they've still got a pencil in hand."

Discipline and self-restraint were evident. The Reagan administration tried to shift the focus from the issues on which Bork was on the defensive, such as civil rights and privacy, to popular Reagan issues, especially law and order. They would make Bork a symbol of tough law enforcement, a judge who would not "coddle" criminals by over-nice insistence upon the rights of defendants—though, in truth, Bork had never taken much interest in the conservatives' law and order agenda. "They could only make the issue law and order," says Lewis, "if we cooperated. We had initially framed this debate, and they then tried to get back in the game. We did not cooperate." Lewis remembers,

> Somebody would eventually stand up and say, 'We never said he was outside the mainstream on law enforcement, we said he was outside the mainstream on women's rights, workers' rights, civil rights.' We stuck to our themes . . .
> I thought that was a high point for the ability of that coalition to exercise internal discipline. Our message was that he was an extremist, that he was outside the mainstream; we had our examples and we kept using them over and over again, and we would not allow ourselves to get picked off, one at a time, on individual issues. That could have not necessarily broken the coalition, because we were all on the same side, but would have broken our ability to frame the message, and we might not have been able to get back in the game.

The greatest test was the coalition's response to the "lynch mob" charges. What the coalition needed was to disappear, at least in the media. That was not so easy. When so many energetic and motivated people converge, there are strong urges to do more, though doing less may be more prudent. The ACLU's Halperin describes the case of the disappearing "news sheet":

There was a proposal that surfaced at the [coalition's Steering Committee] meeting before the first day of the Bork hearings that a sheet was going to be issued every morning called "Bork notes," or something, which was going to be highlights of the hearings that should be pursued in the next day's hearings.

I said, "Senator Simpson will pick this up every morning, and will say, 'Now these are the instructions from the groups to the senators.' " And that ended the argument, because it was clear that he would do that. They had passed out the first day's one, saying, "We want to pass this out." And they were then collected and, I think, mostly destroyed.

"What was important for us," says Wertheimer, "was not to get into a fight with our coverers over whether or not this had been the perfect campaign. We could not force a battle as to whether they were correct or incorrect in their perceptions, because we couldn't win that battle. What was important was to try to minimize it, play it down, and get on to the next business."

The consensus was that those groups attacked should respond with exhaustive, but low-key documentation of their critiques of Bork, but neither individual group leaders nor coalition spokespersons would respond in kind to the White House attacks, nor to Senators Hatch or Simpson, no matter how tendentious they became. "The coalition understood that the pro-Bork campaign was taking out after the messenger because it didn't like the message," says Verveer.

But not all of the coalition's media initiatives were defensive. With the hearings approaching, and attention squarely focused on Bork's anticipated testimony, the White House inadvertently presented Neas and his colleagues with the opportunity to play the politics of excessive—then failed—expectations. Neas explains:

Tom Korologos and the White House, in the weeks preceding September 15, were constantly being quoted as saying Bork would be their secret weapon. Contemporaneous with these comments was the admittedly stunning performance of Ollie North. In the opinion of many, he was the star of the summer and had played the Iran/Contra Committee to a standstill, if not won hands down . . . It was obvious that some of the key administration strategists thought that Bork, who is supposedly witty, urbane, and avuncular, would win senators over.

So we had meetings on this and I spoke to it, Kathy Bonk spoke to it, Ann Lewis spoke to it, and we all said let us make statements consistent with the White House line. We said, "This guy is going to be terrific" . . . We played up the attractiveness of Bork and the expectations.

As Supreme Court nominees go, Bork would be a forthright and responsive witness. But he would not be Ollie North; he would not rivet a nation with his personality and charm or intimidate the senators. And when his dramatic performance fell short of expectations, the perception would grow that he had failed as a witness.

But it would be flaws in the substance of Bork's testimony— and the skillful role played by the senators themselves, as well as the coalition's experts and spokespersons, in exposing and highlighting and framing those flaws for the media—that would help to seal his defeat.

The "framing" strategy of the Block Bork Coalition had remained both fixed and flexible: fixed on the central issues and themes raised by Bork's writings and judicial philosophy; flexible in reacting to problems and opportunities.

There were certainly ways in which the White House and the coalition mirrored each other's strategies: Each side tried to wrest the favorable symbols of the debate from the other. Each sought to coordinate all the voices on its side, to avoid conflicting or inconsistent messages, to mute the alienating outbursts of extremists.

But there were characteristic differences. The White House

"Line of the Day" was an executive directive from the central authority. The lines developed at the coalition meetings were more like a smorgasbord of ideas which each independent organization affiliated with the coalition was free to use or not use, pursuing its own rhetorical delights.

Verveer cautions against attributing White House–style discipline or lock-step cohesion to the coalition's "Line of the Day" formulation:

> There wasn't usually tight spin control on what we were saying. There wasn't a line that was crafted that we all parroted to reporters. *That* was evident in the papers. (We would scream the next morning when "blank" went off and said thus and so, or "blank" went off and said thus and so, or somebody else said thus and so!) There were, of course, general themes or issues we had to address. We'd say, "Now this is one thing we really do want to respond to."

The rigidity of the administration's "Line of the Day" process, in which each day's line was fixed in the White House at its 8:00 A.M. morning meeting, left the White House unable to respond as the day's events unfurled. "We were always a day ahead of the White House," says Eric Schnapper of the NAACP Legal Defense and Educational Fund. "We were always meeting. The White House met the next morning. They could never produce lawyerly documents within twenty-four hours."

The coalition's message began to take shape in the morning hour, gradually evolving and responding to the hearings as the day progressed, only to firm up at the afternoon break, in time for Ralph Neas or Nan Aron or other coalition voices to catch the deadline and have the last word for the evening network news.

But the fundamental difference between the White House line and the coalition's message was that the White House's lines were disconnected from the substance of the debate over Bork's legal philosophy, while the coalition sought constantly to return the focus to the Bork record.

11

THE FINAL ROUND:
Bork v. Bork

For the coalition, the drama of the hearings was played out largely on a four-part stage: at both ends of the grand Senate Caucus Room, in the corridors outside, and in the "War Room."

There were other stages for other players. In the Senate Judiciary Committee anteroom, the senators and their staffs would huddle to discuss substance and strategy before stepping out into the light of the cameras. In Senator Kennedy's conference room across the hall from the hearing room, Kennedy and his allies would convene. And for the White House and Justice Department lobbyists, there were at least two of their own "War Rooms."

While the hearings were in progress, the focal point was the crescent of fourteen senators facing the witness seated at the table before them. At the other end of the hearing room, with the press tables and the cameras in between, was the audience, where the leaders of the coalition sat in clumps of two and three, or stood in clusters lining the walls of the packed room—reacting, sometimes feverishly, in whispers or scribbled notes.

The grandiloquently named "War Room" was actually the corner of a small office two floors down in the basement of the Russell Senate Office Building. More earthy members of the coalition referred to it as the "Boiler Room," and Neas, at his most circumspect, simply, as "Room 115." It was the office of Judiciary Committee Staff Counsel Bill Lewis, who had worked closely with Elaine Jones and others on several other controversial nominations and had served as a committee liaison with the coalition. Here, with a couple of desks, some empty bookcases, and a phone, legal experts from several coalition organizations set up a small, handy, branch "Library of Bork": Every word Bork had written, every report and exegesis of the "Book of Bork," law review articles, constitutional law treatises, court opinions and case notes—everything that would be needed to detect any misstatement, any false shading of the record, any significant omission, any shift in position which hinted of a "confirmation conversion."

It was also a quiet place for the coalition's constitutional law experts to convene and deliberate on the meaning and significance of the testimony—and on the appropriate response. It was organized by two veteran civil rights lawyers and advocates, Elaine Jones and Bill Taylor, who, between them, had fifty years experience in the practice of civil rights law. Its resident creative spark plug was Eric Schnapper, Jones's colleague with the NAACP Legal Defense and Educational Fund.

As the testimony shifted from issue to issue, the War Room would draw upon other legal specialists within the coalition. Bill Schultz of the Public Citizen Litigation Group, for example, knew every Bork vote and opinion as a Court of Appeals judge. Judy Lichtman of the Women's Legal Defense Fund, as well as Marcia Greenberger of the National Women's Law Center, knew his record on women's place (or lack of place) in the Constitution. Janet Kohn of the AFL-CIO was often in residence. "Janet Kohn has been a key player in all the judgeship fights," says Aron. "When they called down to that room for information about a case, Janet immediately got to work, and if she couldn't do it, she knew who to call upon."

Ricki Seidman of People for the American Way, who could place her fingers on even the most remote Bork utterance, managed the operation of the War Room. "It was," says Schnapper, "a logistical convenience. In the ordinary hearing, I would sit at the back of the room with the files in my briefcase, and pass notes." It was also the lawyers' sanctum. Other than coalition leaders Aron and Neas and others, who drew counsel from the experts, "the lobbyists," says David Cohen of the Advocacy Institute, "were not encouraged to loiter."

The coalition was also encouraged to draw upon the information resources of the American Civil Liberties Union's nearby Washington town house headquarters. During the hearings, the ACLU arranged to receive, by direct satellite feed, a verbatim transcript from the official stenographers within two hours of each spoken word (while the "official" transcript was not available to the Judiciary Committee until that evening). This "hot copy" enabled Helen Hershkoff and other members of the ACLU legal department, together with such lobbyists as Jerry Berman and Leslie Harris, to scrutinize each morning's testimony during the committee's noon recess, and to suggest possible follow-up questions by committee members by early afternoon.

The War Room was patterned on a similar operation developed during the nomination hearings of Reynolds for the number three slot at the Justice Department: a back room "truth squad" to monitor and challenge the nominee's testimony.

In the successful effort to deny Reynolds confirmation, the "truth squad" served to alert the committee members and their staffs to testimony inconsistent with his civil rights record. But that was not so necessary in the Bork hearings. As Bill Taylor observes, "There was a limited amount that we could really do, because the members and staff themselves were so well prepared. Often we found that what we did had already been done or was duplicated by the staff. But the War Room did provide a focal point of energy for concentrating very heavily on substance and, really, to respond to the media."

The War Room was useful to those senators on the committee who had limited staff capacity of their own. Several of the staff assistants acknowledge that this close tracking of the transcript proved helpful. Senator DeConcini's counsel recalls, in particular, how useful it was when Greenberger relayed a series of questions responding, within minutes, to Bork's testimony on the Equal Protection Clause.

But the War Room was most useful in helping the coalition frame the import of Bork's testimony for the media. It was "the center," says Neas, of the coalition's media "substantive response tactic. We had to make sure we had our facts straight all the time: if we were trying to undermine Bork's credibility, our credibility had to be unimpeachable."

Real Time, Research, and Reaction

Bork is at the witness table. The Senators are questioning him. Neas and Verveer are standing together against the wall at the back of the room, listening, taking notes. Neas catches an inconsistency, or a subtle change of position, leans over and whispers to Verveer a half-formed retort. Verveer [or someone else] exits, heads for the War Room, confers with Schultz, Schnapper, Taylor.

At the next break declared by Chairman Biden (frequently enough, at least, to allow witness Bork to satisfy his need for nicotine), the scene shifts to the corridors outside the hearing room. Neas and Aron and other coalition leaders stream out to huddle and caucus with Taylor and Jones and others working in the War Room. Depending upon the issue, one or more spokespersons are informally designated to comment to the press. "As soon as there was a break," says Verveer, "everybody was out and available to the press." As Neas recalls,

> What was vital was Melanne, Nan, Althea, Joe, Estelle, myself and others in that [Senate Caucus] room, getting a sense of what was happening and being able to respond immediately. Almost as important was that when something would come up, we could go back to whoever else was in Room 115 and have a strategy meeting.
>
> Whoever the spokesperson was, what counted was our ability instantaneously to get Elaine Jones or Eric Schnapper or Bill Taylor or Judy Lichtman or Marcia Greenberger to help us make a substantive analysis of a statement by Bork or any witness. If appropriate, we could point out inconsistencies with prior statements or how Bork was underscoring what we had been saying all along. Whatever our response, we could always speak with confidence, after conferring with the experts.
>
> Really we had a mobile task force for fifteen or twenty hours a day. It was always evolving and there was always something happening that you could not have forecast at eight-thirty in the morning. The ability to react instantaneously was a large part of our success.

The War Room also served to help restrain the too-hasty tongue. The impulse to commit rhetorical excess was easily triggered by Bork or Bork's supporters on the committee. "Sometimes, one of us was ready," says Taylor, "to go up the spout." After quiet, but intense, moments of reflection and discussion in the War Room, much of that rhetoric was left unuttered. In that sense, says Taylor, the War Room served as "a safety valve."

Gradually, toward the end of the day — or more precisely, toward the moment when the deadline for inclusion in the network evening news approached — the coalition's "Line of the Day" would begin to emerge. And, each day, at about 4:00 P.M., there would be a twenty-minute break, just at the right moment for Neas or Aron and other coalition voices to catch the deadline, and have the last words and pictures in the corridor for the network cameras. "There were times when the statements of committee members dictated what we would be saying," recalls

Neas, "but, regardless of how it came about, by the three or four o'clock TV deadline, or the six or six-thirty newspaper deadline, we had a 'Line of the Day.' "

"The key question," adds Taylor, "was, 'What was the message that emerged at the end of the day?' And that was formulated on kind of an ad hoc basis—sometimes with a smaller group in the War Room, sometimes everybody was there, Senate staff as well. For us that was the key thing."

The War Room was often the scene of spirited debate. On the second day of Bork's testimony—Wednesday, September 16—Bork substantially modified several of his positions on critical issues which had been raised by the coalition.

At the first break, recalls Neas, "We go into [Room] 115 and we say, 'How are we going to handle this?' " One idea was to label Bork's testimony the product of a "confirmation conversion"—like the proverbial deathbed conversion, subject to justifiable skepticism. It was a powerful, framing catch phrase, which would easily capture the headlines and the leads in the nightly news. But Bill Taylor worried that the emphasis on the fact that Bork *had* changed his mind on some issues might suggest that he had truly become more temperate and moderate—rather than that his modified views were an expedient, and that his moderation would likely last only until he was safely confirmed. Taylor also feared that emphasis on Bork's "conversion" would obscure the retrograde views, such as the exclusion of a general right of privacy from the Constitution, to which Bork steadfastly adhered.

"Eric and I sort of battled that out," says Taylor, "but there was collegiality and respect that enabled us to work it out." That Thursday night, Schnapper waited around for the transcript, then stayed up until 5 A.M. sorting out the "New Bork" from the "Old Bork." "This was real time reaction, and real time research," says Schnapper.

Early the next morning, the fruit of Schnapper's toil was distributed: "BORK v. BORK," a trenchant statement and analysis, under the letterhead of the Leadership Conference. It began:

> For the last three days the Senate Judiciary Committee has heard from a nominee who offers views significantly different from the views expressed by Judge Bork prior to September 15, 1987.
>
> What the New Judge Bork now says differs significantly from the Old Judge Bork on free speech, privacy, contraception, and discrimination on the basis of sex. The New Judge Bork has made statements in favor of the civil rights laws, and against restrictive covenants and forcible sterilization, which the Old Judge Bork, in all of his voluminous writings and speeches, never wrote or uttered.
>
> We oppose the confirmation of either the New Judge Bork or the Old Judge Bork. Even the constitutional positions of the New Judge Bork pose an unacceptable risk to many of the rights which Americans widely regard as their birthright.
>
> But we will urge the Senate, in evaluating this nomination, to place primary emphasis upon the positions taken by Judge Bork *prior* to the date on which he was nominated for the Supreme Court. We believe that those statements, made when Judge Bork had little incentive to cast his views in a manner likely to be more palatable to the Senate, are a truer indication of what Judge Bork would do if he became a member of the Supreme Court.

The statement was followed by an annotated seven-page analysis, contrasting direct quotations from the transcript of Bork's testimony with annotated quotations from the "Old Bork," including quotations from conflicting statements made as recently as the spring of 1987.

Neas says, "Now the NAACP Legal Defense Fund, and People for, and others refined that in more extensive documents later, but we had this document before the TV deadlines, well before the print deadlines. That was an example of how we came up with the 'Line of the Day.' It wasn't something that happened at eight-thirty in the morning in a vacuum." And it dominated the weekend stories.

Those who looked to the War Room as a creative resource

agree that much of its creative spark came from Eric Schnapper. "Eric," says Verveer, "described Bork as 'a walking constitutional amendment.' *Eric* was a walking Bork encyclopedia." "Eric was substance," adds Taylor, "it wasn't spin masters."

Schnapper is more modest. "The real power is with the person who could type, and I was the only one who could type (or admit that I could type). Ralph had to issue a statement every day, and I had to type it."

How Equal are Women?

For those unfamiliar with the charged language of constitutional law, Judge Bork, in responding to hard questioning by Senator DeConcini, seemed willing to apply the "Equal Protection Clause" of the Constitution to women as well as racial minorities. He espoused, for the first time publicly, the adoption of a standard which would strike down as a violation of the Constitution any sex discrimination which did not have a "reasonable basis."

This testimony alarmed Lichtman and Greenberger because it was inconsistent with all of Bork's previous statements on the issue, and because his explanation of what he meant by a "reasonable basis" strongly suggested that he would give great deference to sex-based classifications drawn by any local, state, or federal governmental body. Yet they feared that the media would interpret Bork's testimony as the equivalent of agreeing that the Equal Protection Clause applied equally to women.

It was evident to the listening women's law specialists that Bork was stating a new position, different from the one he had articulated in an interview a few weeks before his nomination. Judy Lichtman, Marcia Greenberger, Linda Dorian (of the National Federation of Business and Professional Women), and Irene Natividad (of the National Women's Political Caucus) materialized outside the hearing room before the cameras to pinpoint the change in Bork's position, and the problems his newly stated views still posed for women's constitutional rights.

Within hours of Bork's testimony, they had produced, under the letterhead of the National Women's Law Center, an eight-page memo, "Judge Bork: No Friend to Women's Legal Rights," in which they cited five previous instances, including one the month before he was nominated, in which Bork had insisted that he could find "no principled way" of applying the Equal Protection Clause to women, and that in so doing in at least one case, the Supreme Court had only served "to trivialize the Constitution and to spread it to areas it did not address."

At the impromptu news conference, they discussed Bork's previous record and his testimony as a whole, and argued that women could find little comfort in it. "No amount of selective citation and interpretation," they concluded, "can change Judge Bork's record on women's legal rights from what it demonstrably is — one of deep hostility."

On the fourth day, Bork was questioned by Senator Metzenbaum (D-Ohio) about the *American Cyanamid* case, in which he joined a three-judge decision that the Occupational Safety and Health Act did not ban an employer's "fetus protection" policy, that allowed women to work in a certain plant department only if they were surgically sterilized. Bork responded, "They [American Cyanamid] offered a choice to women; some of them I guess did not want to have children."

"It was only four or five words — a subordinate clause — and if you weren't listening closely, you might have missed it," recalls Schnapper, who heard the response on the radio as he was on his way to the Hill in a taxi. Lichtman heard it from the back of the hearing room. In a few minutes she was on the phone to the ACLU attorney who had represented the women. They, in turn, reached two of the women who had sued American Cyanamid and, with them, drafted two telegrams which were dispatched

to the committee. That same afternoon, Metzenbaum read one
of the telegrams to the committee in open session:

> I cannot believe Judge Bork thinks we were glad to have the choice
> of getting sterilized or getting fired. Only a judge who knows noth-
> ing about women who need to work could say that. I was only 26
> years old, but I had to work, so I had no choice. It is incredible that
> a judge who is supposed to be fair can support a company that does
> not follow OSHA rules. This was the most awful thing that hap-
> pened to me.

The next day Senator Simpson (R-Wyo.) challenged the
authenticity of the telegram: "It would have a greater ring of
clarity if it were prepared by the person, but it was prepared by
her attorney . . . [T]o make it look like some voluntary
wire . . . is offensive to me."

Once again, Lichtman was on the phone. And another telegram came from the two women attesting that no one had put
words in their mouths.

As Lichtman says,

> This provided a vehicle for showing just how outside the main-
> stream he was. This was not a moderate Justice Stevens . . . We
> were not talking about abstract legal and constitutional principles,
> we were talking about women's lives — their reproductive lives, and
> their lives as economically independent family members. We
> showed a candidate for the Court who was capable of little or no
> sympathy, let alone empathy. This was the "Book of Bork" and this
> example breathed life into it.

As Bork concluded his week of testimony, the Senate was at
the center of media attention, and the issue-framing initiative
was assumed not by the coalition spokespersons, but by the
anti-Bork members of the Senate — especially by Judiciary Committee Chairman Biden, who launched his prime-time questioning of Bork by hammering away at the privacy issue. Neither the

Reagan White House, nor Bork's Senate advocates, nor Bork himself was able to shift the focus away from Bork's judicial philosophy and its constitutional implications.

The Sacrifice

> Neas engineered the most effective disappearing act in the history of Washington lobbying.
>
> MARY MCGRORY, The Washington Post,
> October 1987

Mort Halperin, like the ACLU he represents, does not make his mark being avuncular or accommodating. He was in character when he made a brief appearance at the second coalition meeting on July 2. "I offered them gratuitous advice," says Halperin. "I said, 'Look, we're not going to be at any meetings; we don't take positions on nominations. But, before I leave, let me offer you one piece of advice. None of you should testify.' " They all thought I said something totally nuts, and none of them remembered it when it reemerged, and I said it again, that I had said it back then."

Halperin's lecture was premature. The decision to testify or not to testify probably should have awaited — as it did — the outcome of Bork's own testimony. But it is not hard to understand why his colleagues reacted to Halperin's message as if he were a plague carrier. Testifying before Congress is what the leaders of advocacy groups *do*.

From the beginning of the campaign, both the Judiciary Committee members and staff and Block Bork Coalition leaders certainly assumed that figures such as Benjamin Hooks, head of both the Leadership Conference and the NAACP, and AFL-CIO President Lane Kirkland, and thirty to forty other prominent national leaders would be witnesses. Indeed, the committee staff requested that every group make a *pro forma* request to testify in order to preserve maximum flexibility in designing the hearings for the committee leadership.

Testifying was the norm. For some groups, such as the NAACP, to remain silent on such a prominent civil rights conflict was unthinkable. For thirty years, the NAACP had never failed to testify on a civil rights issue. Not to do so was to abdicate responsibility; to fail to meet the expectations of those who looked to the NAACP to speak for them.

For months, the leaders had been preparing, like athletes in training, to take on this champion of the right wing. They were ready. Humility is not a common characteristic of advocacy group leaders; none feared the consequences of verbal combat with the likes of Hatch and Simpson.

For some of the organizations, there were mundane, but not ignoble interests at stake: testimony would provide a national platform for the display of individual organizations and their leaders — their hour in the sunlight. With one appearance, they could satisfy the claims of organizational identification for those grassroots activists who had worked in relative anonymity for months; they could recruit new members; and they could reinforce fund-raising appeals.

That the groups might not testify had begun to emerge as a possible option a few weeks before the hearings. Melanne Verveer recalls:

> It was indeed evolutionary; it didn't come down one magic morning and drop there. I remember Mark Gitenstein, Ralph Neas, and I talking about it — mid-summer, perhaps. It wasn't a new idea, but no decisions were made at that point because it wasn't necessary. Why it was necessary to come to closure on it at the task force meetings (at the close of Bork's testimony) was because one week later we needed to know whether we were testifying or not, and whether or not the political winds had shifted sufficiently to caution us all not to do that.

While all the groups had preserved their right to testimony — and the major groups fully expected to testify — Ralph Neas explains how coalition leaders deliberately postponed final discussions on precisely who would testify until after Bork's appearance:

> Our basic strategy with respect to Robert Bork's week of testimony was to get through that week in a position to win, not to win that first week. We just wanted to preserve all of our possible options so that we would have a chance to rebut his testimony, and to pick up any lost ground that might have occurred during his testimony.

Bork failed to alleviate the misgivings of the undecided senators in his hours before the committee. The right-wing vision of Robert Bork clasped to the nation's bosom, as Lt. Col. Oliver North had been three months earlier in the televised Iran-Contra investigation, was shattered. And those Olympian voices of moral and legal authority who followed in the second week not only struck deep in discrediting Bork's judicial philosophy, but also successfully deflected the mean-spirited attacks of the Bork point men, Hatch and Simpson. Indeed, the Republicans' relentless questioning simply afforded articulate opponents, such as William Coleman, more time to command the nation's center with their powerful message.

As the White House and the Senate Republicans watched their expectations thwarted, they began to perceive that their last hope lay in shifting the focus of the Senate from the flaws in Bork's judicial philosophy to the coalition "lynch mob." They knew that not many of the coalition's leaders were exactly scholars of the Constitution. And even those that were carried institutional baggage that made them more vulnerable to the thrusts of Bork's partisans than the unaffiliated experts who opposed Bork.

Halperin might have been anticipating the unforgettable low moments of the 1988 Bush presidential campaign when he warned American Civil Liberties Union President Norman Dorsen, who was to be the ACLU's witness, what might lie in store for him:

I got a call from my president, as everybody did, saying that he had been telling people that he was going to testify—that he didn't care whether he testified, but many people were telling him it was important that he testify, and so he wanted to know where I stood.

I said, "I have to tell you, I'm doing everything that I can to see to it that you and everybody else doesn't testify." He said, "Why?"

And I said, "Well, Norman, you think you're going to come down here and talk about the Bill of Rights and how important the Court's role is, but let me tell you what the first question is. The first question is going to be, 'Mr. Dorsen, you say that Judge Bork doesn't understand the meaning of privacy in the Constitution. Is that right? Yes! You believe that privacy in the Constitution means that gays have to have the right to marry. Is that right? Yes!' "

I said, "You're going to be talking about abortion on demand, and child pornography . . . [Senator] Simpson has got all that stuff, he's ready to go: 'The groups say Bork doesn't have a mainstream view of the Constitution, and *they* are in favor of a dead fetus after eight months, child pornography flooding the country, gay marriage, and this is the coalition that wants him defeated.' "

He said, "I understand; I understand."

That Halperin's horrific vision was not fantasy was demonstrated by New Hampshire Republican Senator Gordon Humphrey's nasty examination of NYU law professor David A. J. Richards, an expert on privacy law. While Richards sought carefully to discuss constitutional theories of privacy, Humphrey seemed intent upon portraying Richards as a sex or drug maniac. "You feel it is unwise to make prostitution unlawful. Well, that helps us in understanding where you're coming from. Let's turn to drugs . . . "

By the end of Bork's testimony, a handful of Democratic Committee staff and Block Bork Coalition strategists had concluded that testimony by the groups would be counterproductive. Jo Blum of Planned Parenthood remembers the emerging consensus: "For those of us who were standing there watching the hearings it was very clear that things were breaking our way and to prolong the hearings was not politically advantageous, but it wasn't so easy to convince people who weren't standing there every day watching and feeling the political wind."

There is an adage that legislators know well, even if they honor it mostly in the breach: If you have the votes, shut up, sit down, and call the roll. But conventional wisdom is not the exclusive wisdom. While ego and parochial group needs played some role in the reluctance of some leaders to forego testifying, there were serious arguments in favor of testifying. Failure to appear might be interpreted by the media as a concession to the Republicans' characterization of the coalition as a band of "special interests" whose views could not withstand the light of public scrutiny and cross-examination. Worse, after decades of progress in gaining the recognized right to testify in what had once been a closed proceeding, the absence of citizen group testimony could be taken as a precedent, ceding that right in any future judicial nomination hearing.

Coalition leaders flinched at conveying the impression that they had been intimidated and diverted by the politics of labels. Molly Yard, the full-throated president of NOW who does not tiptoe, felt deeply that the decision not to testify was simply political cowardice.

Ralph Nader viewed the hearings as a unique opportunity to reach beyond the nomination, to extend what had become a national seminar on constitutional rights to the launching of a new progressive agenda:

A political struggle over a Supreme Court nominee is a political struggle, and when you have ten pins you want to mow down and you've got terrific bowling balls, you don't just mow down four pins and say "well, that's all we need."

There were all kinds of mobilizations out there. We were getting small businesses and southern senators, we were getting organized labor, and environmental groups. It was really coming together as sort of a pronouncement on the Reagan administration because

Bork, in an incredibly diverse way, represented so many of the bad things about Reagan's policies. When you wait seven years for an opportunity like this you take it for all it has; you turn it into a fissionable reactor.

Nader also believes that the "special interest" imagery could have been diffused by interspersing witnesses from the coalition within the panels of independent legal scholars and experts. But that option was effectively removed by Chairman Biden and his staff, who decided to structure the witness list in such a way so those organizational leaders requesting to testify would only have the opportunity to appear before the committee following the panels.

This conflict could not be resolved by objective data. It came down to a question of judgement: Was the defeat of Bork already so secure that testimony by the groups could provide a political consciousness-raising opportunity at little risk? Or was there still a real possibility that Hatch and Simpson and the other Bork partisans among the committee Republicans could manipulate the groups' appearances to redirect the Senate's animus against the coalition and save the nomination?

Resolving this conflict proved to be the most severe test of the coalition and the strength of its interlocking networks. As Ricki Seidman observed, "Some of the toughest sessions were on the witness issue. They were almost tougher than trying to cajole a senator to vote against the nomination."

The problem for the coalition was that the decision *not* to testify had to be reached by a compelling consensus, if not Joe Rauh's "substantial unanimity." While it was true that Biden, committee chairman and presidential contender, had the authority to deny any group the opportunity to testify, or to choose from among the group leaders, the *political* reality was that Biden could not pick and choose without incurring the undying enmity of those who were denied. It had to be *none*, or (virtually) all.

There were leaders who might—barely—be persuaded that not testifying was the right course, but who would be committing a form of organizational humiliation if the leaders of competitive organizations testified while they did not. How could NARAL explain it to its members, who had devoted three months of their lives to this campaign, if Molly Yard of NOW testified while Kate Michelman did not? And how could Ben Hooks of the NAACP decline to testify if AFL-CIO President Kirkland remained on the witness list? "If one group decided to testify," declares Ann McBride of Common Cause, "it would be a house of cards."

Again, there was no formal decision-making process, no formal Steering Committee agenda, no votes. The process, both within the coalition and with the Judiciary Committee leadership, was informal—almost intangible. But the one overriding rule was that the issue had to be talked through. Elaine Jones conveys this consensus-building process:

> It's not a situation where any one group—I don't care how large it is—can determine which direction the campaign is going to go in. That's something that has to come from the coalition, and no one group can take primary responsibility or credit for whatever comes out. That's just against the rules.

Part of "the Steering Committee group started to discuss testifying," recalls NARAL's Michelman:

> There was real disagreement; so we kept discussing it. One night after testimony—I remember because it went late—a number of us got together in a little room in the ACLU building. Some of the staff from the Judiciary Committee were there because it was important that we come to a final decision about whether we would testify. The Judiciary Committee staff were in a delicate position—their instincts were that we should not testify, that it would do more harm than good, but they didn't want to force that position on the groups

who had been so very important to the campaign, and cause a back-
lash. They wanted the groups to come to that conclusion themselves.

Among those who came to the firm conviction that insisting
upon testifying would be highly risky, if not fatal, were leaders
who had earned the respect and trust of their colleagues over
time. Ernie Dubester of the AFL-CIO played a critical role, taking an early position in support of no testimony—and DuBester
spoke for Lane Kirkland, a giant among coalition leaders. Elaine
Jones may have dampened the zeal of some leaders to testify by
recounting the days of intensive preparations undertaken by
William Coleman—preparations comparable to those for a Supreme Court argument—before he considered himself ready to
face the committee and its "Bork Guard." Judy Lichtman of the
Women's Legal Defense Fund enjoyed the special trust of the
women's groups, and her advocacy of no testimony carried great
weight with them. Ann Lewis remembers being struck by the
fact that it was three or four of the women leaders, in a row, who
first spoke against testifying.

"Neas communicated, with a verbal calm," describes David
Cohen of the Advocacy Institute, " 'no decisions until we're
ready . . . nothing rushed.' " Gradually, a consensus did
emerge, however informal and intangible the decision-making
process was. Althea Simmons, who was one of the last holdouts
pressing for Ben Hooks to testify, describes it:

> We never reached a real coalition consensus on testifying as such.
> It was a day-by-day kind of thing, and you tried to weigh the odds,
> and you make the arguments back and forth as to the advantages and
> disadvantages thereof, and all of us wanted to testify . . . We'd
> send a signal to the committee saying we haven't made a decision
> yet. Everybody had their testimony all written up. So we finally
> decided almost without saying it that we would submit testimony
> in writing and not appear.

Peer pressure proved to be a critical factor. Joe Rauh thought the decision was wrong, argued vigorously against it, but accepted the consensus. Molly Yard and Ralph Nader were never reconciled to either the decision or the decision-making process—which they viewed as shadowy, with neither Biden and the committee, nor the Neas and other central coalition strategists taking responsibility. Their acceptance of the decision was not made any easier by a feeling that the coalition had not freely come to its own decision, that some of the senators and their staffs had "leaned too hard" on the coalition to stop the groups from testifying. Nader characterizes the Bork campaign as "a great victory, but a lost opportunity."

Elegant decision-making it was not. It more resembled the British "muddling through." But of course, the British have muddled through sufficiently well to win a number of serious wars. Senators Hatch and Simpson, after all, were denied the opportunity to make mischief. Despite the tensions, no public controversy erupted to deflect attention from the hearings. No one publicly insisted upon testifying. And, at the close of the hearings, Bork and his flawed constitutional vision—and not the coalition—remained at center stage.

Mary McGrory, in the *Washington Post*, enshrined the coalition's decision as "the Supreme Sacrifice." And she cited, as proof of the wisdom of that sacrifice, the words of Senator Alan Simpson, who called it an "awesome" move. "We were hoping to have Ellie Smeal [former head of the National Organization of Women] up here screaming about abortion rights," said Simpson. "We would have liked to ask Ralph [Neas] too, so we could ask him how many dying organizations have been refueled and larded up their treasuries on this issue. But they didn't come."

The Curtain Falls

On the Saturday after Bork's thirty-two hours of testimony had concluded, as he listened to the week's round-up on National Public Radio, Phil Sparks was convinced that the nomination would be defeated.

Hatch was summing up the week on behalf of Bork, and that was a double negative: First, because everybody understood that Hatch was a conservative ideologue; they had chosen the wrong person to be speaking. Second, instead of promoting "law and order," Bork's conservative credentials, and all the other conservative issues, that just never got started; instead, he was defending Bork's record on women's rights and civil rights. That was a "do not compute": Orrin Hatch can do a lot of things, but he cannot be a spokesmen on those two issues because he has no standing himself.

On Sunday, I called Kathy and I said, "The strategic debate is over. The polls will show next week what happened, but it's clear to me that if Hatch had to defend on these grounds the whole debate for the first week, the debate had been focused exactly where we wanted to be, both by the senators (who had used our poll results) and our public education campaign." That's exactly what happened. The poll results that came out the middle of the second week of testimony, which were devastating to Bork, followed right along the lines of the Kiley survey from a month-and-a-half before.

The rest was managing the whole thing just to make sure that things didn't get out of hand and that we maintained our discipline.

Ralph Neas was also heartened by Bork's testimony, but not quite so certain as Sparks. As the Bork testimony came to an end, he recalls, "I said to Melanne, who was standing beside me, 'We can win this thing.'" But by the following Monday, after the powerful, contrasting testimony of William Coleman and Barbara Jordan, he was able to say, "We are going to win."

The campaign was over, though it would take over three more weeks for the painful process to end. Early on October 1, the day after the hearings concluded, three key southern senators — Bennett Johnston of Louisiana, David Pryor of Arkansas, Terry Sanford of North Carolina — announced their opposition to the nomination. Later that same day, Republican committee member Arlen Specter declared he would vote against Bork. On October 5, Judiciary Committee members Robert Byrd and Dennis

DeConcini said they would vote no, and the next day, Howell Heflin of Alabama joined them.

The Judiciary Committee voted 9–5 to recommend that the full Senate reject the nomination, technically defeating a motion to send the nomination to the Senate with a favorable recommendation.

On the next day, ten more Democrats announced their opposition. As of October 20, fifty-four Senators were publicly committed to vote against confirmation.

The White House continued to condemn the coalition; Judge Bork steadfastly refused to withdraw; his close friend, Leonard Garment, persisted in decrying the corruption of the process — all to no avail.

On October 23, 1987, nearly four months after President Reagan chose to nominate him, a majority of the Senate, including previously uncommitted conservatives John Stennis of Mississippi and John Warner of Virginia, voted to reject the nomination. The final vote was 58–42, the largest margin of defeat for any Supreme Court nominee in history.

12

HARD QUESTIONS

In the aftermath of the Bork campaign there were, and still remain, hard feelings and hard questions. Judge Bork has now left the bench; he travels and speaks, mostly to conservative audiences. He and they are bitter, outraged at his rejection, vowing retribution against those they hold accountable for a great outrage of American judicial history.

In the other corner are liberals who are also bitter. They fear nothing lasting has come of all the energy expended in the effort to defeat the Bork nomination — *except* the residue of rancor on the Right. Three months after the defeat of Bork, President Reagan's substitute nominee, Judge Anthony Kennedy, was confirmed with little opposition or debate. And, as his staunchly conservative votes quicken the rightward march of Reagan appointees O'Connor and Scalia and Chief Justice Rehnquist, many liberals ask, "What, if anything, was gained by this victory?"

Whatever else may be true, Judge Bork was made to suffer a personal tragedy. As Yale law professor Bruce Ackerman rightly accedes, "Even those, like myself, who disagree with Bork

237

both can and should admire the way he has woven theory and practice, reason and passion, into a pattern that expresses so eloquently our deepest hopes for a life in the law. The republic needs more people like Robert Bork. It is a tragedy that the republic should repay him for his decades of service by publicly humiliating him."

So we must ask, was there good reason to challenge Bork, but not to challenge O'Connor, Scalia, or Kennedy? Was any high constitutional purpose served by a confrontation which Bork and others experienced as brutish?

If the effort to defeat the Bork nomination passes that threshold test, more hard questions remain—and they go to the core of our purpose in writing this book.

We have cited *New York Times* Editorial Page Editor Jack Rosenthal for the proposition that "it was the Book of Bork that beat Bork." And we have cited the leadership of the Bork opposition within the Senate itself. Of what importance, then, was the work, however strenuous and splendid, of the "outside" opposition?

The expression, to "Bork" a nominee, bids to enter the public lexicon as a synonym for a crude and reckless campaign of calumny. Is it, after all, an apt phrase? Was the campaign unfair, as Bork and his allies continue to charge? And was the campaign too political, as others troubled by the politicization of the courts fear?

We have chronicled the unfolding of the anti-Bork campaign; now it's time to address these questions.

Why Bork, and Only Bork?

Justice Lewis Powell, whom Robert Bork would have replaced, had been, in Herman Schwartz's words, perhaps the Supreme Court's "single most influential member," and a moderate. By 1987, he had also become its swing vote in holding the Court

precariously to a 5–4 adherence to its modern line of constitutional cases. By contrast, conservative Antonin Scalia, in 1986,
replaced an apparently equally conservative Justice Warren
Burger. That distinction alone would have made the Bork confirmation an historic constitutional event.

We are indebted to Professor Ackerman for also enabling us
to see how it was through the Bork nomination, in particular,
that President Reagan sought to radically transform the Court,
and why it was both right and inevitable that those opposed to
that transformation should draw their line in the dust at Bork.

Like President Franklin Delano Roosevelt, says Ackerman,
President Reagan sought to overturn decades of constitutional
precedent by appointment rather than by constitutional amendment. With each of his successive nominations to the Court, beginning with Sandra Day O'Connor and proceeding through
Rehnquist (as chief justice) and Scalia, Ackerman sees "an esca-
lation in the President's transformative ambitions":

> While O'Connor was a solid professional who held vaguely con-
> servative views, these facts did not account for the President's deci-
> sion to single her out. Instead, he was using her nomination as a
> reassuring symbol to a potentially important voting bloc . . .
>
> [N]either Rehnquist nor Scalia raised the prospect of a Roose-
> veltian transformation with Bork-like clarity. While Rehnquist had
> established his transformative inclinations during his lengthy ser-
> vice as Associate Justice, he had also demonstrated that, without
> reinforcements, he could not lead the Court to make a sharp and sus-
> tained break with the past. Similarly, Antonin Scalia's public views
> of the Constitution were less distinct than Bork's and less distinctly
> transformative in their implications.

Later, Linda Greenhouse of the *New York Times* would contrast Anthony Kennedy's judicial philosophy with that of Bork:

> Judge Kennedy's testimony gave little guidance on how he would
> vote. But his generalities were nonetheless reassuring, even elo-

quent. He accepted the view that the Constitution protects the right to privacy and other rights not spelled out in the text, a concept Judge Bork rejected. And he gently, but unmistakably disavowed the notion that constitutional interpretation can be confined to a mechanical search for the "original intent" of the framers. He spoke of a Constitution with a built-in capacity for growth, of framers who "made a covenant with the future." While Judge Bork appeared preoccupied with what the Constitution should not be asked to do, Judge Kennedy spoke of its potential.

"There are cases after cases," argued Harvard Law Professor Laurence Tribe, "in which Judge Kennedy has shown himself to be far more moderate, writing opinions that Robert Bork would never have penned and reaching results that Robert Bork would never have reached."

In contrast with all these nominees, notes Ackerman, Bork, uniquely, "was a man whose public record suggested that he might possess *both* the transformative vision *and* legal ability needed to spearhead a radical judicial break with the past. If the Senate was ever to raise questions about the constitutional direction in which the President proposed to lead the nation, surely it was *this* nomination that made such questioning appropriate?"

In the End, What Was Accomplished?

Professor Laurence Tribe, one of this nation's preeminent constitutional scholars, brought his intellect and his passion to the effort to defeat Bork. His reward, from the Right, was the vow of a vengeful campaign of retribution should a president ever have the temerity to nominate Tribe to the Supreme Court.

That dim prospect does not seem to have diminished Tribe's enthusiasm, for he has since celebrated the great battle over Bork as "a transformative national experience." Many others who lent their voices and labor to the anti-Bork campaign would agree. But what precisely was transformed? Curiously, perhaps the single most important achievement of the opposition was that the Constitution — as it stood in the summer of 1987 — *was not* transformed, despite the Reagan-Meese assault. As Tribe himself noted, "The right wing lost the constitutional referendum of 1987. That is what galls them most about the loss of Robert Bork. It is not pity for a man who had so long wanted to serve on the Court and whose credentials were so superb. It is pity for an agenda that was dramatically, decisively repudiated."

Former Congresswoman Barbara Jordan, who holds the L.B.J. Centennial Chair at the University of Texas School of Public Affairs, observes:

> The Bork nomination offered an ideal opportunity to test a guiding principle of the American Right: that Americans fiercely oppose much of what the Supreme Court has done since the era of Earl Warren and would welcome the chance to restrict the role of the federal courts. The lasting lesson of the Bork controversy — and what must account for the fury of Bork and his supporters — is that, given the opportunity to rise up against "judicial tyranny" and support the leading advocate of "judicial restraint" and "orginal intent," the American public did no such thing.

And Bill Taylor adds, "The Right's continually pulling at the Bork defeat like a scab says something about the legacy. Clearly they saw it as the death of a dream — of reestablishing white male dominance, Billy Sunday morality."

But it is plain that much *was* transformed: if not the Constitution, then the public vision of the Constitution, and the Senate confirmation process itself.

To millions of Americans, for whom the Constitution earlier had meaning, if at all, as a contentless icon or dry civics lesson, the campaign brought to life their own stake in this "constitutional referendum." For the first time in their lives, many Americans looked hard at their Constitution, and asked themselves what they wanted and expected from it.

In the summer of 1987, Emily Tynes, a black communications specialist, had just completed an intense, grueling campaign for NARAL and was looking forward to a less stressful career as a real estate broker. Her words describing her decision, instead, to plunge into the anti-Bork campaign, are unique, but the sentiments were nearly universal, especially among minorities and women:

> I was from the optimistic generation. I had seen Little Rock; I had seen the schools integrated; I had been in that process and from then on the world was mine. I just could not believe we were back where we started. That's what Bork represented to me. So it was very personal. It was like you do it or you die. I didn't even know how I was going to get paid, but I said, "Here I am."

And the great corporate lawyer and former Republican cabinet secretary, William T. Coleman, Jr., felt compelled by the same force to step forward, or be judged by history for his failure to do so. Bill Taylor remembers: "A federal judge said to me, 'You probably won't do anything more important in your life.' "

Across the country, thousands of non-activist Americans determined that they wanted their privacy inviolate — and were activated! Black or white, they did not want to reopen settled guarantees of civil rights. "Indeed," as National Public Radio legal correspondent Nina Totenberg reported, "the public seemed to support most of the Court's decisions in the areas of race and sex discrimination, free speech, privacy, and even abortion."

Even the politically diverse and uneasy "baby boom" generation appears to have shared a common concern at the threat to their liberties that Bork seemed to pose. Pollster Patrick Caddell noted that privacy issues, such as birth control and abortion, are "quintessential baby boom issues, resonating with the libertarian streak on social issues that unites the generation despite its differences in other areas."

And the South, claims Texas's Barbara Jordan, "has become a force for reconciliation, not reaction."

We would not be justified in reading into the Senate vote an unambiguous plebiscite in support of nearly four decades of Supreme Court holdings and current doctrine. It is noteworthy, however, that despite dark warnings by conservatives of voter retribution in 1988 should the Senate reject Bork, candidate Bush rarely mentioned the Bork nomination in his presidential campaign, and then only *sotto voce*. And "original intent" appears to have dropped from our political agenda along with the welcome passing of Edwin Meese from the scene.

At the very least, as NYU law professor Ronald Dworkin suggests, "The public apparently sensed the constitutional importance of the Senate's decision; and it is part of our constitutional tradition, in such circumstances, that the nation as a whole is regarded as more committed than it was before to the principles that provide the most convincing justification for what the Senate did."

Professor Ackerman predicts that "the personal tragedy of Robert Bork would go down in history as a marker of a *failed constitutional moment*, in which a political movement, after raising a new agenda for constitutional reform, fails to generate the kind of deep and broad support necessary to legitimate a change in the constitutional principles institutionally defended in the name of 'We the People.' "

The Confirmation Process

The conflict over the Bork nomination also changed, for the foreseeable future, the Senate's confirmation process. With an "attentive public" now accustomed to paying great heed to Supreme Court nominees, with televised hearings an established Senate ritual, it is not likely that the hearings for any Court nominee in the near future will resemble "cocktail parties — not con-

firmation inquiries," as Federation of Women Lawyers' Estelle
Rogers scornfully characterized such hearings in the early
eighties.

"I think the Judiciary Committee finally rediscovered the 'ad-
vise and consent' clause in the Constitution," concluded Senator
Leahy (D-Vt.) "And I think that would be the same in the 101st
Congress, whether we had President Bush or Dukakis."

And Joe Rauh has won his 1960s debate with Democratic
liberals, who—in their need to hold back the right-wing assault
on liberal Justice Abe Fortas, nominated by Lyndon Johnson for
chief justice—staunchly maintained that ideology had no place
in Senate "advise and consent" deliberations. As a student of the
Court and the legislature, the Brookings Institution's Robert
Katzmann predicts, "Whatever the intensity of the inquiry, it is
all but certain that ideology will now be taken for granted as an
acceptable subject for questioning." And as Senator Specter
declared on the day of Justice Anthony Kennedy's confirmation,
"We have established in the 100th Congress a very important
precedent that judicial philosophy is relevant and important."

Judiciary Committee Chairman Biden vowed that the committee will henceforth hold nominees to a standard of "open-
mindedness, fairness, and the recognition that constitutional
interpretation must continually evolve."

What Credit Can the Campaign Claim?

It's the difference between the "inside game,"
and the "outside game." There's the assumption that the media coverage would have
been the same without the coalition's efforts,
and that Joe Biden, in his glory, was
sufficient to persuade Senator Specter, or
that Senator Specter was persuaded [simply]
by his own reasoning and reading of the record. That's just not true of politics. The out-

side game, in this case, was very important,
and it was important because it was under
control. It didn't slide off into craziness.
                                    CAROL FOREMAN

We must take care not to claim, for the grassroots campaign of opposition, or the national anti-Bork coalition, too great a share of the credit for this historic "constitutional moment." There were other, large factors.

Of course, the Senate itself, and not the "outside" campaign was the crucible of the contest over the Bork nomination. It was, once again, a Democratic Senate. In 1986, the voters had restored a Democratic Senate majority (54–46 and a majority of the Judiciary Committee members) in defiance of Reagan's plea for support to complete his transformation of the judiciary. That meant that the Judiciary Committee chair, too, was now under Democratic control. That gave Biden the power to start the hearings two months after Bork was nominated, affording the campaign critical time to gain momentum—time that Senator Thurmond, Republican chairman for the first six years of the Reagan presidency, and his Republican committee majority, would never have let pass. "We lost the nomination as of November 4, 1986," commented Bork strategist Tom Korologos on the day before the committee vote.

President Reagan's powers were waning in the last years of his term. His popularity had eroded. He was embattled and weakened by the Iran/Contra revelations and investigations. Thus, though the Senate remained respectful of the president's nomination prerogatives, it was freed of undue fear of Reagan's retaliatory powers.

In the Senate, the defeat of Bork owes much to the intense personal campaigns of Democratic leaders such as Biden, Kennedy, Metzenbaum, Leahy, Cranston, and Johnston. As we have seen, they were the campaign's vital "inside" leaders. Each made his special contributions, from Kennedy's role in calling black leaders to action in August, to Biden's statesmanship and grace, as he withdrew from the presidential campaign because of allegations of plagiarism fed by the rival Dukakis camp and refocused his energies on chairing the committee's hearings and on leading its deliberations.

The care and exhaustive study with which Chairman Biden and most members of the Senate Judiciary Committee, Democrat and Republican alike, prepared for and participated in the hearings lent *gravitas* to their inquiry and deliberations. When Pennsylvania's Republican Arlen Specter, undecided until the close of the hearings, chose to oppose Bork, his decision conveyed the moral force of his informed and scrupulous inquiry to those members of the Senate who remained uncommitted.

Equally critical was the quiet leadership of third-term Democrat Bennett Johnston of Louisiana, who led many of the new southern Senators out of the accustomed southern path of judicial conservatism and deference to the president. David Cohen describes Johnston's announcement of opposition one day after the hearings concluded as a "signal giver" to the uncertain.

It has fallen largely to others to tell the full story of the Senate and the Bork nomination. But to these Senate leaders who led the campaign—and to those who simply carried out their constitutional duties as senators with distinction—must go principal credit for the defeat of the Bork nomination.

A potent outside force, independent of the anti-Bork campaign, were the four members of the American Bar Association's Standing Committee on the Federal Judiciary who found Bork "not qualified," and the one member who voted simply "not opposed." Though eight members of the ABA Committee found Bork "well qualified," the dissent by a substantial minority defied precedent, and therefore, expectations. It thus damaged the Bork candidacy where it was thought to be most impregnable: in the nonpartisan judgement of his professional peers.

Also outside the campaign, though buttressed by its research, were those journalists, such as Linda Greenhouse and Stuart Taylor, Jr. of the *New York Times*, who threaded their way independently through the pro-Bork and anti-Bork paper barrages and took great pains to communicate to the "attentive public" the questions raised by Bork's views and record.

Sympathetic to the campaign, but also independent of it, were columnists such as Anthony Lewis of the *New York Times* and Mary McGrory of the *Washington Post*, who conveyed their informed indignation at Reagan's attempt through Bork to transform the Court.

While the weight of editorial opinion, calculated numerically by numbers of papers for and against, leaned toward support for Bork, the reasoned care of editorials opposing Bork, such as those of the *New York Times*, when contrasted with the shrillness of Bork's supporters, notably the *Wall Street Journal*, gave dignity to the opposition.

The campaign in support of Bork directed by the White House suffered from mutually inconsistent messages: While White House Chief of Staff Howard Baker and the White House's chosen lobbyist, Tom Korologos, were assuring all and sundry that Bork was truly a moderate, Richard Vigurie and other right-wing direct-mail voices were exhorting the legions of the Right to rise up and support the nomination as the last, best hope of conservatism. So conflicting were these forces that, in August, the head of the Heritage Foundation felt compelled to convene a "peace conference." But Bork's supporters never reached consensus on a common message about the identity of the nominee.

Well into September, the White House and Justice Department were so insistent that Bork's credentials, rather then his ideas, must carry his nomination, that they left the field of exploring those ideas largely to the opposition. As our research colleague Phil Simon asserts, "They stayed away from the 'Book of Bork' and focused only on the dust covers."

But it is the judgement of most informed observers that Bork would have been confirmed if it had not been for the hearings. Bork himself testified for thirty-two hours over five days. After him came constitutional experts, law professors, legal historians, former federal officials, and veteran civil rights lawyers. Sixty-two testified in Bork's support; forty-eight against.

Before the hearings, many senators remained undecided, including the four principal targets on the committee—Senators Byrd, DeConcini, Heflin, and Specter. As he testified, Bork harmed himself in two ways. First, in his effort to portray his views as moderated by time and the responsibility of high office, he appeared to some to be opportunistic, trimming his judicial philosophy to court the Committee's approval. He appeared to abandon positions he had reaffirmed within the past few months, and expressed an uncharacteristic respect for precedent. In so doing, he undermined his standing as a fierce but principled judicial advocate, evoking from Senator Leahy the scornful charge of "confirmation conversion." Yet Bork's reformulations did not persuade doubting committee members that he would adhere to precedent once he had been confirmed.

Senator Leahy wrote in his diary on the final day of Bork's testimony, "There's no question in my mind that Bork would come to the Supreme Court with an agenda. Some well-established decisions he would seek to overturn. I think we have as clear a picture of that as we are going to get." And Senator Specter lamented, "He tried to ride two horses and fell from both."

Second, Bork affirmed in the hearings his fundamentally restrictive view of the Constitution, especially the provisions guaranteeing individual rights and liberties. Bork's crimped vision was encapsulated for many in his contrasting, antiseptic response to Senator Simpson's inviting question, "Why do you want to be an associate justice of the Supreme Court?"

Judge Bork's answer was framed in terms of the intellectual challenge of the courtroom, especially the Court "that has the most interesting cases and issues, and I think it would be an intellectual feast . . ."

The New York Times's Linda Greenhouse wrote of another "revealing moment . . . late in the second day of Bork's testimony, when Senator Paul Simon of Illinois, also a candidate for the Democratic presidential nomination, reminded the judge of a remark he made in a speech two years ago: " 'When a court adds to one person's constitutional rights, it subtracts from the rights of others.' Did he still believe that? Mr. Simon asked."

"Well, yes, Senator," Judge Bork replied. "I think it's a matter of plain arithmetic." Greenhouse continued:

> This view of the Constitution as a kind of zero-sum system, in which one party can win only at another's expense, was sharply at variance with the vision put forward by Bork's opponents. They spoke of the Constitution in organic rather than arithmetical terms, as a system elastic enough so that adding to the rights of some did not necessarily diminish the rights of others. Where Judge Bork insisted that the text of the Constitution and the intent of its Framers were the only legitimate guides for a judge, the opponents portrayed the Constitution as a concept of liberty destined to continue growing well beyond the bounds of the text itself.

In fairness, Judge Bork also spoke with deep feeling of his commitment to "maintaining our constitutional structure" as "the most important thing this nation has."

But for most of those who were drawn into the debate, even this passion for "constitutional structure" was not "the most important thing." Though the witnesses who opposed Bork were mostly temperate and scholarly, the conflict invariably triggered their passions, not for "constitutional structure," but for constitutional liberties. And it was with that passion that the Senate and the public resonated.

The nation watched and listened, many viewing and hearing the testimony live, millions of others viewing highlights and reading about the testimony as the leading national news story, night after night and morning after morning, all through the week.

A large number of Americans formed their opinions about

Bork's nomination during the two weeks of hearings; a large majority of the public and of the Senate did not approve of what they saw and heard and read about Judge Bork's views.

In summing up the nomination process, Stuart Taylor of the *New York Times* commented, "those who watched the Judiciary Committee hearings saw perhaps the deepest exploration of fundamental constitutional issues ever to capture the public limelight."

He noted that,

> [M]ost of those who testified against Judge Bork, like many of those who lobbied against him, based their positions on careful analysis of his statements on key issues, and avoided the kind of inflammatory rhetoric into which the more partisan Senators on both sides sometimes slipped. In fact, some of the prominent lawyers and scholars who testified against Bork described his more controversial writings at least as accurately as Judge Bork did in his own testimony.

"Those of us who testified against Robert Bork," observes Laurence Tribe, "made quite clear that we did not suspect him of being personally a vicious, woman-hating, privacy-destroying racist. Despite the accusations of Senators Hatch and Simpson and the others, you will simply not find anything in the testimony that questions Robert Bork's personal views on these matters."

It was the hearings themselves that had the greatest impact on public opinion. Stuart Taylor commented:

> [F]or all the indignation and attention focused by Bork's supporters on these [the opposition's] advertisements, there is little evidence that they have had a major effect on the outcome, any more than did the simplistic and emotional advertisements placed by pro-Bork groups.
>
> Results of public opinion polls indicate that the sharpest swing against the Judge resulted from his five days of televised testimony.

And what of those who still believe that it was really the "Beard of Bork" that beat Bork?

"It would be as serious a mistake to assume that because Robert Bork looked like an old goat on TV, that explained the vote against him," Ann Lewis insists, "as those people I know who still think that the public voted for Ronald Reagan because they found him charming. Voters really do know what they're doing. They did not like what Bork would mean. His demeanor, and I would say especially his answers to the questions, meant he couldn't leap over his unpopular positions by making a personal and emotional connection, but this was not a referendum on red-bearded men."

John Tower, President Bush's nominee for secretary of defense, was attacked for his alleged drinking. House Speaker Jim Wright was attacked for his ethical lapses. But Robert Bork was only attacked for the implications of his ideology. Even popular comedians got the point. In his September 23, 1987 offering of "Current Comedy," Robert Orben wrote, "The way I see it, Judge Bork will have to come up with satisfactory answers to three major problems before he can be appointed to the Supreme Court: Will he change his views? Will he change his philosophy? Will he change his barber?"

If it was the "Book of Bork" that beat Bork, then it was the campaign that forced the Senate to read the book. In our judgement, the principal contribution of the outside campaign was to force the Senate to take seriously its constitutional obligation to examine the Bork nomination. We do not believe the Senate was intimidated or misled by the campaign; indeed, we are satisfied that the Block Bork Coalition contributed to the Senate's and the nation's understanding of Bork's views and their implications for the lives of American citizens.

There is a crude political maxim: the only upright politician is one who is under equal pressure from all sides. President Reagan had already fueled a militant right-wing political constituency in support of his transformation of the Court. So when the anti-Bork campaign, led by Senator Kennedy, signalled its intention *at the outset* to wage a political campaign in opposition to the Bork nomination, it served notice on the Senate that succumbing to inertia or the political pressures from the Right would not be politically painless. And as the campaign progressed, and gained momentum, most of the members of the Senate had reason to believe that a vote for or against Bork would incur roughly equal political costs. This meant each was free to vote as his or her conscience would dictate.

This was perhaps not quite so true with the southern Democrats, the five members of the "class of '86", who had been elected with large black pluralities. As we have seen, no constituency feared Bork more, none was more militant, and none better organized than southern blacks.

It also appeared through the polls, to the surprise of many, that southern whites were not anxious to reopen the wounds of segregation, and that fears for the invasion of privacy resonated deeply among all southerners, black and white alike. Perhaps a conservative southern senator who might otherwise have leaned to support Bork may have been restrained by the wishes of the larger part of his constituency. But if this was politics, it was the politics of reconciliation, not division. How else to interpret the vote against Bork by Mississippi Senator John Stennis, who was retiring and could not have been influenced by narrow political calculation? Stennis and Byrd of West Virginia were the only members of the Senate left who had opposed the 1964 Civil Rights Act.

Having forced the Senate to pay careful heed to the nomination, the campaign's second contribution was the publication and distribution of the unexpurgated "Book of Bork"—to the senators and their staffs, to the Bar and to academia (including the most potent of prospective witnesses), to the journalists and editorial writers, and to the grassroots networks.

While some Senate staff viewed the coalition's research and

paper production as "redundant" and "overkill," this intensive effort helped, directly and indirectly, to achieve a number of critical goals for the coalition.

To begin with, the very intensity and redundancy of the research effort brought to light critical pieces of the Bork record, especially the latest speeches, which might otherwise have been missed. The unique immersion of the coalition's lobbyists and grassroots leaders in the Bork record and its implications built confidence and an authoritative capacity to persuade both senators and the media. The compilation and broad dissemination of original Bork documents satisfied the extraordinary hunger of activists and potential activists, in Washington and at the grassroots, for deep knowledge—which, in turn, transformed concerned citizens into informed advocates.

The legitimacy of a political campaign against a Supreme Court nominee was very much at issue in the Bork campaign, especially given the reputation for legal scholarship which Bork enjoyed. The coalition's research and analytic efforts gave intellectual legitimacy and weight to their campaign. The production of the analyses and reports furnished the framework of constitutional law through which the Bork record could be seen as extreme and off-center. The portrait of Bork's legal mind and inclinations which emerged from the mosaic of his writings and record was so troublesome in itself to so many that most of the coalition's advocates were not tempted to turn to exaggerated or distorted rhetoric. By establishing a role as authoritative information resource to the Senate and the media, the coalition also gained access, credibility, and standing.

In addition—and again working with its Senate leaders—the coalition also helped shape the hearings, helped recruit and educate and prepare witnesses. By subordinating specific issues, such as abortion, within general principles, such as privacy, and by forbearing to testify, the campaign's strategists helped keep the focus of the confirmation hearings on those aspects of Bork's views which most troubled the majority of the Senate.

The national coalition put a premium on the importance of education. Of course the crudest, most simplistic, most inflammatory propaganda can be laundered in the telling as "citizen education." When an advocate says—as most of those working to defeat Bork did—that their central strategy was to "educate" the public to the risks of Bork, the critical observer is entitled to be skeptical. And, surely, the motivating force behind such "education" on the judicial philosophy and record of Bork was to arouse deep concern in the minds of those to be educated.

But, as we have seen, the coalition had great faith in the power of exposing the full range of Bork's legal ideas and opinions to public scrutiny. Again and again, those participants we interviewed testified that the more deeply they read the raw materials, the writings of Bork himself, the more they were convinced of his unsuitability for the Court.

A third important contribution of the campaign was its success in framing the central issue of the conflict in a way that resonated powerfully with the broad American public. It was the campaign that made it clear that this fight was not about whether Bork was an honest or decent man, nor about antiseptic theories of constitutional interpretation. It was about a perceived threat to the advances in human rights made in America since the 1950s. And it asked of all Americans whether they were prepared to refight the terrible struggles of the sixties, which have now largely receded into history. And the answer, as much in the South as anywhere, was no.

Who Were Those Masked Men and Women?

As the battle drew to a close, Merrill Hartson of the Associated Press noticed that the White House was employing its customary fancy rhetorical footwork in characterizing Judge Bork's supporters in one way, and the organized opposition to Bork in another way. All those aflame with the conviction that Bork's nomination would not only reclaim the Constitution but the Bible as well, the president's men hailed as "citizen action groups," and "grassroots supporters." Such activists represented groups including the Conservative Alliance, the Knights of Columbus, the Christian Action Council, the American Farm Bureau Federation, Concerned Women of America, the Moral Majority, and the Ad Hoc Coalition of Conservative and Law Enforcement Organizations.

When it came to those who opposed the nomination, however, they were attacked as nothing but that subhuman species that taints the purity of our democracy, the dreaded "special interests." Robert Bork, himself, immoderately dismissed them as "ultra-liberals, radicals, and leftists." Well who, precisely, were they? In particular, how "Left," how "ultra," and how "special"?

"These 'special interests,' are the constitutional rights and liberties of every American," says Ralph Neas. "They are 'very' special public interests.' "

Those defending these interests were, many of them, mainstream Americans. They included the Florida Federation of Business and Professional Women's Clubs, the Texas Teachers Education Association, the Virginia Black Republican Caucus, Student Future Leaders of Alabama, and a former West Virginia Supreme Court judge. They were the influential Democratic and Republican "Maxi-Club" campaign contributors to Arizona Senator DeConcini, and they were the 600-member Philadelphia Ad Hoc Lawyers' Committee Against Bork, which included at least one partner from every Philadelphia law firm.

The opposition also boasted such "ultra-liberals, radicals, and leftists" as former president Jimmy Carter, Ford cabinet secretary William Coleman, three former American Bar Association presidents, and conservative University of Chicago constitutional law professor Philip Kurland.

They were the elected Democratic state office holders of Texas, and Planned Parenthood members — a third of whom are registered Republicans. They were a former Washington State

Republican Party chairman, black and white priests and ministers, Republican environmentalists, and the Epilepsy Foundation.

In the end, they were, also, fifty-eight members of the United States Senate.

Proof of the Pudding:
From Abortion to Privacy

Historian James McPherson tells us that in the 1840s the abolitionists found that the fundamental immorality of slavery did not strike a sufficient spark of outrage in middle class Americans to kindle political will. "Abolition" was not a polite term. But, McPherson tells us, the abolitionists discovered that the breakup of families, a logical economic byproduct of the slave market, was "the theme most likely to pluck the heartstrings of middle class readers who cherished children and spouses of their own." Hence, *Uncle Tom's Cabin* was conceived.

In 1987, the dreaded "A" word was not "abolition," but "abortion." The great fear of the leaders of the Bork opposition was that Reagan would succeed in portraying the opposition to Bork as sectarian crusaders for abortion rights, leaving much of the middle class unmoved, or hostile. While polls consistently show that a substantial majority of Americans support the freedom of pregnant woman to choose abortion, one fear was that the issue would divide the Block Bork Coalition itself, since many of the groups within the coalition were indifferent or even opposed to abortion rights. Of even greater concern was that prominence in the media of the abortion issue, and of abortion rights advocates, would give credence to Reagan's portrayal of the opposition as a "special interest."

This fear was borne out by early coverage of the opposition. In the *Washington Post* on July 2, Lou Cannon and Edward Walsh reported that "Bork's position on abortion is likely to be a particular lightning rod for opposition to his nomination." On July 6, Stephen Wermiel's article in the *Wall Street Journal* was headlined, "Bork's Abortion Views Looming Larger as Problem in High Court Confirmation." And, on July 8, the *New York Times's* E.J. Dionne reported that the Bork nomination "is pushing the abortion issue back to the center stage of American politics."

The strategy to deal with the "A" word was not to abandon reproductive rights as an issue, nor to seek to silence the pro-choice groups for whom Bork's opposition to abortion rights was, indeed, the central issue. Instead, coalition strategists sought to embrace and subsume "abortion rights" within a spacious principle—more broadly and less divisively calculated, in McPherson's words, "to pluck the heartstrings of middle class readers"—privacy.

How was "abortion" to fade into "privacy"? Through both skill and serendipity. Once again, the "Book of Bork" laid the foundation. As the coalition's research team highlighted the significance of Bork's scorn for the *Griswold* decision, which struck down a state ban on the use of contraceptives, Bork's willingness to permit state intervention in the bedrooms even of those who would not contemplate abortion was raised in bold relief.

But the primacy of "privacy" over the "A" word also reflected a core component of the campaign: the conscious development and implementation of a media advocacy strategy. A critical component of that strategy was the identification of themes, or symbols, such as the defense of "privacy" with universal appeal, and the dogged avoidance of divisive symbols such as the "A" words, "abortion" and "affirmative action."

Ann Lewis describes how the campaign seized upon "privacy" as the salient issue:

> It was the right to privacy that *he* had challenged, so it wasn't that we sat around and thought "we can't talk about abortion, what's an-

other word." He had handed us that because his attack was on the right to privacy. In addition, it was the strongest way to make the case, because when you talk about privacy, everyone has their own private ideas for private behavior. For women, it was very clear what we were talking about—it offered a whole lot of people a chance to talk about sexual behavior without using explicit language. But there were no doubts on what was involved, or again, what the right was.

It worked. By the time of the hearings, the abortion issue had virtually dropped from sight. At the end of the campaign, the *New York Times's* Linda Greenhouse reflected on the evolution of the privacy theme:

> It came to stand for the whole theme of fundamental rights, the concept of an expansive Constitution in contrast to Judge Bork's view that the Constitution was limited by its precise language and the intent of its 18th Century framers. The abortion question itself became subsumed into the broader question of a generalized right to privacy, a concept that politicians were suddenly rushing to embrace.

The Editorials: A Thematic Scorecard

Using the coalition's basic themes as a scorecard, we asked our colleague Phil Simon to survey newspaper editorials commenting on the nomination and the confirmation process to help determine the effectiveness of the symbols opposing forces deployed to characterize the nominee.

As the campaign progressed, the editorial pages became a barometer of the status of the thematic battle. There, in an average of up to one editorial per week for some interested papers, the struggle was played out.

The sample survey identified more than 600 editorials from 226 papers in eighteen states. It included the top twenty-five major dailies in the U.S. and these eight key swing states—

Alabama, Arizona, Florida, Georgia, Louisiana, Pennsylvania, Tennessee, and West Virginia.

The editorials reveal that, while Bork received more editorial support, measured by numbers of supporting editorials, the Block Bork Coalition and its allies in the Senate largely shaped the thematic content of the debate. Thus, even while pro-Bork editorials repeated the White House's messages, they also felt compelled to respond to the charges levelled by the campaign, to explain what Bork was not. Richard Viguerie, the Right's leading media specialist, concluded that "the liberals framed the debate and put Bork on the defensive."

There certainly was no landslide of editorial opposition to Bork in American newspapers. In the eight swing states, where fourteen of sixteen senators eventually voted against Bork, editorials ran heavily in favor of the nominee. The top twenty-five papers in the country were split on the nomination. Opponents did gain crucial support from three influential papers—the *New York Times*, the *Los Angeles Times*, and, grudgingly, the *Washington Post*.

The editorial writers were certainly activated by the conflict. At least forty-three papers published five or more editorials on the topic. Three of the most influential papers, the *Wall Street Journal*, the *Washington Post*, and the *New York Times*, wrote a total of forty-three, often lengthy, editorials on Bork-related topics.

By September, the themes and symbols stressed by the coalition pervaded newspaper editorials around the country, whether they were for or against the nominee. Whatever their position on Bork, the editorials conveyed the sense of a rising tide of opposition.

For example, overarching themes insisted upon by the coalition—including the ideas that the stakes in the battle were high and that the judicial philosophy of the nominee was an appropriate, key question—were accepted as legitimate by papers supporting Bork, as well as by opponents.

The "stakes" theme emerged quickly. On July 3, the *Philadelphia Inquirer* posited that whoever filled Justice Powell's seat "could be positioned to set the course of American constitutional law and justice for several years." The *Wall Street Journal*, a staunch, if not hysterical Bork proponent, agreed that, "the stakes for the Reagan presidency are sufficiently high to warrant a large effort."

Even before the September hearings began, the editorials had begun to ask, "Who is the real Judge Bork?" "Bork's judicial philosophy is what is at issue," explained the pro-Bork *Phoenix Republic* in mid-September. "Who is Robert Bork? Does he really believe in the judicial restraint? Can we be certain that he is in the judicial mainstream?" asked the *Atlanta Journal/Constitution*.

Significantly, the basic misgivings cited with regard to Bork were identical to those crafted by the coalition. The three broad themes most often mentioned were: the stakes of the nomination are high; his judicial philosophy is too extreme, narrow or divisive; and his views on civil rights, women's rights, and privacy are outside the mainstream. Many editorials also questioned Bork's commitment to follow precedent and his "opportunistic" confirmation conversion.

Editorials were preoccupied with Bork's legal judicial philosophy — not his qualifications, as the White House wished. A July *St. Petersburg Times* editorial typified this focus: "Bork is a right-wing extremist who wants to turn back the clock. His views are outside the mainstream of American thought on many issues, such as the right of women to choose abortion, civil rights . . . sexual harassment of women." The *New York Times* wrote that "Judge Bork frightened many blacks . . . because of his rigid view of the Constitution and of Congress's power to safeguard civil rights."

After venting its disquiet at the campaign, the *Washington Post* still urged rejection of Bork because on race, free speech, fair representation and privacy issues, it is not clear that he "would let broader considerations of justice guide him as he handed down opinions . . . " Bork "does not seem to care who is crushed," concluded the *Post*.

One month into the campaign, few anti-Bork editorials dwelt upon the issues of abortion, homosexuality, or Watergate. In July, the *St. Petersburg Times* had cited abortion first among a list of constitutional questions raised by Bork's record. By September, the paper had altered the terms of its opposition: "Personal privacy—the underlying legal issue in the abortion debate —remains the greatest source of concern about him."

Of course, Bork's defenders attacked the "character assassination" tactics of opponents, particularly "special interest groups" and "liberal Democratic senators." Ten of the *Wall Street Journal*'s twenty editorials on Bork lashed out at the "special interest" opposition. The *Journal* castigated those who opposed Bork as "bullies," "hypocrites," "murderous" and "demagogues."

Pro-Bork editorials did not have a monopoly on this theme. Some newspapers which opposed Bork also opposed the tactics of the campaign. The *Los Angeles Times* complained that "Bork's opposition did not distinguish itself with some of the political tactics it employed to defeat him." The *New York Times* lamented "distortions" by opponents and expressed concern that the battle "has at times been reduced to slogan."

But Phil Simon discovered that most pro-Bork editorials devoted as much energy to defending the nominee *on the coalition's terms* as they did to extolling his credentials or excoriating the opponents—indicating how potent the themes used by Bork's critics had become. For every editorial that painted Bork as a mainstream conservative, another pro-Bork paper felt compelled to deny that he was a right-wing radical. The *Tucson Citizen*'s style was typical: "The real Bork is no closed-minded, concrete-cased idealogue of the far right . . . Bork is not 'out of the mainstream' . . . Bork represents no threat to the Court's balance . . . Bork is no racist, sexist or anti-abortion zealot." The *Birmingham News* insisted, defensively, "His rec-

ord as a Federal Appeals Court judge is not one of wild extremism, but one of agreement" with other Court of Appeals judges.

Was it Fair?

When confronted with charges, such as *Washington Post*
columnist Charles Krauthammer's, that the campaign against
Bork was "one of the most mendacious media campaigns ever
launched against a public official," and "the meanest national
campaign of this decade," we might have spent pages critiquing
the intemperate, liberal-baiting, hate-mongering advertising
campaigns which sought to further Bork's cause by attacking the
ethics and patriotism of Bork's opponents, both in the coalition
and in the Senate. Those who recall the Bush campaign's distortions of the ACLU will have a sense of the debased level of public discourse that characterized the pro-Bork ads.

Such exercises in comparative mendacity may be marginally
useful in responding to such startling assertions as those of *New
York Times* columnist William Safire, who claimed that the character assassination media strategies of the Bush campaign were a
direct response to the low standards pioneered by the Bork opposition. It might be shown that it was the Right, led by the twisted
genius of direct mail provocateur Richard Viguerie, that pioneered in lowering the level of political discourse. But that would not
satisfy those genuinely troubled by accusations that Bork was
caricatured by the campaign opposing his confirmation.

The fundamental difference between the Bush presidential
campaign and the anti-Bork campaign was that those who
crafted the Bush attack on the ACLU *knew* that Democratic contender Dukakis had disavowed the very ACLU positions with
which the Bush campaign had tarred him. By contrast, the anti-
Bork campaign based its fears on Bork's own words and legal
theories.

The paid advertising issue, especially, leaves even some participants in the anti-Bork effort discomfited, especially those constitutional lawyers who had participated in earlier, more genteel campaigns. They fear that paid advertising, no matter how scrupulous, coarsens the confirmation process. Others have no objection to paid ads in principle, but feel that certain ads did not fairly characterize Bork's record. Still others believe that the ads were proper and marginally useful, but not worth the ammunition they gave Bork and his proponents. And some believe the ads fairly communicated well grounded fears about Judge Bork.

So we are left with the question: Was the campaign to oppose Bork fairly conducted?

Of course, there were rhetorical excesses and oversimplifications. Especially reprehensible were the handbills circulated by the Alabama state coalition, echoing Senator Heflin's slurs on the nominee's reputed agnosticism. Ironically, one of the few indefensible characterizations of Bork occurred a year after the nomination was defeated, during the second Bush-Dukakis presidential debate, when Dukakis coolly lumped Bork in with the "sleaze" parade of indicted Reagan officials. But we found few examples of such gross distortion; we found none originating in Washington from the members of the national coalition.

Jeff Robinson, who served as chief counsel to Senator Specter, a prime target of the campaign, viewed the anti-Bork effort as substantive, and fair:

> For the most part, what the groups were out there doing was presenting fair representations of complex legal concepts to people, and saying, "We think this is what it means, and we think this is awful, and we want you to support us in thinking that."
>
> I think the coalition had a huge part in getting that story out to the media, and distilling the information in a way that the media could understand it and present it, which is a tough job.

Post-nomination assaults on the fairness of the campaign invariably overlook the role and quality of the hearings, which were the culmination of the campaign, its final and central act. Yet, in those hearings, no witness for the opposition challenged Bork's integrity or truthfulness (as they had Rehnquist's). No one challenged Bork's intellectual ability; no one accused him of moral or ethical failings. Though the campaign argued strenuously that a Bork confirmation would set back racial progress through the impact of his judicial philosophy, none of the campaign material we reviewed labelled Bork a racist. It was Bork's own constitutional writings, and his defense of these writings, that was the subject matter of the campaign.

Even the most intemperate of Bork's supporters on the Judiciary Committee could not find grounds for challenging the fairness or thoroughness of the hearings. The ranking Republican senator, Strom Thurmond, praised Biden for conducting the hearings in a "fair and reasonable manner." (So scrupulous was Biden that his behavior weakens Nader's "nicotine fit" theory, for he humanely provided periodic "smoking breaks" during Bork's trying testimony.)

In response to a question raised by Senator Simpson, Bork ally Lloyd Cutler testified:

> I think the terms of the inquiry are perfectly fair. I think it is appropriate for the senators to raise these questions and worry about these questions as long as in the end the majority take a long view, a view based on the admitted inaccuracies and imperfections of judging how a particular nominee will turn out to be when he gets to enjoy the appointment during his good behavior, and is independent from then on.

And Senator Hatch, one of Bork's most ardent supporters, commented later, "I thought that it was a very high, intellectual proceeding and experience. I think most of my colleagues felt that way, too."

As for the charge by others that the anti-Bork campaign revived "McCarthyism," Alexander Cockburn of the *Nation* responds:

Sen. McCarthy bullied witnesses, refused them opportunity to speak or to defend themselves, sent them forth from the hearing room into ruin. He ruled by innuendo, by distortion, by lies. Judge Bork did not leave the hearing a ruined man but one afforded every courtesy, every opportunity to explain, clarify, retract.

Still, it was the paid advertisements that triggered the greatest outrage. And fair-minded observers, such as the *New York Times*'s Stuart Taylor, did find that some of the ads "painted a frightening portrait, based upon exaggerations of and highly creative extrapolations from his past statements."

Taylor's criticism was directed especially at a NARAL full-page newspaper ad which began with the warning that Bork would seek "to wipe out every advance women have made in the 20th century." The ad asserted that "Robert Bork's writings and his record demonstrate a hostility to rights most women would consider fundamental, from personal privacy to the equality of women and men before the law; and he's threatened to overturn any Supreme Court precedent that stands in his way."

But it was PFAW's "Gregory Peck" television ad which drew the most fire, for appearing to allege that Bork favored not just the reasoning but the results of decisions, such as the preservation of poll taxes, which he insisted were dictated only by his constitutional principles.

What the ad actually said was that "he defended poll taxes and literacy tests, which kept many Americans from voting." The response by People for the American Way was that, indeed, "Bork's statements clearly indicate that as a judge, he would defend a state's ability to enact a poll tax".

The ad also noted that "Bork opposed the civil rights law that ended 'whites only' signs at lunch counters." That assertion was attacked, not because it was untrue, but because Bork later changed his mind. It should be noted, however, that this change of mind was part of an earlier "confirmation conversion," which took place in 1973, as Bork sought Senate confirmation as solicitor general. He did not, however, repudiate his earlier assertion that the civil rights laws were based upon a principle of "unsurpassed ugliness." His acceptance of the law was based not upon newly found principles of justice, but upon the pragmatic ground that the law worked.

"The bottom line was fact," insists PFAW's David Kusnet, and describes the elaborate fact-checking process:

> The issue people had been instrumental in doing that first draft, and once we boiled it down, it went back to them for fact checking. You know, here's this high-profile group with a lot of enemies, that takes on the administration and its nominee for the highest court in the land, in this high voltage debate. We know that we damned well better be able to defend every word that we say. We put it through the wringer. It went through at least a half-dozen people, from a professional librarian who won't let a word go by unless she sees it documented somewhere she respects, to issue experts like Ricki [Seidman] and Melanne [Verveer]. They consulted with others, including David Cohen and Bill Taylor. I wouldn't have dared to say, "Let's put this in, because it sounds a little better." We may be one of the few organizations in town that has a *New Yorker*–style fact-checking department going over our TV and radio spots. It might be the only TV spot of that measure of success in history that began as a research paper, and went through a fact-checking department. The bottom line was not rhetoric; the bottom line was fact.

But doesn't the simplification and compression necessary to "present the themes" necessarily involve distortion and manipulation? Kusnet responds:

> No matter how profound or detailed or substantive an idea you have, it ought to be possible to reduce it to a simple idea. I worked for several years for suburban newspapers, and learned news style and headline writing. Even if you have a six-part series of articles and each of them is fifty paragraphs long, you still ought to be able to write a headline over it, and write a lead for it. It doesn't do full justice to it, but it ought not distort it. Bayard Rustin was a great civil rights leader who built all kinds of movements around complicated

ideas and knew you had to boil them down. He once told a visiting delegation who took an hour to explain a complicated welfare reform strategy, that "If you have an idea that takes several hours to explain, then I don't think you have much of an idea."

Suzanne Garment invoked brutal rhetoric in attacking the Peck ad: "This entire spot was composed of false innuendoes and outright lies . . . slander . . . mendaciously confused . . . errors and lies." She did not, however, match up these charged words with specific assertions in the ad.

Arthur Kropp, executive director of PFAW, and Bill Taylor responded, citing extensive evidence from Bork's record to support each charge, and concluding that, "Mrs. Garment is simply wrong on her facts . . . [T]he ads require no apology. The hurt they caused was the sting that the truth sometimes inflicts."

David Cohen recalls that those within the coalition who were planning to use paid advertising in the campaign agreed early that every assertion would be documented "to meet the zone of acceptability for feisty ads.'"

It is not our purpose, and it is beyond our expertise, to referee arguments over the fine points of the Bork record. But so much fiery rhetoric from Bork and his supporters attends the subject of the paid ads, and the Peck spot in particular, that it is plain that more than mere partisanship is at work.

In the end, the judgement of fairness seems to depend largely upon the prism through which the observer views the sum of the parts of the Bork record, and Bork himself as a judge and as a human being.

There are those who believe, as Bork insists, that the pattern of denial of rights that flows from his written arguments and judgements are the unavoidable, even painful product of his search for "neutral principles" with which to maintain the "constitutional structure" of the framers as a bulwark against arbitrary or tyrannical judges of the Left or Right. They naturally view any suggestion that he desired or welcomed those denials of rights as deliberately misleading.

On the other hand, there are scholars, such as Professor Philip Kurland, who, reviewing the entire opus of Bork's writings, conclude that his constitutional theories mask his true preferences. Bork's "original intent," argues Kurland, "is not a jurisprudential theory, but, like Nixon's 'strict construction,' and Roosevelt's 'back to the Constitution,' it is merely a slogan to excuse replacing existing Supreme Court judgments with those closer to the predilections of their expounders." "Bork's current constitutional jurisprudence," Kurland concluded in his testimony, "is essentially directed to a diminution of minority and individual rights."

Such critics note that Bork's claim to "judicial restraint,"—to be guided solely by the dictates of the Constitution's founders or of the legislators—is undermined by his actions when the plain will of the legislature violates his own vision of morality. So when Judge Bork views the evident congressional intent in enacting antitrust laws as misguided, he disdains to follow the will of Congress. But he is not inclined to do so with respect to legislative denials of privacy and other individual rights.

There are other critics who conclude, with Shirley Hufstedler, that Bork's lifelong "quest for certitudes" served largely to enable him to avoid "having to confront the grief and the untidiness of the human condition." They note that Bork's outrage—expressed in such passionate terms as "unsurpassed ugliness," "unprincipled," "indefensible," "pernicious," "utterly specious" —has always been directed at the extension of rights to vulnerable citizens, never their denial.

Which is the true Judge Bork is unknowable. The question of fairness relates not to whether the fears expressed by the Bork opponents would certainly have been realized had he been confirmed, but whether they were fairly grounded in the Bork record and his articulated judicial philosophy. By this standard, it is our judgement that the campaign waged by the anti-Bork coalition was fundamentally fair.

Both the White House and the anti-Bork campaign did indeed employ highly compressed symbols and themes in the nomination contest. But we agree with journalist Renata Adler that it was the White House that resorted to "defactualized" symbols, while the campaign elevated the public dialogue by invoking symbols fairly connected to Bork's record. The campaign employed symbols, says historian Jeremy Brecher, that "you could get your mind around."

We leave the last words on unfairness to former member of Congress Barbara Jordan, who responded directly to Krauthammer's charges of "mendacity" and "meanness":

> Krauthammer faults those of us who opposed Judge Bork for using paid advertisements to take our case to the people. But we told nothing but the facts: Bork did oppose the Civil Rights Act of 1964; he did oppose the one person, one vote decision; he did defend literacy tests and poll taxes, which kept millions of Americans from voting; he did rule in favor of a company that gave its women employees the gruesome choice of getting sterilized or getting fired; and, even during his confirmation, he denied that American citizens have the fundamental right to privacy.
>
> If Charles Krauthammer really equates concern with justice with the crassest negative campaign tactics, then I respectfully suggest he just doesn't understand the depth of feeling that accompanies a desire for equality and justice. And when I think back to my constituents who were disenfranchised by policies Bork condoned and enfranchised by a decision he condemned, I realize that they could teach the learned Krauthammer a lesson about what's fair and what's unfair in American politics.

Was the Campaign Too Political?

Twenty-seven nominees to the Supreme Court have been rejected or failed to take their seats. According to Robert Katz-

mann of the Brookings Institution, a scholar of the Court and the
Senate, "most rejections were linked to political objections."
That includes the Senate's rejection of George Washington's
nominee for chief justice, John Rutledge, on grounds no grander
than the Senate's pique with Rutledge's public opposition to the
Jay Treaty.

Still, some observers of the Court, no fans of Judge Bork, express deep unease about the mass politics of the Bork opposition. Some liberals who deplored the Right's media-hyped attack in California which brought down liberal justice Rose Bird
and her colleagues saw the Bork campaign in the same, vul-
garizing light.

Suzanne Garment, a staunch Bork proponent, argued that
while there has always been "insider politics" in the judicial
selection process, the vice of the anti-Bork campaign arose from
the decision "to cross the line between the insider politics of judicial selection and the constituency politics of a national political campaign."

And columnist William Safire's complaint was that the
"liberals, abetted nationwide by a hyper-politicized American
Civil Liberties Union, killed the nomination of an eminently
qualified judge . . . in an unprecedented 'rolling vote' in the
media that undermined the traditions of the Senate . . . "

Now the injection of mass citizen participation into the judicial selection process may or may not be a good thing. But let
there be no mistake about it: It was Reagan the candidate and
Reagan the president who injected politics into the Court and
the Bork nomination. It was Reagan who pleaded with the
voters to give him Republican senators who would vote for
justices to transform the Supreme Court. In the days preceding
the Bork nomination, Senate Democratic Leader Robert Byrd
and Ralph Neas, among others, had warned the White House
that the Bork nomination, above all others, would provoke a political battle.

As University of Minnesota law professor David Bryden argues, "the rejection of Judge Bork . . . sent a message that was as much anti-political as political. [The Senate] asserted a more political role for [itself], but it also warned presidents and potential nominees to be less overtly political."

Still, there is no question that citizen groups and citizens around the country are more likely in the aftermath of Bork to pay attention to—and, where alarmed, to mount the political ramparts in opposition to—a Supreme Court nominee.

Robert Bork believes that it was not just left-wing agitation that beat him, but a flood of left-wing advertising dollars. Al Kamen of the *Washington Post* reported on March 27, 1988: "In Bork's view, a 'massive coalition of ultraliberal and left groups . . . poured $10 million to $15 million,' into a negative advertising campaign of 'lies and distortions' . . . a 'blitzkrieg' of negative advertising that set public opinion against him.

None of the expenditures by any party to the Bork controversy are public; no one we asked could supply solid numbers. We suspect that the combined totals of funds spent by the far Right in their massive direct-mail campaigns, as well as paid ads, and by the White House and the Justice Department in their mobilization in support of the nomination, dwarf the expenditures by the anti-Bork opposition.

Our estimate is that the combined total of print and broadcast ads by members of the anti-Bork coalition did not exceed $2,000,000. Of course, the campaign incurred other out-of-pocket expenses, some of which—such as PFAW's heroic xeroxing and mailing bill for publishing and disseminating the reports and analyses and excerpts from the "Book of Bork" to coalition members, the media and others—were substantial, though hardly amounting to millions of dollars.

For purposes of rough comparison, in the 1988 California referenda issue advertising campaigns, the insurance industry spent $70,000,000 on advertising to defeat an insurance initiative supported by Ralph Nader, and the tobacco industry, with

Bush media genius Roger Ailes, spent $20,000,000 to defeat a twenty-five cent cigarette excise tax increase. That was in one state. And they both lost.

Media buys did not buy Bork's defeat.

Still, the question remains: Was the national mobilization against Bork good for the Constitution and the Court, or does it threaten to undermine the independence and integrity of the Supreme Court?

We believe the answer lies in the constrained nature of the political challenge mounted by most participants in the campaign: it was, for the most part, not a single-issue campaign (like the California Right's attack on Rose Bird's refusal to impose the death penalty). No narrow, specific stand by Judge Bork—not on abortion, any pending civil rights issue, women's, environment, or consumer issue—was made a litmus test of acceptability by the coalition. The steady focus of the campaign, instead, was Bork's fundamental judicial philosophy and the broad implications of that philosophy.

Thus, the anti-Bork campaign engaged citizens in a grand debate over competing visions of society: of human rights vs. property rights; of unrestrained state and majoritarian power vs. individual and minority rights; of the permissible limits to free speech; of the sanctity of the home and the bedroom.

How can we say to these citizens, "It's O.K. for senators to inquire into such grand issues; it's O.K. for 'insiders,' for legal elites to participate—but don't even *try* to explain what's at stake to the public"?

Linda Monk, a Washington writer on constitutional issues, responded in the *Washington Post*, one week before the start of the Senate hearings, to two political scientists who had called for the depoliticizing of the nomination process. "Both law and politics," she wrote, "are at heart about what society values and the choices it is willing to make among competing values." She concluded:

To discourage citizens from participating in the confirmation process of a Supreme Court Justice flies in the face of what the Bicentennial of the Constitution is all about. Bork's confirmation hearings are scheduled to begin on Sept. 15; the bicentennial of the signing of the original Constitution is Sept. 17. There's no better way to celebrate that occasion than for citizens to let their Senators know their views on Bork's nomination, whether he should be interpreting the Constitution for the next few decades. It sure beats reading about the Constitution on the backs of cereal boxes.

Does a more open and aggressive hearing process impose a "political litmus test" on judicial nominees, as Republican Whip Senator Alan Simpson fears?

The Brookings Institution's Katzmann quotes the young William H. Rehnquist, writing in the *Harvard Law Record* of October 8, 1959, in response:

> It is high time that those critical of the present [Warren] Court recognize with the late Charles Evans Hughes that for one hundred seventy-five years that Constitution has been what the judges say it is. If greater judicial self-restraint is desired, or a different interpretation of the phrases 'due process of law' or 'equal protection of the law,' then men sympathetic to such desires must sit upon the high court. The only way for the Senate to learn of these sympathies is 'to inquire of men on their way to the Supreme Court something of their views on these questions.'

Former Chief Justice Warren Burger, no liberal, came to the Senate to testify in support of Bork. Nonetheless, he hailed the process. The hearings, he told the committee, "are going to help our [Constitutional Bicentennial] Commission's five-year plan or program of a history and civics lesson for the country, for ourselves, because it shows the process at work. So, although I have heard some criticism of the operation, I do not share that criticism. I think this is, on the whole, when we take the net result, good for the country."

As for the future use of political advertising and the potential therein for distortion, it seems clear to us that the process will be largely self-correcting. Though they have staunchly defended the truth and integrity of their ads, those who used them in the Bork campaign have plainly been bruised by the intensity of the criticism — and by the seizure of the ads by the Right as a symbol of the corrupt methods of the Left. No one in the coalition believes that ads were central to their success.

"In looking at the question of paid ads from a future perspective," reflects PFAW's Melanne Verveer, "you would at least have to consider as a factor the reaction you were going to get from the other side for using them. If you believe you have something to say and this is the most effective medium, go with it; but first carefully weigh the possibility of adverse response and the merits of going forward."

"I wouldn't rule out ads again," Ricki Seidman adds. "To insulate against this sort of future criticism, there might be a different way to do it: state the record, either from editorials, from noted experts, from the nominee's own writings, without putting in some interpretative wording of our own that was the cause for some criticism. Not that I think it was wrong, but maybe that's something we learn from."

Perhaps the generic lesson is best expressed by Kathy Bonk: "I've always been a believer that the media should attract attention to the message, not the medium. You don't want to have media that overpowers the message and becomes the issue itself."

Finally, Bork's defeat, and the organized citizen outrage it provoked, may well make future Supreme Court nominations *less* political. As NYU law professor Dworkin observes, if future presidents behave as Reagan behaved, "their nominees will almost certainly face political opposition . . . But that lesson may itself lead future presidents toward less confrontational appointments; and the shared sense of the danger that Supreme Court appointments have already become too political may encourage consensus rather than controversy."

13

A TASTE OF EMPOWERMENT

> The Bork model is a real model. It's a model
> for how you talk about the issues; it's a
> model for working together; it is a model for
> successful involvement.
>
> KATE MICHELMAN

Was the Bork campaign truly a model? A blueprint for the progressive politics of the 1990s and beyond? And did it herald grand progressive alliances to come?

There is no shortage of skeptical voices, even among those most active and nostalgic about the Bork campaign, who believe nonetheless that only the "red-bearded menace," the particular broad threat of a Bork-led constitutional revolution, could have brought so many together in such harmony and common purpose.

But there are others, and we are inclined to share this view, who believe, with Laurence Tribe, that the Bork campaign was truly "a transformative experience" for many of its participants —a transformative experience which promises to change the nature of future citizen campaigns in ways both large and small.

We base this judgement on a series of qualities that, coming together, made the Bork campaign different from any within recent experience:

- While the conservative challenges posed by Reagan for most of the eighties tended to fragment and divide the progressive community, the Bork campaign promoted a transcendent unity.

- *While many seventies and eighties issue campaigns* tended to be either Washington-centered and highly professionalized, or strong in grassroots energy but strategically weak, the Supreme Court fight succeeded in integrating both "inside" Washington-based leadership and "outside" networks and coalitions throughout the country.
- *While citizen advocates* have been chronically reluctant to acknowledge the need for professional issue advocacy skills, the Bork campaign reached out for a full complement of professional lobbyists, organizers, media specialists, and other issue advocacy professionals.
- *While conservatives* nurtured their leaders in the upper reaches of the Reagan administration, the anti-Bork effort proved a crucible for enriching the ranks of Democratic Party leaders skilled in guiding and releasing the energies of autonomous citizen activists.
- *While the Reagan era* had led many would-be activists to despair of progressive change, those who participated in the Bork campaign experienced a renewed sense of civic empowerment and hope.

From Divisiveness to Unity

For much of the 1980s, under massive assault by the Reagan administration and its mobilized constituencies, civil rights, women's, consumer, and environmental groups fought desperately—and separately—on diverse fronts to preserve the gains they had made in the sixties and seventies. And sometimes they found themselves vying for the attention of overloaded liberal legislators, or competing for segments of a shrinking federal budget.

Demands for the redemption of rights by Hispanic and women's groups did not always mesh with the priorities of black civil rights leaders; and the strong alliance forged in the sixties between Jews and blacks had been tested. But by focusing on the core values and principles underlying specific issues, not the issues themselves, the Bork campaign brought old allies back together and forged new, and in some instances highly unlikely, alliances.

To a greater extent than in any campaign in recent memory, this unity of purpose led the participating leaders and groups to subordinate personal and institutional interests to the common goal. Of course, the millennium did not arrive with the Bork campaign. Ego needs and institutional "turf-mindedness" and "column inches envy" did not disappear. There were dissenters; there were those outside the consensus who believed that not all participants were treated equally or fairly; there were those inside the consensus who argued that free spirits who took their own counsel and set their own course of action without much regard to the consensual plan of action jeopardized the final vote.

But for the most part, egos and turf battles were held in check as the stakes rose and the odds against Bork's confirmation tightened. Sheri O'Dell of NOW saw this intensity in action:

> People worked beautifully together out in the field, and they did whatever they thought was going to work. It was more, "how are we going to get this guy's vote," than "who's going to get credit for what." Getting credit for something doesn't always take second place, but in this instance it did. People did think they had a chance to win it, and there really was an urgency. It was, like, "we *have* to win this one."

Bill Robinson, executive director of the Lawyers' Committee on Civil Rights, said, "You get massive coalition efforts when

the stakes are truly high and there is an ultimate goal that everybody can subscribe to and understand why they must submerge
their individual and organizational interests." This was just
such a time.

"People that had never met before, and organizations that
would never have considered working together before, all got
together and did what needed to be done," says Texas organizer
Mike MacDougall. "It was really remarkable."

Dr. Gwen Patton, historian of the Alabama New South Coalition, writes;

> For the first time ever, Black and White Alabamians publicly
> joined together . . . Such strong statements of unity from an
> Alabaman cross section of Black and White representatives in labor,
> politics, small businesses, social-justice programs, clergy and
> women organizations have never been made, not even during and
> after the successful 1955–56 Montgomery Bus Boycott, nor the 1965
> Selma-to-Montgomery Voting Rights March.

In Texas, after the vote, members of the state coalition met to
explore the possibilities of joint action in the future on other issues. The power of coalitions no longer seemed an illusion to
many who participated in organizing the first grassroots campaign over a judicial nomination. Jewish lawyers and law
teachers and NAACP community activists, white male labor
leaders and feminists, libertarians and politically liberal baby
boomers, consumer advocates, environmentalists, and small
business leaders—all came together in common purpose to defeat Bork.

Months after Bork's defeat, a member of the National Conference of Black Lawyers in Seattle confessed amazement at
finding himself at a fundraiser for the Seattle NARAL affiliate,
an involvement he never would have contemplated prior to the
Bork battle.

In chapter 2, we recounted the development of a new relationship, a relationship of trust and sharing, between NARAL's Kate Michelman and the NAACP's Althea Simmons. Many such new relationships were forged in the campaign, and new levels of trust were gained among those who had previously worked together formally in coalition, but actually at arms length.

As Bill Taylor observed, "No battle brought more diverse groups together. That's part of the legacy, because once people have worked together and found that they can work together, it provides a basis for doing so again."

"Tens of thousands of citizens," says Ralph Neas, "struggled passionately . . . and were bonded!"

The campaign gave meaning to the seldom realized ideal of "community." "I think I was the youngest professional involved in the whole national campaign," says NARAL's Richard Mintz, "and I consider myself incredibly fortunate, because it was an opportunity for people like me to learn . . . I don't know what other opportunities can provide that same kind of experience, and the fact that I was working with Phil Sparks, Ralph, and everybody else was invaluable experience. Up until then I had never had a sense of community, and that is what the Bork campaign did for me."

Brock Evans of the National Audubon Society reflects upon the Bork campaign with strong emotion:

> The history of it all struck me—the forces of one powerful arm of the progressive movement, appealing to the others for help. It wound me back and back and back, to almost twenty years before, when Ralph Nader and some others were the instigators of another historic meeting, a gathering of some of our communities, at Airlie House, September, 1969 . . . really the birth of the great body of environmental laws we have now woven around the places we love.
>
> All of us were finally together again, as we had not been since the Consumer Protection Act—and before, since that earlier rising tide of environmentalism. It was good to be back together again, and I hope it continues.

Integrating "Inside" and "Outside," Networks and Coalitions

By the Reagan years, faced with a hostile administration, intimidated liberals in Congress, and a somnolent press, public interest issue advocates in Washington were forced to recognize that a Washington-centered campaign on a contested national issue, cut off from a national constituency, was like a head with no body: all brains, no brawn. Simultaneously, the leaders of grassroots movements came to understand that national mass movements, such as the nuclear freeze campaign, could not translate their political force into systemic change without at least shared leadership with Washington-based allies and strategists. A grassroots campaign with no Washington base for intelligence gathering and strategic coordination was like a headless body; all brawn and heart, no brain.

In the Bork campaign, the "inside" leaders and lobbyists reached out in full partnership to the "outside." Clearly, the leaders of the anti-Bork effort in Washington knew that citizen action throughout the country was essential to defeating Bork, and they invested resources, time, and respect in developing bridges to the field. And, while the political force and much of the creativity of the campaign came from outside, the grassroots campaign was nourished by the intelligence, resources, and counseling of the Grassroots Task Force and the "desks" in Washington.

"The campaign could not have succeeded," says Florida coalition organizer Frank Jackalone, "if there hadn't been such a creative, reciprocal relationship between the coalition in D.C. and the Florida coalition, because the other side had a very ambitious and scientific campaign going on in favor of Bork, with lots of big money interests and fundamentalist church groups heavily involved."

As David Cohen of the Advocacy Institute concluded, "The administration never could quite make up its mind whether to play the inside or the outside game; the coalition worked both the inside and outside game—and each reinforced the other."

So most of those who participated in the Bork campaign came away with an appreciation for the rewards, as well as the demands of effective networking and of building a winning coalition. They learned that what was required to successfully challenge the White House with a just cause was not mysterious: the engagement of vast networks of activists on a national scale under the umbrella of a richly layered coalition of organizations.

They learned that networks of advocates are the sinews of a movement, and coalitions are its skeleton; that networks build strength and unity by connecting individual activists, enabling them to engage in joint action and to draw upon each other's knowledge, experience, and judgment. They learned that, when properly tended, networks can aggregate the energy of lone activists, reinforce their commitment, empower them, and sustain them through discouraging times. And they learned that successful networks operate at a high level of trust and reciprocity and rely on a process of faithful exchange which builds and strengthens the more it is used.

Joining the networks of activists that made up the Bork campaign was rewarding, not just because it helped lead to Bork's defeat, but also because of the satisfactions that flowed from working together with like-minded people. The networks that sustained the Bork campaign furnished support and recognition. They were a form and a source of psychological affirmation, helping overcome the sense of powerlessness and despondency that can discourage even the most deeply committed advocate over time.

And the participants learned about the power and the limitations of coalitions. By joining in coalition, their own organizations more effectively combined their resources and energies to advance the common goal. In the past, working separately and without coordination, their organizations too often duplicated the efforts of potential allies, and sometimes worked at cross purposes. Under the umbrella of a coalition, each organization became part of a greater whole that could speak with a unified and amplified voice.

"There may be a lot of opposition or a lot of energy out there to fight a wrong if we can just find a structure to mobilize it," says Texas organizer Jackie Jordan-Davis. The integrated national networks and coalitions of the anti-Bork campaign furnished just such a structure.

From Purity to Professionalism

Volunteer activists tend to doubt the purity of commitment of professional lobbyists and organizers. Activists "in the field" are prone to view Washington-based professionals as but one step away from selling out to the seductions of Gomorrah on the Potomac. Progressives with roots in social service professions look upon the new cadre of public interest media specialists as a symptom, rather than part of the cure, of our social ills. And those who are drawn to social causes by a personal need to "bear witness" tend to place low priority on *winning*. David Kusnet of People for the American Way observes:

> Even in the eighties, losing is much more a part of the folkways of the Left than of the Right. It's almost a kind of pacifism; we're not sure we want to do what it takes to win. We're not sure we want to do what it takes to reach a large number of people; we're not sure it's ethical to talk about something for only sixty seconds. It speaks well of people that they take very seriously what they do, but it can diminish their effectiveness.

While the general public tends to look down on all lobbying as a low form of political life, public interest lobbyists tend to look down upon media advocacy specialists as an even lower form of life, an unhealthy mutation spawned by Madison Avenue out of corporate public relations. Emily Tynes expressed what she perceived to be the underlying attitude of the traditional lawyers and public interest advocates: "What *we* do is substance; P.R. is the nasty thing those people have to do to manipulate."

Among issue advocates who come out of social service traditions, or the protest politics of the 1960s, media advocacy remains suspect. Kusnet observes:

> There's always a kind of ambivalence about TV, especially among knowledgeable policy people, probably mostly among people who are left of center. Advertising and the use of the electronic media are just much more a part of the culture of the corporate sector and the Republican party and the Right than it is of the Left.

These suspicions did not simply evaporate in the Bork campaign, but they were transcended by the possibility and the desire to win, and by the recognition that only a full-scale, contemporary political campaign could beat Bork. One coalition leader recalls the warning of their foremost Senate ally and leader, Ted Kennedy: "This campaign can't be done on the back of an envelope." And that meant reaching out for the professionals.

"You have to integrate successfully your lobbying, substantive, media, and grassroots strategies," say Neas. "If you fail with respect to one component, most likely your campaign will fail." Media professionals were as essential as community organizers.

Although Reagan and the Bork supporters made some headway with the media in turning the focus away from Bork and onto the "special interest" lobbies, the consistency and breadth and aggressiveness of the coalition's media advocacy overwhelmed the "special interest" counterblast in the media.

Thus one of the most significant achievements of the Bork

campaign was the heightening of appreciation for the importance of media strategy. Though many of the most sophisticated
lobbyists have known it for years, there will no longer be any
doubt that media strategy must be an integral part of a campaign
at all stages, and that it cannot be divorced or subordinated to
the issues research, the lobbying, the grassroots organizing, or
any other aspect of the campaign. The Bork media campaign,
summarizes Phil Sparks, "was blissfully simple—but labor intensive!"

AFSCME's Henry Griggs concludes:

> [The history of the Bork campaign] speaks to the need for each or-
> ganization to have a really focused program on training and improv-
> ing media skills at the grassroots so that they can mobilize effec-
> tively. Some organizations are better at that, but it was clear that we
> had to reach targeted areas, and the national spokesperson is not go-
> ing to be the person with the time to do that. Some of these organiza-
> tions had affiliates in a lot of states, and some of their field people
> had basic media skills, were more effective, and came up with
> stronger messages. You can't do it without spending some time and
> effort in training your grassroots organizations.

Coalition leaders do not take kindly to the suggestion that the
campaign emulated the White House or the Right. "I don't see
why we should give them credit," responds Ann Lewis tersely.
"I've been in campaigns for public opinion before."

Phil Sparks of AFSCME, on the other hand, takes pride in
learning from the techniques of the Right—and besting them:

> We tried to learn the lessons of the New Right. I had read all their
> books, and I read all the books about them, and I had been on the
> receiving end of what they do. I think we have mastered their mass
> communications techniques and improved on them—because we
> still have one thing they don't generally have: a highly motivated,
> grassroots organization. To match that with our public education,
> research, and lobbying efforts made us more formidable than they
> were. I wrote Ralph Neas a letter afterwards, and I said it was finally

good to outfox the fox. That was the most fun for me, to beat them in that way.

It's true, of course, that advocates on both sides of the ideological divide learn strategy, if not substance, from each other. The Reagan White House did not invent, though they may have perfected, the art of crafting and disciplining all voices to adhere to one unitary media theme each day. But the anti-Bork campaign certainly represented state-of-the-art advocacy for the public interest community.

What the coalition did *not* learn—from the Reagan White House or Madison Avenue—was to remove substance from image. There was a direct line from the deep research on the "Book of Bork," through the extracted summaries of the Bork record, through the themes memos, to the campaign's issues and messages. And the message was the same in the Senate lobbies as on the local talk radio shows.

The polls, the refining of the message, the consciousness of symbols and labels helped the coalition to discard or subsume issues and themes which did not resonate with greater majorities of Americans. But those themes that emerged were not false or disingenuous. Those who feared the loss of the right to have an abortion did fear—and had reason to fear—Bork's threat to the larger right of privacy. The broader symbols simply placed the narrow concerns of individual groups within a broader constitutional and value framework to which the greater majority could and did relate.

Lobbyists, organizers, researchers, and media specialists with diverse skills—ranging from reconciling potentially hostile coalition members to crafting media "bites"—were all needed and all welcome. The Leadership Conference had never hired community organizers in a campaign before. The Block Bork Coalition's lobbyists, already skilled through experience in media advocacy, recognized the need and the place for media professionals.

As AFL-CIO lobbyist Ernie DuBester remembers, it all came together:

> Lobbying, media messages, . . . they were always actively going on by different organizations independently while still working cooperatively within the sphere of the coalition. That was the beautiful thing about it . . . They reinforced one another.

As Marcia Greenberger of the National Women's Law Center says, "There was a political maturation of the public interest community like I've never seen, and I've spent most of my adult life working on it."

A New Generation of Leaders

It is sweet irony that one of Ronald Reagan's most lasting legacies may be his stimulation of a new generation of citizen leaders, who rose up in the 1980s to join with an earlier generation of leaders in resisting his vision and his policies. And it was the Bork campaign that battle tested and strengthened the largest cadre of such leaders.

We are not writing of charismatic leadership, of man-on-a-white-horse leadership, of towering figures — of a "Z," a Lech Walesa, a Martin Luther King, Jr. Of the Bork campaign's leaders, Ted Kennedy, Ralph Nader, Jesse Jackson, Rev. Lowery, Ben Hooks, and Molly Yard were perhaps the best known and most capable of rallying citizens to their personal standards, and they each played an important leadership role. But as leaders in the Bork campaign, they were among equals, dozens of equals. And many important leaders remain little known, but no less ready to lead again.

Ralph Neas comes closest to being the central leader, but Neas's particular genius lies in aggregating a collective leadership of complementary skills. The warrior leader is often seen as isolated and lonely in command. Neas's leadership, by contrast, is communal; he is the great convener, the leader who reaches out for other leaders. And in the Bork campaign, as we have seen in every chapter of this book, he and Aron and others in formal leadership positions readily found others able to share leadership tasks and responsibilities.

There were *intellectual leaders*, spark plugs of knowledge and ideas, like Bill Taylor, Eric Schnapper, Walter Dellinger, and Janet Kohn—and the towering witnesses against Bork, like William Coleman.

There were *network leaders*, reaching out and drawing in diverse webs of other groups and activists like Nan Aron, Althea Simmons, Elaine Jones, and Antonia Hernandez.

There were *mobilizers of resources*, those who worked through large organizations, able to cut through institutional inertia, like Ken Young and Gerald McEntee, who helped channel organized labor's commitment into the mobilizing of union sources.

Some also served as the *voices of public morality*, latter day counterparts to the old testament prophets, including Barbara Jordan, and Ralph Nader.

There were historically *wise leaders*, especially Joe Rauh, and Fred Wertheimer, who brought to bear the learning of past experience.

There were *conveners and doers*, those who could bring people together comfortably and cut though resistance to get the job done, like Judy Lichtman and Joan Claybrook (whose constructive presence was often drawn upon even as her more severe colleague, Ralph Nader, was distancing himself from the coalition's strategy).

There were *leaders in communications*, helping to recognize and seize the opportunities presented by the mass media, like Ann Lewis, Kathy Bonk, Phil Sparks and Nikki Heidepriem.

And there were many whose skills were multi-layered. David Cohen is an example. "I called him a lot," says Melanne Verveer.

He's everyone's mentor and guru. If you were going to have an important meeting with a few people and you wanted some wisdom and depth, you called David and asked him if he could be there. He has been through so many battles—he's a legislative strategist; he knows how to talk to the media; he is very sensitive to senators and their peculiarities and very sensitive to coalition politics; he knows how a public interest group works. He could have been a high-powered, highly paid consultant, but he was at the disposal of the groups to use as we saw fit. He could tell us how we looked when we didn't know ourselves how we looked.

Joe Rauh singled out Melanne Verveer as "a smoother of the way." With quiet authority, Verveer, as we have seen, was looked to by her peers for her uncommon strengths as lobbyist, strategic planner, media resource, problem solver, harmonizer, and as the one who could be counted upon to *follow through* to its conclusion any task she undertook.

There are those—and they are not all women—who believe that this campaign did so well in building consensus because so many of its leaders were women, not only in the women's groups but in all elements of the campaign. Ann Lewis observes:

> Women were major players in setting the strategy and implementing the strategy at the state-by-state level. The way the structure was developed and the emphasis that was put on everyone staying informed, for example, were ways in which the women who had developed the coalition worked with one another and set that model for this campaign.

This is hardly surprising. Feminist psychologists, such as Prof. Carol Gilligan of Harvard and Dr. Jean Baker Miller, find strong evidence that women tend to recognize the critical importance of cooperation and that they also tend to place a high value on mutuality and caring in relationships.

One acknowledgement of the essential role of the younger women leaders was the fact that when the Steering Committee began meeting on a daily basis, their starting time was moved up from 8:00 A.M. to 8:30, to accommodate those who had to make sure that children were safely in the hands of school or day care.

Perhaps most important, these leaders, men and women, with whom we are most familiar because they operate in Washington where we know them, are mirrored in their leadership skills by hundreds of their counterparts, who sparked the state and local coalitions throughout the country — leaders like Georgia's Rev. Tim McDonald, Pennsylvania's Frances Sheehan, Florida's Frank Jackalone, Washington state's Frank Shoichet.

And, though each brought a different array of talents to the campaign, they each reflect those essential qualities and attitudes which John Gardner, the founder of Common Cause, has characterized as the essence of democratic leadership:

> Leaders don't invent motivation in their followers, they unlock it. They work with what is there. Of course, "what is there" is generally a great tangle of motives. Leaders tap those that serve the purposes of group action in pursuit of shared goals . . .
>
> They release energy rather than smother it, motivate rather than deaden, invite individual initiative rather than apathy . . . And it's the task of the leader to keep hope alive. It is the ultimate fuel. [Gardner wrote this long before Jesse Jackson enshrined it.]
>
> Such leaders . . . understand the wants and purposes and values of their people, and they must know how to overcome the inertia that afflicts most of the people most of the time.

From Despair to Hope and Empowerment

There is, among the campaign's leaders, a realistic recognition that the factors which combined to make the Bork campaign a success may not ever reoccur. The Bork nomination was, after all, a challenge to the mainstream, and liberals and progressives far more often find themselves *challenging* the mainstream.

Still, in the Bork victory, many who had lost hope for almost a decade tasted victory and a sense of empowerment. And they found strength and reinforcement and joy in the sheer numbers and diversity of their fellow citizens drawn together in common purpose. Ann Lewis, who is no political novice, talks of her surprise at the renewed sense of empowerment which the Bork campaign gave even to political veterans:

Shortly after the vote on Bork, I went to a meeting of the Democratic National Committee, and found an air of pride over this victory that I had not seen in a long time. Essentially what I heard was people saying, "We did it! We won it! This proves we can win it!" Stronger, in fact, than the vote for the Senate [in 1986], because it was, to them again, an affirmation that by changing the makeup of the Senate, they had changed the consequences to their lives, and when I get that kind of reaction from Democratic National Committee members, that's a very strong signal to me.

[It affected] Democrats across the board—and I attended a Democratic Women's Caucus, where people were coming up to me to tell me of the role they played in the anti-Bork coalitions out in the states. It really was something to be proud of, because it meant standing up for your principles and winning, and they felt they hadn't been able to do that for a while.

The campaign also provided, according to Lewis, "a new visibility, a new effectiveness for the civil rights community." And Lewis also notes that many who had never experienced political efficacy before first tasted such power in the Bork campaign:

When I think of groups that got energized around this issue and learned a lesson about being effective, I think of BPW [the National Federation of Business and Professional Women]—again, a very solid, mainstream organization. [They] had not been active before in judicial selection; [BPW, which] is not considered a major civil rights organization, got deeply involved in this one. These were issues that they cared about and understood. In the course of getting involved in the integral coalitions in their states, [they] met a new group of people, liked those associations, are still proud of the role they played in the Bork defeat.

Rev. Lowery of the Southern Christian Leadership Conference avers "The Bork defeat is indicative that the civil rights movement is alive and the era of activism is not concluded."

Joe Rauh, at seventy-eight the grand dean of civil rights activists, now believes that "the great tide of liberalism" that ebbed in the Reagan years seems ready to come in again. Rauh, who had been in fragile health for several months prior to the Bork nomination, relays his wife's judgment that the Bork campaign saved his life—the nomination by fueling the fires of his outrage; the campaign, his hope.

As the great psychoanalyst and humanist Erich Fromm tells us, hope is "a decisive element in any attempt to bring about social change." He likens hope to "the crouched tiger" which is always ready to jump "when the moment for jumping has come." In the Bork campaign, the moment came. We believe the tiger of an American progressive movement is crouched and ready to jump again.

Chronology
of the Bork Opposition
HIGHLIGHTS FROM JUNE THROUGH OCTOBER 1987

HIGH ANXIETY

June 2 - At the annual Law Day Luncheon sponsored by the Alliance for Justice, civil rights leader Joseph Rauh predicts that Supreme Court Justice Lewis Powell will resign, and an opponent of civil rights constitutional advances will be nominated by President Reagan. Rauh urges those attending to mobilize to oppose the nomination, calling the summer "our window of vulnerability . . . for [the] Supreme Court."

June 26 - Justice Powell steps down from the Supreme Court. It is "Black Friday" for concerned public interest activists who anticipate that D.C. Court of Appeals Judge Robert Bork or Senator Orrin Hatch of Utah will be the likely replacement.

June 27 and 28 - Over the weekend leaders of civil rights organizations inform White House Chief of Staff Howard Baker that a Bork nomination would precipitate a full-scale battle.

June 29 - Concerned civil rights groups and women's organizations meet informally to formulate an anticipatory strategy and launch a comprehensive look at Bork's record. Senate Democratic Whip Alan Cranston urges Senate Democrats to form "a solid phalanx" of opposition if the president nominates an ideological extremist to replace Justice Powell.

June 30 - Leaders of forty organizations meet to organize and set as an interim goal, a Senate "freeze," seeking assurance from members of the Senate that they will withhold either support or opposition to the nominee until the confirmation process has run its due course.

OPENING SALVOS

July 1 - President Ronald Reagan announces his choice of Robert H. Bork. Forty-five minutes later, Senator Edward Kennedy charges, in the Senate, that "Bork's America is a land where women would be forced into back-alley abortions, blacks would sit at segregated lunch counters . . . " Many groups hold news conferences and issue press releases stating their concern or outright opposition.

July 2 - Eighty organization leaders and lobbyists overflow the Leadership Conference on Civil Rights conference room at the formal organizing meeting of the Block Bork Coalition. Preliminary analyses of Bork's record are distributed and the central campaign themes are suggested.

July 4 - Over the Independence Day recess, constituents meet with senators asking them to forebear taking a position on the Bork nomination.

July 5 - Senator Packwood (R-Or.), staunch defender of the Supreme Court's 1973 decision legalizing abortion, vows to wage a filibuster if Bork does not agree to accept the key reproductive rights decision, *Roe v. Wade*, as settled constitutional law.

Independence Day Weekend - Key coalition organizations, including the National Education Association, National Association for the Advancement of Colored People, National Abortion Rights Action League, Planned Parenthood, all pass formal resolutions of opposition to the Bork nomination. (Within the next several weeks, at their national conventions, the National Organization for Women, the Southern Christian Leadership Conference and other groups join in formal opposition.)

July 7 - The Senate Judiciary Committee officially receives the nomination of Robert Bork to be the 104th Supreme Court justice. At the third meeting of the anti-Bork coalition four task forces are formed: research/drafting, lobbying, grassroots, and media.

July 8 - Senate Judiciary Committee Chairman Joseph Biden determines that confirmation hearings will not commence prior to the August recess but will begin September 15. Chairman Biden meets privately with six representatives of the coalition to inform them of his intention to lead the opposition. He predicts, "This is going to cost me the [presidential] nomination."

July 13 - The national Grassroots Task Force meets for the first time. A list of target states for mobilization is developed.

July 15 - Other coalition task forces hold their first meetings. Senate Minority Leader Robert Dole estimates that it is "50–50" whether Bork will win Senate confirmation, and Alan Cranston's whip count claims 45 opposed; 45 in favor; 10 undecided.

July 23 - Joseph Biden's hour-long floor speech briefs a coequal role for the Senate in the judicial nomination process, and argues that the nominee's ideology is a proper matter for Senate inquiry.

July 30 - Thirty state delegations at the National Conference of State Legislatures record opposition to the Bork nomination; eighteen support the president's choice.

SENATE SUMMER RECESS AND MOBILIZATION

August 1 - Common Cause board votes to oppose the nomination.

August 2 - 1,200 grassroots organizers and activists attending the national meeting of Citizen Action in Chicago hear rallying speeches by Senators Cranston and Kennedy, Ralph Neas of the Leadership Conference on Civil Rights and Ricki Seidman of People for the American Way.

August 3 - Coalition leaders conduct detailed critiques for the media of the just-released White House paper, "Materials on Robert H. Bork," which portrays the nominee as well within the mainstream of constitutional jurisprudence.

August 4 - The Alliance for Justice convenes a forum on "How to Organize Your Campus" for congressional summer interns who will soon return to college. Yale Law Professor Paul Gewirtz's seminar on the Senate's "advise and consent" role is held for Senate staff.

August 5 - The NAACP Legal Defense Fund report on Bork's views on precedent is distributed to Judiciary Committee staff. Both the NAACP Legal Defense Fund and People for the American Way collaborate on the selected "Thoughts of Judge Bork."

August 6 - The coalition's Steering Committee meets at the National Education Association, one of the few coalition members which has a room large enough to accommodate the participants, who now number between 80 and 100 per meeting. A 123-page report by Public Citizen Litigation Group is released, which concludes that D.C. Circuit Court Judge Bork consistently voted to support government action or inaction when challeged by individual citizens or public interest groups, but not when challenged by business.

August 9 - Forum on the Bork nomination, co-sponsored by the Alliance for Justice and the Federation of Women Lawyers, is held in San Francisco for lawyers attending the annual convention of the American Bar Association.

August 11 - Senator Biden in a speech at the annual ABA convention warns that "if Judge Bork has meant what he has written for the past thirty years and had his view prevailed, America would be a fundamentally different place than it is today."

August 13 - A "message memo" drafted by political consultant Nikki Heidepriem for the Alliance for Justice highlighting the central themes of the campaign is circulated at a coalition meeting.

August 13–17 - Pollster Tom Kiley, under contract with AFSCME, surveys over 1,000 voters and concludes that conservative southern whites are troubled, just as liberals, by Bork's positions on civil rights, privacy and individual freedoms.

August 15 - Pollster Harrison Hickman briefs the coalition on the results from focus group surveys conducted for the National Abortion Rights Action League. The surveys indicate growing public awareness of the Bork controversy.

August 17 - The thirty-five-member executive board of the AFL-CIO formally votes to oppose Bork, vows a "no-holds-barred battle" and releases a report focusing on Bork's views regarding workers' rights and labor law.

August 18 - The National Women's Law Center releases its thirty-nine-page analysis of Bork's judicial record, finding therein "unparalleled hostility to women's rights."

August 28 - Survey results of the Kiley poll are circulated and, drawing on the extensive polling data, the coalition's Media Task Force generates a three-page "themes memo" distilling five central themes.

August 29 - Police, prosecutors, and public interest lawyers hold a press conference charging that Bork's views on criminal justice are unclear. The conference is designed to counter President Reagan's meeting the day before with officials of law enforcement groups in which he characterized Bork as a "law and order" judge.

OVERTURE TO THE SENATE HEARINGS

August 31 - The American Civil Liberties Union abandons its customary neutrality in fights over judicial nominations and, the following day, releases its "ACLU Report on the Civil Liberties Record of Judge Robert H. Bork."

September 3 - Senator Biden issues an exhaustive rebuttal to the Reagan administration's "Briefing Book" on Bork's record. The Judiciary Committee Chairman claims the administration distorts Bork's record in an effort to portray him as a "mainstream jurist."

September 8 - The 131-page report titled "The Bork Report: The Supreme Court Watch Project's Analysis of the Record of Judge Robert H. Bork" is released by the Nation Institute.

September 9 - The influential American Bar Association Standing Committee on the Federal Judiciary, which began evaluating nominees in 1948, does not reaffirm the unanimous "exceptionally well qualified" rating it gave to Bork when he was selected for the D.C. Court of Appeals. Four of the fifteen members of the ABA committee vote Judge Bork as "not qualified" and one votes "not opposed."

September 10 - The anti-Bork coalition distributes to most Senate offices its "Background Book Briefing Papers."

September 11 - Representatives of twenty-two national women's groups with a combined membership of 2.6 million hold a news conference in Washington, D.C. urging the Senate to block the appointment. Nearly half of the organizations had never before opposed a Supreme Court nominee. Common Cause releases its report, "Why The U.S. Senate Should Not Consent to the Nomination of Judge Robert H. Bork to be Associate Justice of the Supreme Court."

September 13 - Anti-Bork demonstrations are held in Minnesota, New York, and Washington, D.C.

September 14 - 1,200 attend the Monday morning "Funeral for Justice" in Philadelphia. A statement of opposition, signed by ninety-one prominent attorneys of the Lawyers' Committee for Civil Rights under Law, concludes that Bork's nomination "jeopardizes the continued vitality of civil rights and liberties long enjoyed by all Americans."

SENATE CONFIRMATION PROCEEDINGS

September 15 - A *New York Times* op-ed column written by leading Republican civil rights lawyer William T. Coleman, Jr. makes his case against the nomination. Televised Judiciary Committee hearings begin with Bork's testimony. The "Gregory Peck" TV spot, prepared by People for The American Way, and newspaper ads by the National Abortion Rights Action League and Planned Parenthood Federation of America opposing confirmation, are run.

Sept 16–19 - As nominee Judge Robert Bork continues his testimony, Committee member Patrick Leahy (D-Vt.) coins the term "confirmation conversion" to characterize Bork's apparent change of position on certain issues.

September 18 - The NAACP Legal Defense Fund and People for the American Way Action Fund release "Bork v. Bork: A Comparison of Judge Bork's Confirmation Testimony with His Previous Speeches and Articles." PFAW also releases its forty-page analysis, "Lessons Learned at the Confirmation Hearing: Judge Bork's Testimony Raises New Concerns."

September 21 - Panels of prominent lawyers and constitutional scholars begin to testify for and against the president's nominee. 100 law professors, including seventy-one constitutional law professors, and thirty-two law school deans urge the Senate to reject Bork.

September 23 - The Association for Retarded Citizens and twenty-two other disability groups urge Senate rejection.

September 25 - Environmental groups, including the Sierra Club, Greenpeace, Natural Resources Defense Council, and Friends of the Earth announce their opposition.

September 29 - People for the American Way responds to Senator Hatch's attack on anti-Bork print and TV ads with "Hatch's '67 Flaws': Flawed."

September 30 - Hearings end with the last of the 112 witnesses. Anti-Bork groups submit written testimony. Nearly 2,000 full-time law school faculty members submit a letter of opposition to the nomination. Majority Whip Alan Cranston reveals his latest vote count: 49 against, 40 in favor and 11 undecided.

THE WILL OF THE SENATE

October 1 - Three southern Democrats, Bennett Johnston (La.), David Pryor (Ar.) and Terry Sanford (N.C.) announce their opposition. Committee member Arlen Specter (R-Pa.), reveals his decision to vote against Bork. Senator Cranston revises his vote tally announcing now that 50 are opposed to Bork, 40 in support and 10 remain undecided. The Leadership Council on Aging, a consortium of ten large senior citizen groups, urges Senate rejection.

October 2 - Senator Boren of Oklahoma is the first Democrat to announce his support for Bork. A letter of opposition signed by 102

"Pillars of the Bar," consisting of prominent lawyers from more than thirty states, is delivered to the U.S. Senate.

October 3 - The National Abortion Rights Action League releases its report, "Opposition to Bork: The Case for Women's Liberty."

October 5 - Two other "swing" Democrats on the Judiciary Committee, Dennis DeConcini (Ariz.) and Robert Byrd (W.V.), declare their opposition.

October 6 - Senate Judiciary Committee votes 9–5 against Robert Bork. Previously uncommitted Alabama Democrat Howell Heflin joins seven other committee Democrats and Republican Arlen Specter in voting no.

October 7 - Ten more Democrats announce their opposition.

October 8 - Ernest Hollings (D-S.C.), is the second Democrat to announce he will vote for Bork.

October 9 - Judge Bork discloses that he will not withdraw but will insist that the full Senate vote.

October 13 - Senate Judiciary Committee issues its report (Exec. Report 100–7) recommending rejection of the Bork nomination.

October 21 - Senate debate begins.

October 23 - By the largest negative margin in history on a Supreme Court nomination, the Senate rejects the Bork nomination, 58–42. Many state coalitions hold press conferences publicly applauding those senators who voted against confirmation, and initiate praiseful "letters to the editor," especially to those conservative southern newspapers which had criticized their senators' votes against Bork.

Appendix A: Cast of Activists

[The organization noted beside each individual reflects his or her affiliation at the time of the campaign.]

Nan Aron – *Alliance for Justice*
Hope Babcock – *National Audubon Society*
Jerry Berman – *American Civil Liberties Union (ACLU)*
Jo Blum – *Planned Parenthood Federation of America*
Kathy Bonk – *National Organization for Women (NOW) Legal Defense and Education Fund*
Karen Bosch – *Arizonians for a Just Supreme Court*
John Buchanan – *People for the American Way (PFAW)*
Nancy Broff – *Alliance for Justice Judicial Selection Project*
Jim Brosnahan – *San Francisco attorney*
John Clay – *Lawyers for the Judiciary (Illinois)*
Joan Claybrook – *Public Citizen*
David Cohen – *Advocacy Institute*
Jonathan Cuneo – *Committee to Support Antitrust Laws*
Linda Dorian – *National Federation of Business and Professional Women (BPW)*
Norman Dorsen – *American Civil Liberties Union (ACLU)*
Ernie DuBester – *American Federation of Labor and Congress of Industrial Organizations (AFL-CIO)*
Hazel Dukes – *National Association for the Advancement of Colored People (New York)*
Annie Eberhart – *Foreman & Heidepriem*

Brock Evans – *National Audubon Society*
Faith Evans – *United Church of Christ*
Burt Foer – *Melart Jewelers*
Carol Foreman – *Foreman & Heidepriem*
John Frank – *Arizona lawyer*
Paul Gewirtz – *Yale University Law School*
Janlori Goldman – *American Civil Liberties Union (ACLU)*
Marcia Greenberger – *National Women's Law Center (NWLC)*
Henry Griggs – *American Federation of State, County and Municipal Employees (AFSCME)*
Bill Hamilton – *Planned Parenthood Federation of America*
Morton Halperin – *American Civil Liberties Union (ACLU)*
Leslie Harris – *American Civil Liberties Union (ACLU)*
Nikki Heidepriem – *Foreman & Heidepriem*
Antonia Hernandez – *Mexican American Legal Defense and Educational Fund (MALDEF)*
Helen Hershkoff – *American Civil Liberties Union (ACLU)*
Benjamin Hooks – *National Association for the Advancement of Colored People (NAACP) & Leadership Conference on Civil Rights (LCCR)*
Mike Hudson – *People for the American Way (Texas)*
Frank Jackalone – *Florida Consumers Federation*
Elaine Jones – *NAACP Legal Defense and Educational Fund*
Jackie Jordan-Davis – *Texas organizer*
Lane Kirkland – *American Federation of Labor and Congress of Industrial Organizations (AFL-CIO)*
Janet Kohn – *American Federation of Labor and Congress of Industrial Organizations (AFL-CIO) & Leadership Conference on Civil Rights (LCCR)*
Arthur Kropp – *People for the American Way (PFAW)*
David Kusnet – *People for the American Way (PFAW)*
Ann Lewis – *political consultant*
Judith Lichtman – *Women's Legal Defense Fund*
Rev. Joseph Lowery – *Southern Christian Leadership Conference*
Mike MacDougall – *grassroots organizer*
Mimi Mager – *Leadership Conference on Civil Rights (LCCR)*
David Marlin – *Washington, D.C. attorney*
Noelle McAfee – *Public Citizen*
Bob McAlpine – *National Urban League*
Ann McBride – *Common Cause*
Rev. Tim McDonald – *Southern Christian Leadership Conference*

Bob McGlotten – *American Federation of Labor and Congress of Industrial Organizations (AFL-CIO)*

Kate Michelman – *National Abortion Rights Action League (NARAL)*

Richard Mintz – *National Abortion Rights Action League (NARAL)*

Mario Moreno – *Mexican American Legal Defense and Educational Fund (MALDEF)*

Ralph Nader – *consumer advocate*

Irene Natividad – *National Women's Political Caucus*

Ralph Neas – *Leadership Conference on Civil Rights (LCCR)*

Debra Ness – *National Abortion Rights Action League (NARAL)*

Sheri O'Dell – *National Organization for Women (NOW)*

Joel Packer – *National Education Association (NEA)*

Jenny Pfizer – *National Abortion Rights Action League (NARAL)*

Robert Pitofsky – *Georgetown University Law School*

Michael Ratner – *Center for Constitutional Rights*

Joseph Rauh – *Leadership Conference on Civil Rights (LCCR)*

William Robinson – *Lawyers' Committee on Civil Rights under Law*

Estelle Rogers – *Federation of Women Lawyers*

Leonard Rubenstein – *Mental Health Task Force*

Eric Schnapper – *NAACP Legal Defense and Educational Fund*

Bill Schultz – *Public Citizen Litigation Group*

Linda Schwartz – *grassroots organizer*

Herman Schwartz – *American University Washington College of Law*

Peck Scott – *American Federation of State, County and Municipal Employees (Minnesota)*

Ricki Seidman – *People for the American Way (PFAW)*

Frances Sheehan – *National Abortion Rights Action League (NARAL)*

Frank Shoicet – *Washington state attorney*

Althea Simmons – *National Association for the Advancement of Colored People (NAACP)*

Phil Sparks – *American Federation of State, County and Municipal Employees (AFSCME)*

Nancy Stella – *People for the American Way (PFAW)*

Berry Sweet – *National Abortion Rights Action League (NARAL) (Arizona)*

Bill Taylor – *Leadership Conference on Civil Rights & People for the American Way*

Laurence Tribe – *Harvard University Law School*

Emily Tynes – *communications consultant*

Melanne Verveer – *People for the American Way (PFAW)*

Dick Warden – *International Union of United Automobile Workers (UAW)*

Fritz Weicking – *Citizens for Tax Justice*
Mary Weidler – *Alabama organizer*
Fred Wertheimer – *Common Cause*
Pat Wright – *Disability Rights Education and Defense Fund*
Molly Yard – *National Organization for Women (NOW)*
Durwood Zaelke – *Sierra Club Legal Defense Fund (SCLDF)*

Appendix B: Alphabetical Listing of Organizations

Representative Sampling of National Groups
Opposed to Bork

Alliance for Justice
American Association for Counseling and Development
American Association of University Professors
American Association of University Women (AAUW)
American Civil Liberties Union (ACLU)
American Federation of Government Employees
American Federation of Labor and Congress of Industrial Organizations (AFL-CIO)
American Federation of State, County and Municipal Employees (AFSCME)
American Jewish Congress
American Nurses Association
Americans for Democratic Action
Americans for Religious Liberty
Americans United for Separation of Church and State
Association for Retarded Citizens – United States
Black Women's Agenda
B'nai B'rith Women
Catholics for a Free Choice
Center for Constitutional Rights
Center for Population Options
Children's Defense Fund

Church Women United
Citizen Action
Coalition of Labor Women
Common Cause
Communications Workers of America
Disability Rights Education and Defense Fund
Epilepsy Foundation of America
Federally Employed Women
Federation of Women Lawyers
Friends of the Earth
Hadassah
International Association of Machinists
International Ladies' Garment Workers Union
International Union of Electronics, Electrical, Salaried Machine and
    Furniture Workers
International Union, United Automobile Workers of America (UAW)
Jewish Women's Caucus
Leadership Conference on Civil Rights (LCCR)
Mental Health Law Project
Mexican American Legal Defense and Educational Fund (MALDEF)
Mexican American Women's National Association
Na'Amat USA
National Association for the Advancement of Colored People (NAACP)
NAACP Legal Defense and Educational Fund (NAACP/LDF)
National Abortion Rights Action League (NARAL)
National Association of Protection and Advocacy Systems
National Association of Social Workers
National Black Caucus of State Legislators
National Black Leadership Roundtable
National Coalition for Women and Girls in Education
National Coalition to Abolish the Death Penalty
National Conference of Women's Bar Associations
National Council of Churches
National Council of Jewish Women
National Council of La Raza
National Council of Senior Citizens
National Education Association (NEA)
National Federation of Business and Professional Women's Clubs/USA
    (BPW)
National Federation of Temple Sisterhoods
National Gay and Lesbian Task Force

National Institute for Women of Color
National Lawyers Guild
National Legal Aid and Defenders Association
National Organization for Women (NOW)
NOW Legal Defense and Education Fund
National Urban League
National Women's Health Network
National Women's Law Center
National Women's Political Caucus
Natural Resources Defense Council
9 to 5, National Association of Working Women
Oil, Chemical, and Atomic Workers
Older Women's League
Organization of Chinese Americans
People for the American Way (PFAW)
Planned Parenthood Federation of America
Project on Equal Education Rights
Project Vote!
Public Citizen
Rainbow Lobby
Religious Coalition on Abortion Rights
SANE/FREEZE
Seafarers International Union
Service Employees International Union
Sierra Club Legal Defense and Education Fund (SCLDEF)
Southern Christian Leadership Conference
Union of American Hebrew Congregations
United Church of Christ (UCC)
United Food and Commercial Workers International Union
United Mine Workers
United States Student Association
United Steelworkers of America
Voters for Choice
Women's Legal Defense Fund
YWCA of the USA

Bibliographical Essay

The germ of this book was a class project in a course at New York University Law School on public interest non-litigative advocacy. In the Fall of 1987, just as the Bork campaign was reaching its climax, Michael Pertschuk, together with a group of the students in the class, decided to follow the course of the campaign to see what they could learn from its strategies, its techniques, its triumph—or failure. At the students' request, Pertschuk agreed to write a monograph on the campaign, an overview of the project.

As it is said, one thing led to another. Two months after the defeat of the nomination, Wendy Schaetzel volunteered to help organize the data collection and arranged a three-day series of debriefing interviews of Block Bork Coalition leaders. Remarkably, for most of the leaders interviewed, the interviews proved the first opportunity to reflect at length and to share the lessons learned in the heat of the campaign. No one had yet thought to systematically capture, before they faded, the memories which made up the collective oral history of one of the most significant campaigns in U.S. political history.

The interviews proved riveting and rich in the unrecorded lore of issue campaigning. Each of the students began to interview other campaign participants, but the demand of classes and the distance from New York led Pertschuk and Schaetzel to undertake more interviews on their own. By November, 1988, they had conducted formal inter-

306

views with over seventy coalition strategists and grassroots activists. These interviews form the foundation of the book. (The more than 1,000 pages of interview transcripts will be housed by the Manuscript Division of the Library of Congress.)

Schaetzel conducted a comprehensive periodical literature search, and began to comb the major organizational participants' files for campaign materials and memoranda. The lobbyists, legal experts, and activists whom we interviewed generously (and trustingly) shared with us internal memos, mailings to affiliates, press releases, reports analyzing the Bork record, leaflets, editorial memos, polling data, advertising copy and documentation, vote tallies, and coalition correspondence with national groups involved in the anti-Bork campaign; copies of letters sent to senators, packets of material on Bork's record earmarked for Senate staff, and memoranda directed to those reporters on the Bork beat. We had the chance to review the summaries drafted by local coalition leaders, which in some states were weekly or monthly reports detailing the latest activities and developments in the field.

Robert Bork's twenty-five year paper trail including all his articles, speeches, and even his most recent interviews was readily available to us at the Alliance for Justice, the American Civil Liberties Union, and People for the American Way. Each also maintained comprehensive periodical clipping files available to us. Common Cause, for example, gave us access to their complete set of newspaper editorials on the Bork nomination.

Bork's testimony before the Senate Judiciary Committee runs for the first 861 pages of the published hearings. Reports on the nominee's record and judicial philosophy submitted by the NAACP Legal Defense and Educational Fund, the National Women's Law Center, Public Citizen and other studies cited in our book are reproduced in their entirety in the fourth and fifth volumes of the printed hearings.

The full text of letters and telegrams of opposition from law school faculty and constitutional scholars are also included, as are many of the key newspaper and magazine articles which we cite, such as Renata Adler's "Coup at the Court" in *The New Republic* and Lloyd Cutler's *New York Times* op-ed, "Saving Bork from Both Friends and Enemies."

In addition to the comprehensive contemporaneous background analyses published by *National Journal, Congressional Quarterly, Legal Times,* and other legal periodicals, we benefited from several longer features, particularly Professor Robert Dworkin's two articles in *The New York Review of Books* on August 13 and December 17, 1987,

Elizabeth Drew's column in the *New Yorker* on November 2, 1987, Professor Bruce Ackerman's "Transformative Appointments" in Volume 101 of the *Harvard Law Review*, and Senator Leahy's diary, "Judgment Days" which was published in the April 1988 *Washingtonian* magazine.

The article we have most cited was written by an ardent Bork supporter who had much insight into, but little good to say of the campaign. Suzanne Garment's polemic, "The War Against Robert H. Bork," published in the January 1988 issue of *Commentary*, raised important issues of fairness and integrity which greatly helped us frame our analysis, though we largely reject her characterizations of the outside opposition.

For those interested in the judicial selection process under Reagan, two works which we found most enlightening are: *Packing the Courts: The Conservative Campaign to Rewrite The Constitution* by Herman Schwartz (New York: Scribner's, 1988), and Laurence Tribe's *God Save This Honorable Court: How The Choice of Supreme Court Justices Shapes Our History* (New York: Random House, 1985).

Index